Just in Time

Neuroscience and the Temporality of Aesthetic Experience

G. Gabrielle Starr

The MIT Press
Cambridge, Massachusetts
London, England

The MIT Press would like to thank the anonymous peer reviewers who provided comments on drafts of this book. The generous work of academic experts is essential for establishing the authority and quality of our publications. We acknowledge with gratitude the contributions of these otherwise uncredited readers.

This book was set in Stone Serif and Stone Sans by Jen Jackowitz. Printed and bound in the United States of America.

Library of Congress Cataloging-in-Publication Data

Names: Starr, G. Gabrielle, 1974– author.
Title: Just in time : temporality, aesthetic experience, and cognitive neuroscience / G. Gabrielle Starr.
Description: Cambridge, Massachusetts : The MIT Press, [2023] | Includes bibliographical references and index.
Identifiers: LCCN 2022042808 (print) | LCCN 2022042809 (ebook) | ISBN 9780262048040 (hardcover) | ISBN 9780262374187 (epub) | ISBN 9780262374170 (pdf)
Subjects: LCSH: Aesthetics—Psychological aspects. | Neuropsychology. | Visual perception. | Neurosciences and the arts.
Classification: LCC BH301.P45 S73 2023 (print) | LCC BH301.P45 (ebook) | DDC 111/.85—dc23/eng/20230210
LC record available at https://lccn.loc.gov/2022042808
LC ebook record available at https://lccn.loc.gov/2022042809

10 9 8 7 6 5 4 3 2 1

For my children. You are the best gift I have ever received.

Contents

List of Figures

Preface

> I could not take my eyes from her face, which grew larger as she approached, like a sun that it was somehow possible to stare at and that was coming nearer and nearer, letting itself be seen at close quarters, dazzling you with its blaze of red and gold. . . . I saw her leave the station and go down the hill to her home; it was broad daylight now; I was speeding away from the dawn.[1]
>
> —Marcel Proust, *In Search of Lost Time*

A beautiful face flashing in a window can haunt you for a lifetime. In Proust's novel *In Search of Lost Time*, a young Marcel stares out the window as a milkmaid recedes into the distance, carried away by time and the tempo of his train's accelerating motion. He will not see her again; even if he did, the perfect combination of light, the time of day and year, and a child's frame of mind as he speeds into the countryside will never recur. And so, Proust reminds us, the experience of beauty is dynamic; it is precious, and we are lucky if we can ever repeat its perfection again. One thing the experience of the beautiful seems to call for is extension—we want it to last longer; we want to hold on to it, to recreate, and never, ever to lose it. Beauty in that sense is like a child sleeping in one's arms: perhaps this is what Plato meant when Diotima, Socrates's mentor, claims we all wish to give birth in beauty.[2] Thus, we create. We restore. We curate. We call for aesthetic life to be one of shared participation, not isolation.

However, if we are so fortunate as to experience aesthetic power once, how can we ever study it? And how can we learn how beauty and its kin—sublimity, awe, shock, delight, melancholy, joy—unfold in time? It is easy to naturalize any experience of the beautiful because being open to aesthetic pleasures is fundamentally human. It feels right. I remember singing to my son when he was just a few months old. I managed to hit the right note; the song was "Somewhere Over the Rainbow"; he'd never heard me do it so fluidly and clearly. He stopped nursing, opened his eyes, and with his mouth made a little, precious *O*. He knew; I knew. In that moment, we shared something strange, pleasurable, and perfectly just for us.

Thus, moment to moment, aesthetic experience can blossom, from art, from an interaction, nature, thought. But what is the "natural" time course of such an experience, if there is one? The answer to that depends on the timescale you wish to explore, and what kinds of experiences you care about. Given the range of evidence that even brief encounters with objects may have consequential, real, and differential effects, it seems apparent that behavioral and neuroscientific explorations of aesthetics have something important to teach. It is thus critical for those who care about aesthetics to be open to the engagement of the very brief as well as the longest scales of aesthetic life. Neuroaesthetics can help explain even lifelong encounters—from the emergence of taste in the young, to changes in and durability of taste as we age.

Yet neuroaesthetics has its limits. It is often undertaken in unusual settings—labs, with loud, powerful, and expensive equipment; with mobile, sometimes heavy, head-mounted EEG; while staring at a computer screen in a darkened room; or on the quick, open-access model of Amazon's MTurk. We often don't study engagements with artworks in their entirety, or we manipulate components of an original to test one facet of a whole. Individuals are often tested on their own, not in the rich cultural contexts in which we have many daily aesthetic experiences. Of all the challenges neuroaesthetics faces, however, the most crucial involve temporality. All the other elements I mentioned above can be mitigated by altering or combining experimental conditions. For example, one can contrast labs with galleries; EEG technology has advanced and is now much lighter weight and less cumbersome; and so on. But the question remains of what kind of timescales matter most in aesthetics: can the relatively brief timescales of neural processes and the measures we use for them truly capture some part of what is essential to aesthetic life? And how do we model aesthetic experiences over time? This book focuses on these questions, taken alongside the genres we engage and the goals we bring to them, to offer a novel understanding of what neuroaesthetics can do.

Aesthetic experience is ultimately, in my view, about how and why humans learn. Over the course of this book, I will ask you to dwell alongside me with works of art—music, painting and photography, as well as literature—as I inquire into how, because of the way you learn, art can make you feel. Cross-disciplinary work requires patience and humility, and it is always a work in progress. Thus, throughout this journey, I hope you will bear with me: at times I will linger on concepts from neuroscience and the arts that may be new to some readers but old hat to others. They were all new to me, as I have wandered through fields I continue to find inspiring. I hope you enjoy joining me in these pages.

Acknowledgments

It gives me great pleasure to be able to acknowledge individuals and institutions who helped this book become a reality. Much of the empirical research cited here began with a generous grant from New York University to create a Global Institute for Advanced Study on Aesthetic Experience and the Brain. Members of that group are incredibly generative, generous, thoughtful, and brilliant colleagues, including David Pöeppel, Amy Belfi, Anjan Chatterjee, Denis Pelli, Helmut Leder, Andrea Halpern, Rob Hopkins, Felicity Callard, Edward Vessel, Natalie Phillips, and Lauren Vail. I am deeply grateful to Pomona College, where I was able to continue this work. Sam Glick is a peerless supporter. I also thank David Tanenbaum and the research committee at Pomona for underwriting part of this research. Friends and colleagues Christina Ciambriello, Avis Hinkson, Robert Goldberg, José Rodriguez, Maria Watson, Seth Allen, Mark Kendall, Stephanie Navarro, and Alexandra Rodriguez have been a pleasure to work with. Marilyn Perkins is an ace research assistant and illustrator. Kyla Wazana Tompkins and Kevin Dettmar are superb interlocutors. Thank you to Phil Laughlin at the MIT Press for being a hard-core editor.

I am grateful to be able to reprint portions of this book that appeared in slightly different forms elsewhere: "Form and Perception: Wallace Stevens and Cognitive Perspectives on Aesthetics," *The New Wallace Stevens Studies*, edited by Barry Eeckhout and Gül Bilge Han (New York: Cambridge University Press, 2021), 148–158; G. Gabrielle Starr and Amy M. Belfi, "Pleasure," in *Further Reading*, edited by Matthew Rubery and Leah Price (New York: Oxford University Press, 2020), 282–293; Edward A. Vessel, Asye Ilkay Isik,

Amy M. Belfi, Jonathan L. Stahl, G. Gabrielle Starr, "The Default-Mode Network Represents Aesthetic Appeal That Generalizes across Visual Domains," *Proceedings of the National Academy of Science* 116, no. 38 (2019): 19155–19164; Amy M. Belfi, Edward A. Vessel, Aenne Brielmann, Ayse Ilkay Isik, Anjan Chatterjee, Helmut Leder, Denis G. Pelli, and G. Gabrielle Starr, "Dynamics of Aesthetic Experience Are Reflected in the Default-Mode Network," *NeuroImage* 188 (2019): 584–597; Edward A. Vessel, Natalia Maurer, Alexander H. Denker, and G. Gabrielle Starr, "Stronger Shared Taste for Natural Aesthetic Domains Than for Artifacts of Human Culture," *Cognition* 179 (2018): 121–131; and "Aesthetics and Impossible Embodiment: Stevens, Imagery and Disorientation," *Wallace Stevens Journal* 39, no. 2 (2015): 157–181. I have included materials and methods for scientific papers in the appendix to enable readers to quickly check them; however, please consult the originals above for full context and citations.

Good friends mean everything; Amy M. King, Natalie Friedman, Christopher R. Miller, Karen Krahulik, Skip Gates, Dawn Davis, Kat Tait, Molly Ott Ambler, Bill Ambler, Tina Mullick, Tasneem Bahtia, Tracey Letteau, Brendt Stallings, Per Dahlin, Val Smith, Xavier Gabaix, Tom Carew, Matthew Santirocco, John Beckman, Devorah Lieberman, Mary Peck, Bob Gaines, Gigi Dopico, and Katy Fleming make my life better. Andre Fenton helped me think through Markov cycles over a barbeque one muggy day—thank you, Andre, for upping my game, for your generosity and friendship. I also had the great benefit of the careful and knowledgeable eyes of five anonymous press readers; thank you! As always, any mistakes are my own.

Finally, to Leah, Ryan, Hailey, and Caden: be good! And I thank my husband, John Harpole, our children, Georgie and Eli, and my mother, Barbara Starr, for helping to keep home happy while lots of work was done.

Introduction: Aesthetic Time and How We Use It

I would wager that in your own experience there is no single timescale that describes aesthetic life. Sometimes the briefest moment dilates, opening seemingly out to the edge of time. One summer, I stood mesmerized as an osprey floated on a thermal rising over the water. I'd seen this bird before, but never did it take me with such majesty. The span of its wings seemed almost to paint a path over the water as it turned to dive, striking for fish that flashed silver in the light. The bird was young, and just practicing for now. Soon it would be out on its own, its parents heading off for warmer climes.[1]

That experience is in part a series of moments—perceptions, then memories. This perceptual experience of beauty lasted only a few seconds, and it initiated an aesthetic experience that may never emerge as a work of art. In its unpredictability and fleetingness, such an experience is hard to study empirically, even as it may be richly open to description. Thus, as I seek to fix that moment in mind and heart, I have sought echoes in artworks that I know, and I will continue to seek them just to have access to that powerful past sight. The closest I have come is a sonnet by nineteenth-century British priest and poet Gerard Manley Hopkins:

> As kingfishers catch fire, dragonflies draw flame;
> As tumbled over rim in roundy wells
> Stones ring; like each tucked string tells, each hung bell's
> Bow swung finds tongue to fling out broad its name;
> Each mortal thing does one thing and the same:
> Deals out that being indoors each one dwells;
> Selves—goes itself; myself it speaks and spells,
> Crying Whát I dó is me: for that I came.[2]

Each image of this poem, from visual flash to bell's toll, flows by as Hopkins seeks to connect the beauty of an animal, insect, or object to its innermost essence, its most true self. However, far from being timeless, each image is fundamentally temporal. The lines, meter, and rhythm have a duration and sequence that, in the logic of the poem, are essential to its beauty. Take the tongues that, in swinging "fling out broad [each bell's] name": towns and parishes could be identified at many times in England's history based on the timing, sequences, or notes of church bells (in London, St. Paul's Cathedral had one bell that rung in A-flat, and another in E-flat; Big Ben's bells ring in G-sharp, F-sharp, E, and B). Such tolls echo, then vanish, and the identity and clarity of each note in time is echoed in the poem itself. Hopkins's rhythm rings its own changes (sequences of bells identifying times, prayers, or particular liturgical moments) using the technique often called "sprung rhythm," where, as marked above, unusual accents lengthen, shorten, or interrupt existing rhythmic patterns.

The suddenness of these changes is crucial. As Hopkins shifts attention from the beauty of the bird and the world around it, he uses the volta—the transition between ideas that is characteristic of most sonnets—to heal the disruption often understood in the West to be a fundamental split between outer and inner life ("What I do is me: for that I came") by linking what is visible to humans and that which is visible only to God:

> I say móre: the just man justices;
> Keeps grace: thát keeps all his goings graces;
> Acts in God's eye what in God's eye he is—
> Chríst—for Christ plays in ten thousand places,
> Lovely in limbs, and lovely in eyes not his
> To the Father through the features of men's faces.[3]

It is hard to think of timescales more distant: the flash of a bird in the light and the eternity of the Godhead, the minutes it might take to read the poem and its persistence in the life of an individual or culture. For me, thus, this poem is not just about how beauty shines forth in the world; it is also about how beauty exists in time.

Being drawn to the preservation of the beautiful, as well as a recognition of the paradoxes of the timescales at which beauty exists and in which we encounter it, is fundamental in much of Hopkins's poetry. Take "Pied Beauty":

Glory be to God for dappled things—
  For skies of couple-colour as a brinded cow;
    For rose-moles all in stipple upon trout that swim;
Fresh-firecoal chestnut-falls; finches' wings;
  Landscape plotted and pieced—fold, fallow, and plough;
    And áll trádes, their gear and tackle and trim.

All things counter, original, spare, strange;
  Whatever is fickle, freckled (who knows how?)
With swift, slow; sweet, sour; adazzle, dim;
  He fathers-forth whose beauty is past change:
    Praise him.[4]

The visual delay that comes with the stretch of white space on the page—or equally, the pause of a good reader at the poem's final colon and line break, leading to the closing jubilee of praise—these pauses point toward so many characteristics of aesthetic life. Waiting. Wanting. Feeling. Thinking. Ending. Remembering. Renewing. Even forgetting. So how do we learn what those varying experiences mean and how they work?

It is difficult to define aesthetic experience in all its breadth, from the pleasing to the disturbingly astute, funny, melancholy, and even boring or bittersweet. Aesthetic experience is hard to define in part because we don't have words for some of its most powerful expressions: "beauty" covers some of its scope but not all. More than this, what counts as aesthetic experience changes over the history of a culture, an art form, or an individual. The closest I can come is to borrow the language of John Dewey, who argues aesthetic experience happens when something that we see, hear, feel, think, or imagine pushes us toward "appreciating, perceiving, and engaging" with the world more deeply.[5] An aesthetic experience means the "intens[ification of] the sense of immediate living."[6] Under its influence, we don't just live—we thrive.

In this book, I engage with works of art that have for me made good on that promise of intensified life. Each of the works I have chosen will not do that for everyone, but I hope every reader feels at least some kinship with the experiences I describe, and that you feel at least one moment of aesthetic power as you read or look along with me. Thus, I began this book with anecdotes and literature that offer exemplars of a human being in thrall to beauty. In these instances, one might see how aesthetic experiences can be categorized by what they enable, most especially how we can deploy the feelings that beauty or art generates to make meaning of the world. The arc of a bird's wing in the sky triggers intense, searching feelings, stops me in my tracks, leaves me to wonder. The clarity of sight that emerges as a kingfisher's wings catch the light speaks to Hopkins of the sufficiency of God's creation—its exactitude and the singularity and sufficiency of each creature unto itself. Writing may arrest these moments of thrall, offering them for extended examination. However, that kind of temporal dilation and fixation is not *necessary* to aesthetic experience. What it does is to point out the ways in which aesthetic experience seems to affect the temporality of perception itself.

In this book, I combine behavioral psychology with the methods of neuroscience, alongside the humanistic forms of critical and philosophical inquiry to uncover some of the dimensions of how beauty happens in time. One might think the question of time is fundamentally different for objects that have an arrow of temporality that is progressive and extended—a poem, a film, or a piece of music—or as ephemeral as a bird on the wing. Yet in all these cases time becomes fundamentally, subjectively manipulable, as one dwells on a moment, freezes it in memory, and savors it.

To help determine to what extent these kinds of events might be truly distinct from other kinds of aesthetic moments, let's take something in between: American artist Jasper Johns's quest for visual regeneration in his *Target* series (1955–61). Johns was drawn to seriality, experimenting with the American flag as a leitmotif and going on to work with the graphical and semantic complexity of numerals, letters, and the names of colors. *Target with Plaster Casts* (figure I.1), one of the first two in the dozens-long series, is a remarkable mixture.[7] It blends the painterly precision of carefully sculpted rings with the rough work of collage (newspaper lies underneath layers of encaustic paint) and the plaster casts of body parts.

The work foregrounds sets of contradictions. The first set of tensions and conflicting demands is semantic, emerging with the questions of whether the target is a *what* (the bull's-eye) or a *who* (the isolated body parts nestled within each box atop the painting), a style (abstraction or expressionism) or a system (the elite world of galleries and exhibitions). The second set of contradictions is perceptual, and it combines two elements: the contrast between the relentless circularity of the target at the center, with the angularity of a square canvas, stretched tightly to each corner; and the perhaps perplexing dimensions and colors of the plaster casts, which are neither

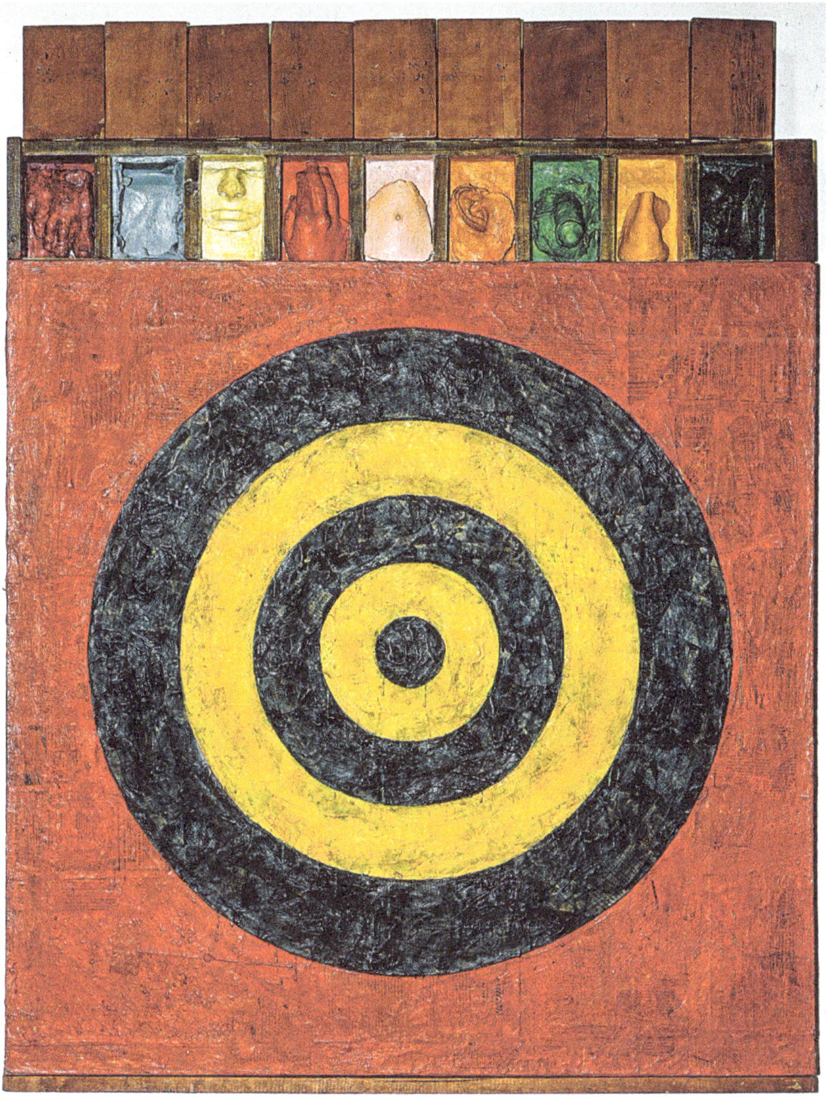

Figure I.1
Jasper Johns, *Target with Plaster Casts*, 1955.

bound by elemental shape (square or circle) nor by the general two-dimensionality of the rest of the work.

Each element of *Target with Plaster Casts* suggests something that lies just out of visual containment. Try it: focus your eyes on the target, and the plaster casts go out of sight. Look closely at the casts, deciphering forms from the color-on-on-color blur, and you will see parts of bodies that shift the register from the graphic and semantic simplicity of targets and concentric rings onto aging feet, genitalia colored wildly, and boxes one might wish simply to close. (This is a version of Troxler fading, an effect discovered in the nineteenth century, which depends on the way the retina is structured to create our field of vision.[8] The timing with which areas in the visual field enter into focus is dependent on differing brain regions: the parietal cortex and frontal cortex, and on average with neurotypical—that is, not subject to injury, illness, or atypical development or connectivity—patients, it takes about seventeen seconds for peripheral features to fade.[9]) While there is little in the way of a prescriptive temporal sequence in which one must proceed through Johns's work (though one might focus first on the most legible symbol, the target), experiences of the work are nonetheless temporally extended. Johns goes on to foreground temporality not just through a single encounter but as something fundamental and expansive, placing each target in a larger sequence.

Later that same year, Johns transforms the conditions under which viewers might engage his work. *Green Target* (figure I.2), in its monochromatic splendor, is a stark revision of other pieces.[10] The target itself seems elusive, almost a will-o-the-wisp, inviting the viewer to come find it: it may be of some use for a marksman, but little for a beginner.

This is, with a knowing wink perhaps, the closest any of the *Target* paintings comes to a textbook idea of the beautiful: as William Hogarth puts it, beauty in its simplicity "*leads the eye a wanton kind of chace.*"[11] This experience of beauty is one of pursuit, both perceptual and mental, as one follows a line or idea wherever it leads. For Johns this time, however, viewers are running in circles, and complexity masquerades as simplicity.

One of the last of the series, *Target 1961* (figure I.3), offers a different kind of return to simplicity, as well as a different set of perceptual affordances (ways of engaging that are perceptually generated by features of the objects).[12]

This target is marred and streaked by admixtures of colors. If *Green Target* were hiding, this target is fading away, and thus it foregrounds different interpretative possibilities (being tired out, weathered, at the end of its use). Different sensory possibilities emerge as one might take the invitation to sit at play with the work. This piece seems particularly set up to mislead with

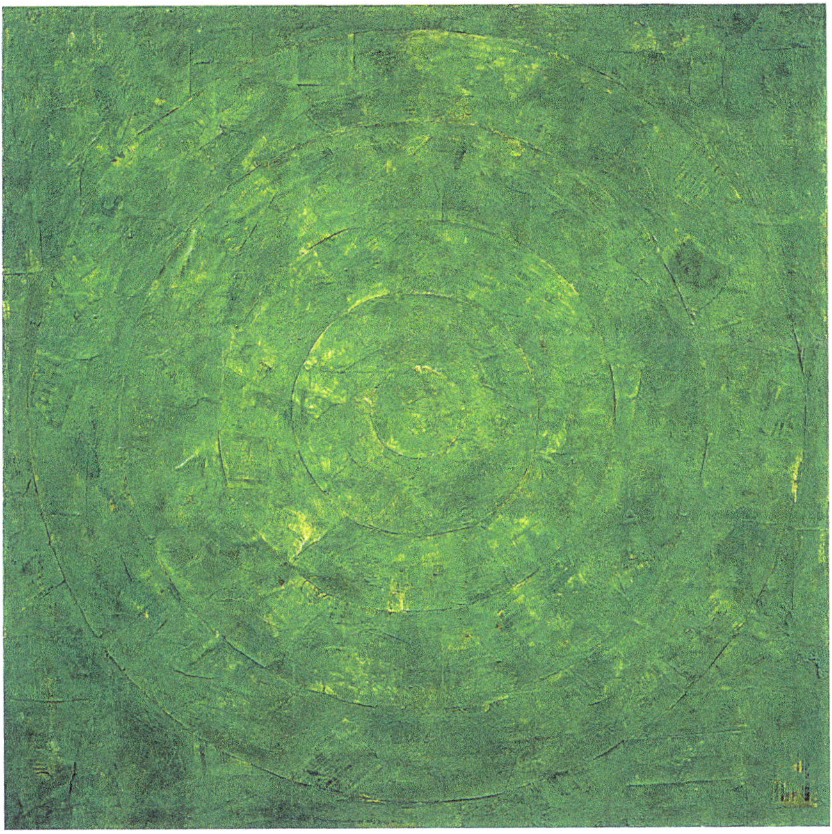

Figure I.2
Jasper Johns, *Green Target*, 1955.

its simplicities; for example, can this target truly be symmetrical when the weight of the pigment changes so quickly, patch by patch? Johns made much of his career by pressing viewers to perceive, anew, deeply familiar and semantically weighted figures from numbers to targets or flags. But in this case, he seems to ask what is left of perception once its object has been scraped away; are we now supposed to unsee or forget the target and approach the layered paint as mere abstraction?[13]

Responding to the various perceptual possibilities generated by these works is fundamentally spatiotemporal, and highly individual; my responses, even stripped down as they are here, offer a peculiar sort of guided tour. When I sketch details of response, I do not do so normatively,

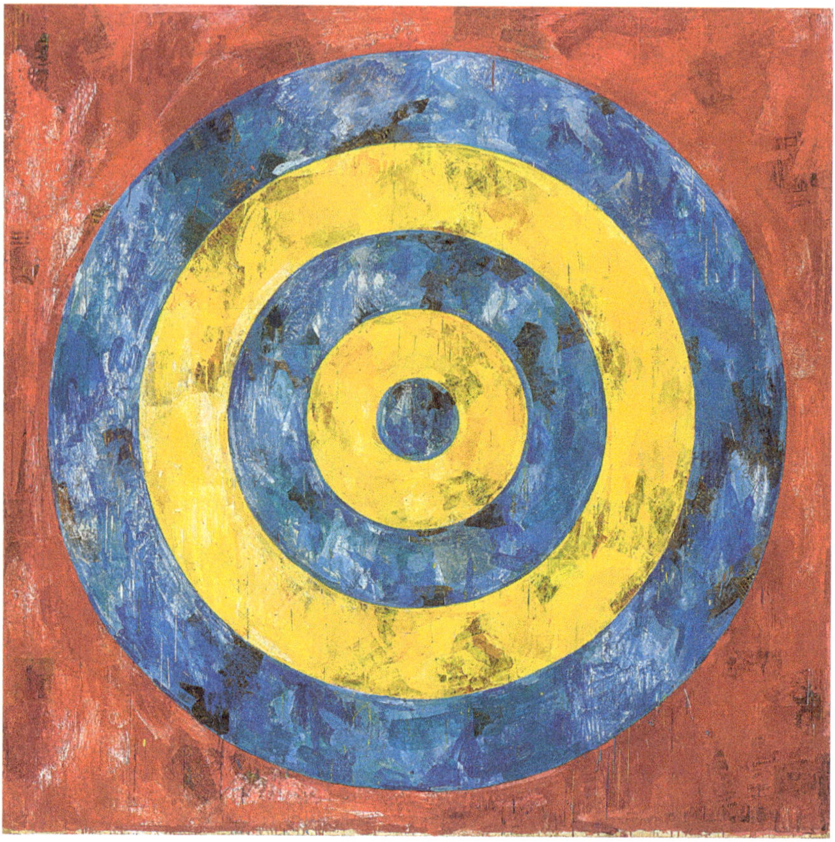

Figure I.3
Jasper Johns, *Target, 1961.*

suggesting their universality or even their frequency for others. Rather, I do so to illustrate possibilities and identify variations. The very multiplicity of interpretive and affective possibilities is important, because even for a single viewer the range of ways in which one can engage with a given artwork is startling. Each of the lenses one might bring to the painting carries different routes for pleasure, disturbance, disruption, curiosity. How can this be? Part of the answer comes with how aesthetic experiences overall are structured—in particular, with how individuals enter into them.

In that spirit, let's turn to another version of aesthetic experience, one that manipulates the *Targets* yet still strikes them true. Following the 1978

Paris exhibition of Johns's work at the Centre Pompidou, surrealist writer Alain Robbe-Grillet made his own unique aesthetic object in response to his experience of Johns's art; he creates something like a first-person detective story, centered around a prison cell, in which objects from the Johns collection appear and disappear through a judas (a small hatch within a door) as the continued darkness disrupts the narrator's sense of time and deprives him of everyday sensations. Robbe-Grillet's *Target* memorializes both the description and transformation of Johns's art, as he connects each ring of the targets (*With Plaster Casts* and *Green*) with other objects in the collection.[14] The narrator vacillates between curiosity, fantastical interpretation, and surface reactions to shape and form. However, at one point, with some exasperation, he confronts the realization that perception is paramount:

> When [a] thoroughly twisted wire made its appearance in my cell, dangling from the extended arm through the wide-open judas, I believed that I was dealing with some bizarre kindness on the part of my guards: although altered by cruel distortions, this was undoubtedly a rudimentary coat hanger, like the ones found in third-class hotels and with which—after suitable alterations—I would be able to hang my jacket from one of the hooks securing the remains of the broken mirror to the wall. I must henceforth accept the obvious: in reality the deformations imposed on the object form the numeral 7. (32–34)

Whatever alterations or deformations of objects or of reality may be wrought in art, there is a limit. From a perceptual standpoint, *Green Target* (or that with plaster casts) remains both a representation of and perhaps a veritable target; the plaster casts represent body parts; numbers emerge unbidden as we stare at a canvas, for we can't (in general) un-know what we have learned so fully; and our perceptual lives can only be resisted in aesthetic experience for so long. The number seven is hard to unsee (figure I.4).[15]

Unlike Robbe-Grillet, who uses Johns's objects as a jumping-off point for his own aesthetic creation, I wish, in bringing these four *Targets* together, to emphasize several things. First, the experiences I describe here (including those Robbe-Grillet details) evolve over differing timescales—some in mere seconds (or less), others in minutes, hours, or over repeated engagements across many years. Given these timescales, it is reasonable to expect that empirical investigations tuned to them, whether they are seconds or hours, will have value in exploring aesthetic life. For example, in one study I undertook with colleagues, we found that with looking at reproductions of artworks for one, five, or fifteen seconds, average self-reported peak

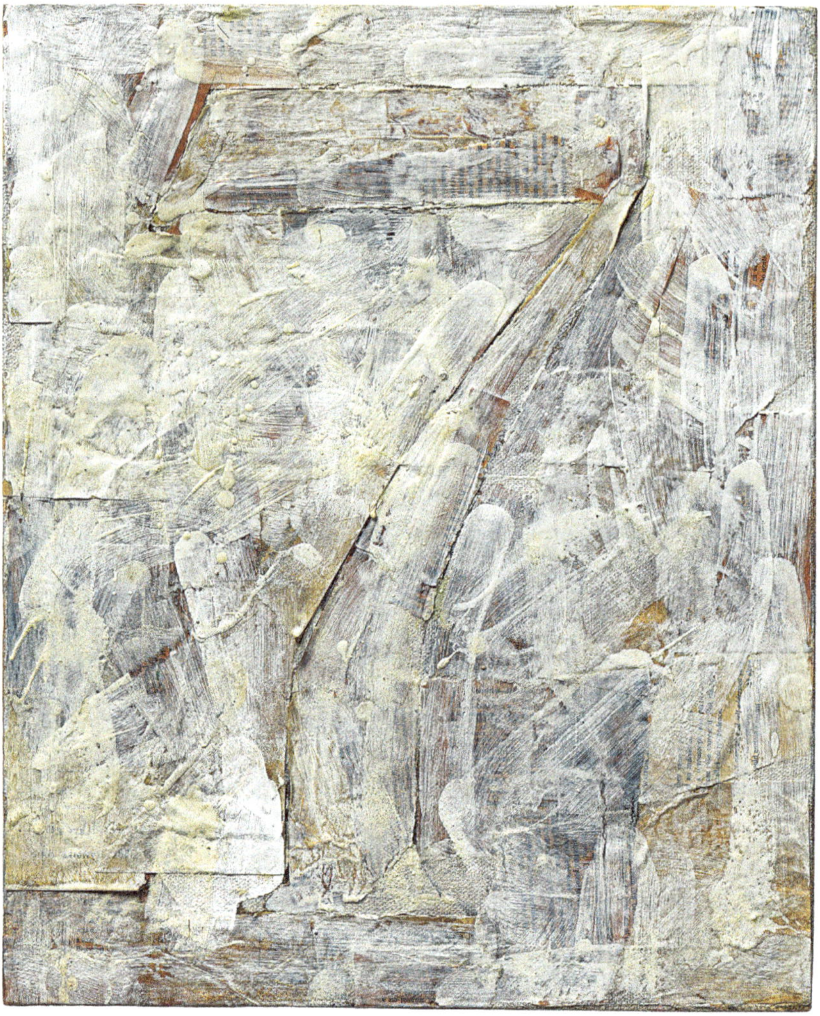

Figure I.4
Jasper Johns, *Seven*, 1955.

pleasure increased with longer looking.[16] But it took at least five seconds for some typical brain responses correlated with aesthetic pleasure to emerge, including default-mode network activation and spikes in the basal ganglia associated with reward (some significant differences emerged, too, which I will discuss later on). There is clearly a disjunction between conscious experience and neural processing, but the fact that even with only one second to look, behavioral indices of pleasure emerge points back to the realization Robbe-Grillet can't resist: conscious perception opens doors of aesthetic perception, and sometimes they don't close quickly.

In these and other ways I will explore, empirical approaches can render clues about experiences of the beautiful and about the temporal dimensions of aesthetic experiences as a whole—experiences that can go beyond beauty or mere liking to include transporting feelings of sorrow, awe, horror, or boredom.[17] As Jeorg Fingerhut and Jesse Prinz point out, "there is no English word for the kind of pleasure that arises in response to beauty, nor any agreed upon theory of beauty," thus, let's "assume for this discussion that beauty is a superordinate concept that refers to a variety of more specific formal properties such as elegance, grace, balance, graphic impact, and so on. . . . [And] each of these may have its own emotional tone. What they share in common is that they are sensory pleasures."[18] As I consider the variety of aesthetic pleasures, in this book I draw on a range of empirical studies to model the time courses of aesthetic experience, from work that follows the development of aesthetic taste in children and changes that come with age or impairment, to work that follows the time course of immediate neural responses, or work that explores the time course of visits to a museum.

Aesthetic Time and the Uses of Art

To understand more about the principles that enable productive empirical investigation alongside humanistic analysis of aesthetic experience, let's begin with posing a complex question: what is art for? I contend that art serves four core functions for its audiences: a social function that centers around communication and community; a developmental function, engaging the sense of self and the relations of self to others; an exploratory and epistemic function that enables feelings of pleasure and displeasure to generate new kinds of curiosity and knowledge; and an emotional function, which provides outlet for and willful alteration of mood and other affective states. Each of these contentions can be explored experimentally, as well as through more traditional methods of humanist investigation. And each of these "uses of art" has key temporal dimensions that help unlock their dynamics. As I will argue, aesthetic time comes down to how you use it.

Art as Social Medium

One way we use art that helps determine the timescale of our experience involves social interaction. Ellen Dissanayake argues that the arts emerge from the human drive for mutuality, a force that shapes the earliest moments of infants outside the womb: the arts help make people "aware of their common humanity" because their "antecedents . . . evolved to enable our human way of life in relationship with others."[19] The case for art's sociality is perhaps most familiar with music. Music-making is a communal activity; for the majority of human existence, music listening has been communal too. From lullabies to hymns, funeral dirges to pop ballads, music prompts and helps organize social interaction. From a physiological level, the social interaction mediated by music is coordinated in part through phenomena known collectively as entrainment, where individuals and even groups engage in synchronized motion. These moments of synchronization can operate at a broad level, such as dancing together or keeping a beat, but also can be found at the neuronal level, where, for example, auditory cortex fires rhythmically with musical meter.[20]

Music also directs social interaction, not just prescribing what is done—singing, dancing, speaking—but by whom, where, when, and how.[21] Gary Tomlinson argues that the practices of music-making and listening (collectively, "musicking") evolved through the development of cultural archives: "Passed through generations, accumulating cultural systems can give rise to their own internal [physiological] development tendencies and vectors, depending on the cognitive, bodily, and environmental constraints they involve."[22] Taken broadly, "music itself is . . . a crucial aesthetic technology that we regularly employ to deepen social intimacy and to train the young in communicative practices essential to their social being. In short, music enhances and refines our affective capacities and empathic relatedness. It plays a critical role in shaping our sociality."[23]

However, while shared human sensory architecture enables and promotes some aesthetic effects while making others nearly impossible, individual taste varies significantly, especially for artifacts of culture.[24] Thus, rather than arguing for universal taste as the sign of the social nature of art, I argue (along with other scholars) that art provides a social site—a meeting place for human interaction. As Nicklaus Lehman describes, "the work of art is produced *exclusively* for the purpose of communication, and that it accomplishes this goal or fails to do so by . . . *using perceptions contrary to their primary purpose.*"[25] In other words, in the case of music, the temporal nature of sound is deployed alongside elements like pitch and timbre, not for the purposes of locating moving objects or identifying elements of our surroundings—but, let's say, for the purposes of evoking shared emotion among a group of people, provoking thought, or making you get up and dance. A variety of timescales emerge here, from the tiniest of tempos, to the length of a song, the time span of a concert, dance, or a festival, and the development of a human life. Each of these is subject to empirical engagement as well as humanist analysis, as we will see.

From the perspective of the artist, the communicative function may be an exclusive purpose, to use Luhmann's phrase (a version of the idea of art as expression), but I doubt it. Certainly, from the perspective of a viewer, reader, or listener, communication looks very different. While there is no true language of art—no basic paradigm of communication that functions purely linguistically—art engages humans in conversation. Think, for example, of the connections that emerge as individuals stand in animated discussion before a work on a gallery wall or argue over the ending of a film. These connections respond to the vibrant call that art issues and are among the reasons people return to art repeatedly as we move through life.

So far I have written about time as we experience it phenomenologically. However, there are human timescales of which we are not consciously aware, even though they form the warp and woof of life. The neuroscience of time has much to resolve. On one side there is the question of response timing—the coordination of output in motion, for example. Yet it appears, as well, that there are significant differences across the timing of input: "different sensory processes keep their own time, [so] that the Now of vision might not coincide with the Now of hearing, or even that the Now of color perception might dissociate from the Now of motion detection. Taken together, the evidence implies that we should talk of subjective *times*, in the plural."[26] If you've ever been in a car accident or gotten a hard blow to the head, you may have experienced this—you can't see, but you can hear, or things just seem to run out of order. Being around an explosion can feel this way, too, when a concussive wave distorts hearing and assembling a coherent subjective experience is nearly impossible.

The processes required for binding sensory data together also shape humans' understanding of time. Different elements perceived by a single sense can be processed across a distributed neural architecture: for example, motion and color have to be reintegrated into a complete percept for vision, as do frequency and timbre for sound. The more complicated the integration, the longer this process takes. We are talking fractions of a second, but for finely tuned actions every moment counts. For this reason the nervous system creates shortcuts to connect and organize crucial components of perception and behavior so that essentials don't get lost in the gaps. One of the most important of these shortcuts is "intentional binding," a term Patrick Haggard and colleagues introduced to describe the phenomenon whereby imputed causes are experienced as slightly closer in time to their effects (and vice versa) than are two events or perceptions that are understood to be unrelated.[27] While it is well known that humans can respond to events that happen below the threshold of consciousness (as with visual or auditory priming), the discovery that the timing of experience has small-scale flexibility (on the order of 50–75 milliseconds) when it comes even to basic inferences about cause and effect underscores the fact that human experience does not simply unroll, full-speed, in a forward direction.[28]

Typically, neuroscientists (and many philosophers) engage with five key aspects of time: subjective duration, memory, futurity, timing (or temporal coordination), and whether or not our fundamental mechanisms of perception are calibrated to something like an atom of time (a small, indivisible increment) or what might be understood as a sliding window (where we assemble something like the sequences you see as you ride along in a car, looking out at the scenery). We will return to these components in chapter 3; here I want to note that another way we might understand temporality is in how we might share in it. For example, the interactions of individuals as they engage with artworks may involve neural synchronization. Recent work in neuroscience has used intersubject correlations to better understand how human beings interact with each other and with our environments. For example, human brains (at least for individuals who are neurotypical) process visual and aural input (short films) in similar ways; researchers have used the neural responses of one individual to successfully predict firing patterns in others. In other words, "individual brains 'tick together' in synchronized spatiotemporal patterns when exposed to the same visual environment."[29]

Building off these techniques, Greg Stephens and colleagues have shown that such neurocoupling may also underpin communication between human beings: in one experiment, individuals listening to a speaker telling a true story about their life showed neural activity mirroring that of the speaker. The closer they were together in their understanding of the story, the more closely mirrored was their neural activity:

> because the speaker's production-based processes mostly precede the listener's comprehension-based processes, the listener's neural dynamics . . . mirror the speaker's neural dynamics with some delay. Conversely, when listeners use their production system to emulate and predict the speaker's utterances, we expect [and found] the opposite: the listener's dynamics . . . precede the speaker's dynamics. However, when the speaker and listener are simply responding to the same shared sensory input (both speaker and listener can hear the same utterances), [we predicted and found] synchronous alignment. Finally, . . . the extent of coupling between a pair of conversers [predicts] . . . the success of communication.[30]

Yet more crucially, emotional responses to music also involve neurocoupling. Participants in one study who showed synchronized firing also showed correlations with their own continuous ratings of valence—positive or negative emotional response—and arousal—here, intensity—of those responses.[31] If neural coordination like this underpins some of our ability to function socially, it is likely that it also might key into some of the social dimensions of art.

Even as art serves as a site of social gathering, conversation, or shared (not to say homogenous) experience, the intensity of some aesthetic experiences may be such that they seem to take over everything one sees or hears. This, as I will discuss later, can influence how we perceive their duration. As much as the display of beauty for Gerard Manley Hopkins, for example, is about the inner essence of a thing, aesthetic experience can seem to take command of one's own inner life too. A character in Donna Tartt's novel *The Goldfinch* richly describes such a moment:

> "You can have a lifetime of perfectly sincere museum-going where you traipse around enjoying everything and then go out and have some lunch. But . . . If a painting really works down in your heart and changes the way you see, and think, and feel, you don't think, 'oh, I love this picture because it's universal.' 'I love this painting because it speaks to all mankind.' That's not the reason anyone loves a piece of art. It's a secret whisper. . . . An individual heart-shock. Your dream, [Eudora] Welty's dream, [Jan] Vermeer's dream . . . [A] really great painting is fluid enough to work its way into the mind and heart through all kinds of different angles, in ways that are unique and very particular. *Yours, yours, I was painted for you.*"[32]

Alva Nöe argues that such interconnectedness between the artwork and its viewer comes because art is what he calls an "organized activity." An organized activity is "primitive and basic, . . . requires delicate and evolving cognitive skills, . . . [and] has something like the structure of turn taking"; it is not orchestrated by only one party; it "has a function" and "is also, at least potentially, a source of pleasure."[33] In this way, the experience of art is organized—and fundamentally social.

Art and a Social Self

Beyond a philosophical or phenomenological perspective about how aesthetic experiences might feel as people interact with art as social objects, there is evidence that the ways that the sense of self is constructed involve the engagement of self- and other-oriented areas of the brain, and that these areas are selectively activated with intense aesthetic experiences. Phenomenal, subjective consciousness of an experience may have temporal effects, especially in terms of how we assemble our own self-narratives (e.g., I am; I came from; I grew; I used to; Now I; and so on). Evocative representations of this problem emerge in René Descartes's *Meditations*. He wonders who the person is who is sitting by a warm stove in his pajamas, watching and feeling wax as it melts. How does he know who he is at a single moment or over time?[34] A century or so later, David Hume, in section VI of *A Treatise of Human Nature*, wonders how we know we are the same person when we wake up as when we went to sleep? Or when we are thirty as opposed to five?[35] These concerns are ancient. In book VII of the *Nichomachean Ethics*, Aristotle, for example, questions whether a person is capable of being accountable for what they did while intoxicated—were they in their right mind? were they their real selves?[36]

The temporal dimensions of aesthetic experience as both social and subjective, personal, and unique are intricately connected to self-perception and self-awareness. There is mounting consensus that a sense of self is partially dependent on and supported by a group of interconnected brain regions first identified by Marcus Raichle and colleagues as the default-mode network (DMN). For example, regions of the canonical DMN have been shown to be involved in imagining or judging the perspectives of other people, as well as making judgments about oneself or individuals similar to oneself.[37] More recently, there is an emerging view that there may be not just a single DMN but two different functionally connected networks involving the same or similar sets of brain areas.[38]

The DMN and the social imaginaries—the concepts of self in relation to others—it helps support are developmental; normally these brain regions knit together slowly, emerging in mature form only nearing the end of adolescence. While structural connections between some of these areas exist in childhood, functional connections are weak and irregular, and task-related deactivation (such as appears in adults) does not regularly occur. Over time, structural connections between regions in the DMN become stronger and more coordinated. With later adolescence, for neurotypical individuals, networked default-mode regions both deactivate on some demanding, externally focused tasks, and function at a (higher) baseline during tasks involving self and social reasoning.[39] In other words, it is reasonable to understand this process of increased functional connectivity as one biologically enabling the development of children as increasingly self- and socially aware.

The involvement of the DMN in engaging with aesthetically moving visual art is increasingly well established, and suggests that systems for self-reference and self-awareness are selectively attuned to aesthetic experiences.[40] While typically, during a visual evaluation task, the canonical DMN (as defined by Raichle, Fox, Gusnard, and others) dips below its resting baseline state, the response pattern for intensely moving aesthetic responses involves an initial dip with a quick return to baseline.[41] Because only extremely moving artworks elicit this response, the DMN may be part of a mechanism underpinning something like the feeling Tartt's character describes—the moment when an artwork, outside you on a wall, enters into your consciousness and seems almost a very part of you: mine, mine, this was created for me. This is indeed a puzzle. While one might, along with Tartt, expect that self-resonance matters in aesthetic experience, it is not clear why one would expect that only strong experience hits at the core of the self.

In approaching this puzzle, it is worthwhile to note that different kinds of art may evoke different kinds of social imaginaries and different ways of conceiving of the self. For example, as Joel Krueger argues, "Music is a kind of social scaffolding. Music affects the cultivation of primitive social skills like interactive turn-taking and the temporal coordination of bodily movement and affective expression," and for children, the connection with a caregiver or parent through music "is 'scaffolding' guiding the child's communicative endeavors and supporting its burgeoning social intelligence."[42] For these reasons one would expect that music might have differing neural engagements in areas involved in social cognition or self-cognition than does visual art. One might further argue that the different ways in which one approaches music—the differing uses to which music is put—involve differing social functions: singing in a choir carries a different kind of sociality than does listening in a concert hall. Musical genre may matter as well: a hymn calls on a different kind of belonging (or its absence) than does a love song. Taking another art form, silent reading of poetry for pleasure has social and personal implications that are different from those of music. Each set of engagements feels different and calls on different neural networks, as I will show a bit further on.

It is reasonable to assume, as well, that different levels of social engagement call on different timescales for development, pleasure, and understanding; new experimental techniques can thus help uncover new dimensions of the ways social interaction is built into some aesthetic experiences. Neuroscientific investigation always wrestles with questions of normativity, and in recent years researchers have focused increasingly on individual differences and neurodiversity. In this vein, a tool that establishes synchronic, time-, behavior-, and stimulus-locked responses could enable us to explore fine distinctions. For example, given that the DMN has been implicated in some aesthetic responses, it is curious that connectivity in the regions that comprise it changes significantly from childhood to adolescence and adulthood. Neurocoupling experiments across developmental stages could help elucidate the role of the DMN in aesthetics. For example, one might establish baseline paired responses for conspecific individuals around reading and listening to a poem (like Hopkins's "Pied Beauty," say), and contrast these with the same individuals paired across age groups. In the absence of fully functional default-mode connectivity, one would expect to see differences in shared response (perhaps with more reliance on representations of one's own emotions, and less inhibition and a longer duration of emotional response for older individuals).[43]

Art and Emotion

How we feel about art can determine the time course of our engagement with it—how long we spend in an encounter, how frequently we return to an object, how often we think about it, and how we remember it. Analyzing the emotional component of aesthetic response has a long tradition in philosophy and science, dating back to Aristotle in the Western tradition of philosophy and to William James in psychology.[44] More recently, researchers have investigated the intensity of physiological and neural responses to the arts. Some of the most well-developed research in neuroscience on art and emotion comes with music, where effects such as the chills and other physiological phenomena linked to emotion have been repeatedly demonstrated.[45] Increasingly, work on poetry and metaphor has also shown physiologically powerful reactions.[46] Visual art, too, has emotional power.[47] These phenomena have been well documented; so here, I focus on one crucial problem: the ways *emotional responses* intersect with or might be distinguishable from *aesthetic pleasure*.[48]

As I will argue in chapter 1, part of the connection between emotion and aesthetic pleasure emerges because art can be motivational. Human beings go to art not just to feel or think, but at times to be *taught* how to feel, how to think, and what to do. This is one of the historical arguments for satire: by causing us to laugh at our own follies and errors, satire might teach us to be wiser than those whom we learn to ridicule. Such an idea of emotional education may also be part of the appeal of reading about love or mourning; it helps train and calibrate our emotions.[49] Or so at least we might hope. Still, emotional responses to the arts do not give access to the fullness of human experience, even as they can be a powerful tool of education. Take the abolitionist movement, where figures like William Cowper, Frederick Douglass, Sojourner Truth, and Harriet Beecher Stowe sought to evoke intense emotional responses to move humans to action to save their fellows. Such power might come in rhetoric, as in Truth's 1851 oratory:

> Look at me! Look at my arm! I have ploughed and planted, and gathered into barns, and no man could head me! And ain't I a woman? I could work as much and eat as much as a man—when I could get it—and bear the lash as well! And ain't I a woman? I have borne thirteen children, and seen most all sold off to slavery, and when I cried out with my mother's grief, none but Jesus heard me! And ain't I a woman?[50]

Yet something close to universal suffrage only became a reality in the United States in 1965. Empathy can only do so much.

Whether emotions and pleasures in art can motivate beyond the printed page is one thing. But affective responses have a further effect: the ability to alter the perception of time, through the dilation of mood, the sense of transportation to a new state, or the felt suspension of normal progression.[51] As Patrick Colm Hogan writes, emotion-provoking "incidents seem to narrow emotions to almost timeless points. Stories expand them to long-term projects, which may unfold over years or even decades."[52] Given the increasing use of continuous behavioral measures in neuroaesthetics, there are emerging ways to chart the time course of aesthetic responses, both in terms of subjective experience and neural activity. Now, for example, we know that pleasure from beauty lingers, while it may dissipate more quickly in different kinds of pleasurable engagement (e.g., savoring the taste of sweetness).[53] Being bored with one thing does not mean the end of aesthetic life (or life at all for that matter, no matter what one's children might say). We disengage from one thing and turn attention to something else. This is why, as I will discuss later, the questions of motivation and the hierarchies that motivations enable in aesthetic experience deserve more attention than they have generally received.

Art Helps Us Find Generative and New Knowledge through Pleasure

In the past, I have argued that aesthetic experiences give access to new knowledge by alerting us to what we value about the world.[54] Here I argue that art can generate subjective shifts in attention that elevate features of the artwork, features of the world, or features of ideas and emotions that had not previously been noted or understood. Art helps us orient ourselves in complex landscapes, actual or imagined, individual or cultural. One way this happens is through pleasures. As Amy Belfi and I have described, and as I will argue in greater depth in chapter 2, intense aesthetic pleasures may belong to the class of hedonic experiences that, in the words of Barbara Fredrickson, help us "broaden and build."[55] Indeed, some psychologists identify two kinds of pleasures, one of which focuses attention relatively narrowly on a goal and its satisfaction. The second kind includes those pleasures Fredrickson identifies; they direct attention beyond satisfaction of a particular, narrow goal or aim, to exploration—finding new goals, new information, and new possibilities.[56]

Many cognitive neuroscientists have argued that aesthetic pleasures may function in ways that don't map directly onto goal-oriented behavior, especially goals linked to basic biological needs and primary (unlearned) reinforcement mechanisms (e.g., hunger or thirst); there are other goals that matter to human beings. However, each of the "functions" of art I lay out in this introduction may be understood in relation to a goal. For example, in the words of Irving Biederman and Edward Vessel, humans are "infovores," and aesthetic experience may feed that hunger—though it is not the only kind of experience that may feed our need for information (I will argue later in this book why aesthetic experiences may be particularly important to how humans learn).[57]

To begin to understand how this might work with visual aesthetics, note that there are distinct response profiles that help distinguish aesthetic responses from other rewarding experiences.[58] Thus, human beings tend to share aesthetic taste in visual images of faces and places, agreeing on visual pleasure at a very high degree. However, as we look at objects that are more clearly the result of culture and human intervention, like architecture or visual art, tastes and pleasures significantly diverge.[59] This latter behavioral point is not just true of visual pleasure: the levels of shared pleasure for poems—haiku and sonnets—are more similar to those for visual art than for landscapes and human beauty.[60] As I will show in chapter 2, this distinction between "natural" and "artifactual" pleasures can help us define more closely what we mean by aesthetic form. We come to know or understand features of a work of art that speak to design—to the kinds of pleasurable or displeasurable interactions that can emerge when we engage with a work of art—by experiencing unexpected pleasures as we rub up against them. Form, I will argue, emerges only in contact with an audience and as a question of experiences of pleasure over time.

Art, Experience, and Time

Aesthetic experience has a variety of relations to the subjective experience of time; in part as a result of the functions of art I have outlined, aesthetic experiences of art exist in multiple temporalities, ranging from the now of an encounter to moments of anticipation, a future point of retrospection, in addition to broadly cultural, synchronic, and diachronic engagements. Objects can alter and fundamentally shape our experiences by calling upon aesthetic engagement (evocation of emotion, engagement of memory, piquing conversation). The arts also shape experience by calling on motion. Art can make you move with a beat, entraining one person's experience to another's. This is not the case with music alone: dynamic visual scenes may call on the motor cortex and potential action, even as static scenes might encourage viewers to imagine approach.[61] Evidence also supports the idea that dynamic scenes may evoke more pleasure than static ones (perhaps unsurprising for a species of sight hunters like us!).[62] Motion is the physical manifestation of the passage of time, and by bringing our bodies to life and movement, aesthetic experience calls on us to do more than simply hear, touch, or see: we experience the fluidity of sensation as action. I will explore this further in chapter 3, as I discuss the ways in which motivation shapes aesthetic time.

The relationships between aesthetic experiences and the goals that motivate them have important temporal implications. A range of experiments have shown that expected reward makes time seem to stretch out. For example, Michel Failing and Jan Theeuwes used an "oddball" task to demonstrate that a percept seems to last longer if it is associated with a reward.[63] Participants were presented with a set of regularly timed and uniformly colored disks; at irregular intervals, a differently colored disk appeared. The participants were told they could receive a monetary reward for correctly indicating the amount of time the oddball was presented. The greater the reward, the longer the subjective duration of the oddball disks' appearance on-screen. Thus, salient objects—those with potential for reward—can seem to last longer. This can't be the whole story, however, as the frequency with which we engage specific, rewarding objects to help pass the time suggests the opposite: time often subjectively speeds up.

The idea that multiple, rapidly occurring inputs may slow down time was most fully developed by A. D. Craig, who argues that the anterior insula may establish a "buffer" that becomes filled with salient information. Once full, the buffer can no longer efficiently feed information forward, and time seems to slow as the speed with which we able to understand what is happening is slower than the rate at which key events occur.[64] In this view, time is largely linked to the need for tim*ing*—processes aimed toward action and distributed across other brain regions as we seek to coordinate a response to what confronts us or what we feel.[65]

With aesthetic responses, it's also important to note that the way we spend time is influenced by the fact that powerful engagements can be hard to find. Indeed, evoking intense aesthetic response in lab conditions is more reliable when people bring in objects they find beautiful, rather than engaging primarily with objects selected by experimenters.[66] And in daily life, whether we are flipping through musical tracks or gazing from one museum piece to another, only a fraction of what we see might focus our attention or pique our interest, much less evoke strong sensations. Most often, then, we are probably in search of aesthetic pleasures rather than experiencing them.

Thus, there are a variety of temporal issues that urgently need discussion around aesthetics. For neuroaesthetics, the central issue may be that of experimental time. With modern imaging methods, the window of investigation is short, a matter of second or tens of seconds. As I hope to show, this is important, for neuroscience enables us to explore timescales to which we otherwise have little or no access. We also can more fully explore processes that are available to perception, like memory, whether it is working memory (the very recent past) or the longer durations of autobiography. We can turn attention to the time of an artwork itself (e.g., the duration of a film or piece of music) and the duration of excerpts too. Notably, while experimental manipulations often regulate viewing time, they also may require the use of excerpts rather than whole pieces in order to control conditions of exposure or produce enough statistical power to allow confidence in findings. However, beyond experimental manipulations, aesthetic experiences may in fact be brief outside any laboratory: my osprey across the sky, for example, lasted only seconds. We also regularly dip in and out of a book, pause a film, or listen to only the first movement of a sonata.

So, aesthetic time is multisided: it may be that aesthetic experience is marked by its general absence—time slows or stands still; that the special nature of aesthetic experience extends its felt extensity as well as its subjective duration long past the disappearance of an object or musical note; or it may, just the same, make time fly. Aesthetic experiences will, I argue later, vary in part by how they interact, by valence, socially, by a neural or other organic system, and in a variety of other ways that comport with the varying motivations we bring to them. If aesthetic experience can lead to reward, it in some way satisfies a goal, whether conscious or not. And by definition, one of the key dimensions of reward and motivation has to do with the speed at which we accomplish our aims.

In general, it is useful to think about the perception of time in terms of differences in adaptive behavior. At the millisecond, a different kind of adaptive behavior is necessary than at the longer timescale of days or years, either in memory or anticipation. When we think of smaller timescales, timing is linked to action coordination. We must be able to synchronize responses to very small changes and nuances to be successful. But this also emerges in longer timescales, where memory comes into the here and now to help us focus on learned patterns, understand salient information, and continually refine actions as we move forward in the world in which we live. Long-term interactions may involve different mechanisms across sensory modes and other contexts (e.g., social, survival). This is important to aesthetics, as I will show.

Aesthetic time influences perception, conscious reflection, memory, history, and unrolls across a variety of time windows subject to experimental analysis. These multiple levels of temporality are interactive. Time can be understood, for example, as one of the substrates of neural processing in that there is a time-delimited dynamic relationship between neuronal activity and what is available to perception. Neurons can only transmit data at regulated rates (and there are maximum rates of transmission that if exceeded can cause cell death); in this economy the extraction of patterns is crucial. Neurons and the networks they produce extract signals from noise; a single event is nearly impossible to decode, but what is understandable as signal emerges because it has a discernible pattern. Patterning allows manageable extraction of usable information from a stream of otherwise unformed data.

Research across different domains has shown that affect and preference also influence perception and time. For example, in a cleanly designed paradigm, Tina Roeske and colleagues presented individual participants with birdsong and asked them to determine the tempo: "extracted tempo choices . . . appeared to rely on an individual, independently preferred tempo rather than on actual temporal properties of the stimuli," so that "participants' aesthetic judgement was not biased toward any particular rates: listeners appreciated all presented tempos, including not only rates exceeding typical *human* rates, but even ranging from half to double the original *birdsong* tempos."[67] Aesthetic experience influenced the pattern extracted from sound, and thus, in detectable ways, *pleasure was able to shift the experience of time*. Notably, there's not any way for those listening to know that their preferences had altered their perceptions—time simply "shifted" as pleasure shaped it.

Aesthetic time runs in cycles; experience yields pleasure as an outcome, and that pleasure can go on to shape the temporality of experience going forward. I will argue that aesthetic time is thus sensitive not just to rewards but to risks too. Aesthetic pleasures change our orientation to the world around us. In the following chapters, I explore multiple levels of temporality and how they intersect with aesthetic pleasures. There is much that unifies or affiliates aesthetic experience across the arts and across sensory modalities, including involvement of emotion systems, sensations and physiology of reward, a vocabulary and institutions of appreciation, the generation of imagery, and more.[68] However, there are important ways in which the arts differ in guiding, engaging, and opening aesthetic experience too.

Chapter 1 of this book lays out some general principles of pleasure. It describes mechanisms by which pleasure can influence perceptions of the duration of aesthetic experience and influence timing in individuals' responses to different genres of art. Key concepts here include intensity, which I define operationally as a rapid rate of change from an affective baseline. I also introduce the idea of "goal time"—a time course bounded by the identification of one or more goals, their satisfaction or frustration, and even the substitution of a different goal or goals set in their place.

Chapter 2 examines how attention to features of an artifact may be directed by pleasure, and I argue that combining internal and external monitoring (self and environment) produces a salience map—an overall perception of how an object *feels*. This appetitive or affective map is what I mean by aesthetic form; this is form as it is perceived and constructed by an individual reader, viewer, or listener. From this complex construction—the idea of what matters in a poem or a painting—individuals may identify new possibilities for exploration, whether of ideas, perceptions, or emotions. I also argue that the existence of aesthetic experience itself reflects the necessary outcome of the vast diversity of goals available to human beings as we evaluate the choices through which we learn.

Chapter 3 further develops the idea of goal time for aesthetic experiences and puts forth a set of models that include brain states unavailable to an individual's own perception, conscious thoughts, and feelings. The model of aesthetic time I offer in this chapter synthesizes the concerns I have outlined above. I won't discuss all of the temporal aspects of aesthetic experience; rather, I will focus on processes of self-monitoring (both conscious and unconscious) and the ways that our prioritization of aspects of aesthetic experience determine how that experience, in any particular instance, unfolds. The model begins with a baseline that is interrupted with an aesthetic encounter. Affect may steal upon us, but its recognition is an irruption, and the passage of time is marked subjectively by an explosion of feeling. This could be a physiological experience like the chills, but it also could be an emotion defined by something like surprise, excitement, joy, or fear. The rhythm of the event is determined by interacting with features of the object at hand. But it is also determined by internal (mis)matches—to, say, expectations or moral/ethical beliefs—and by adjustment of our goals based on this process of comparison and our success or failure in attaining what we desire.

The concluding pages take readers back to artworks, using the kinds of humanist analysis that are part of aesthetic discourse, to fill in some of the details that a cognitivist schematic can't describe. It is my hope that these moments, not just at the close of the book but throughout it, provide further windows into the possibilities of aesthetic experience, the time they take, and the ways they draw our attention to how time doesn't just happen to us, but how we take control of time. Thus, I explore the temporality of engagement with the arts not only as the course of a particular artwork (say, the duration of a song, the length of time it takes to read a poem, or how long one spends looking at a mural) but rather the time course of aesthetic experience as it differs across the arts as well as in different kinds and contexts of encounters with them.[69] Aesthetic response in this view is not just when the artwork is present to the senses, but before and afterward too. This book is therefore in part about what may happen when the lights go out, the book is closed, or the musicians go home. However they happen, aesthetic responses seem to meet us where we are, and if they work, they happen just in time.

1 On Pleasure, Motivation, and Aesthetic Time

Pleasure is an outcome, as well as an origin. Humans are pleased because of (or at times in spite of) something that happens to or within us. The affective dimensions of aesthetic responses include emotions, rewards (as well as their absence or opposite), and pleasures (and their absence or opposite), and disentangling them is complex. In 2014, several colleagues and I launched a multidisciplinary aesthetics and neuroscience research collaboration. Our team included members from a variety of fields and with diverse specializations: philosophical aesthetics, literature, psychology, vision, visual art, hearing, music, psychophysics, neurology, and neuroscience.[1] Our first two-day meeting was nearly consumed by a single question: what was our key behavioral dependent measure? More specifically, what should we be asking about when we inquire about aesthetic responses? Pleasure? Emotions (positive or negative)? Liking? Appreciation? Beauty? Curiosity? Understanding? Or something else entirely?

The discussion was lively, with many of us insisting that aesthetic responses have a complexity that makes a question like "How much did you enjoy this artwork?" seem painfully reductive. We also had a long discussion about whether aesthetic responses exist on a continuum from positive to negative, or whether they are best described on some other set of axes. In some ways we were replaying a long-standing argument about aesthetic pleasure, an argument redounding not just to the character and feel of these pleasures but to the oft-contested view that they are fundamentally distinct in kind, especially compared to those closely linked to evolutionary drives or learned goals. While some (for example, theorists like Edmund Burke and William Hogarth or psychologists like Steven Brown) have sought to normalize aesthetic pleasures, others (not just philosophers like Immanuel Kant and George Santayana but also behaviorists like Winfried Menninghaus—who is also a literary critic) have claimed that aesthetic pleasures are fundamentally distinct. In the foundational version of this case, the *Critique of Judgment,* Kant argues that beauty requires more than "mere" liking: liking emerges when we find something agreeable at the moment and for ourselves; beauty, on the other hand, emerges when we claim that what we find pleasing should be universally so.[2]

In this view, because aesthetic pleasures are "disinterested" and do not rely on the attainment of what are commonly thought of as appetitive goals (goals satisfied by quick consummation, like thirst, hunger, sex), when we judge something as beautiful, pleasure is a sign of a kind of freedom. Kant argues that it signifies the independence of the human mind from the kind of necessity (the if-then of causation, the coercive power of needs for survival, and so on) that takes precedence in the natural world. Aesthetic judgments involve pleasure at encountering the world as if it were made in accordance with human needs and likes, even though it's more like the other way around: the world is not made in accordance with our needs, but rather in accordance with laws independent of our beliefs or desires (yes, Virginia, gravity is real, but—sorry—there is no Santa Claus), and our needs develop from these laws.

However, if aesthetic pleasures occur without satisfying a particular need, that would make them nearly unique in human experience; it's not surprising that my colleagues and I argued. However, what was revealing for me was where we landed in our quest to identify a summative term for powerful aesthetic experience—and it wasn't "beauty." We fully expected diverse emotions to fall under the rubric of aesthetics; we fully expected diverse neural systems to be active across modes, including areas for reward, areas involved in positive and negative emotions, and regions associated with pleasure (e.g., dopaminergic pathways). Given that diversity, it was striking that as we discussed the extant experimental literature, it seemed that in whatever ways the central questions of a summative response were posed, respondents interpreted them similarly: across differing studies, behavioral responses are surprisingly consistent, and neural correlations resolve closely as well. For example, in one of the earliest fMRI studies of visual aesthetics, Kawabata and Zeki assumed we make a bipolar assessment of the beautiful and the ugly: however, even as understandings of the networks and evaluations involved in aesthetic assessment have evolved, the areas Kawabata and Zeki identified for positive aesthetic evaluation have been shown, repeatedly, to be substantively involved in aesthetic judgments.[3]

In our own group we ended up asking a variety of questions across different experiments, including requesting participants to give continuous responses to a range of questions, spanning from indicating "the pleasure you receive from [an] image," to identifying "how enjoyable or aesthetically appealing" they found a poem, "how aesthetically moving" they found an artwork, "how much [they] like" a piece of music, and how "powerful, pleasing, or profound" they found a work of art.[4] Even though "pleasure" can be a loaded term, especially as powerful aesthetic experience may involve negative emotions—perhaps most especially sadness—pleasure remains a key component of what it *feels* like to be moved by art.[5] In all of these differing questions, we were seeking the same phenomenon—the strength of the aesthetic attraction of an object or the power of an aesthetic experience. Over these experiments we saw similar responses (most notably, significant individual differences in which *objects* were more compelling, yet many behavioral and neural responses to objects identified as powerful were similar). Indeed, Aenne Brielmann and Denis Pelli have shown a linear relationship between pleasure and beauty, and that the highest average pleasure is necessary for the highest beauty ratings.[6] As has been observed across the field, powerful aesthetic responses, however they are admixed, solve in part to pleasure; this is true even when we are not conscious of having made an aesthetic judgment at all.[7] Still, a bit like Potter Stewart, associate justice of the United States Supreme Court, people seem to know aesthetic pleasures when they feel them.[8] What we don't know intuitively is how pleasures affect experiences of time, and how the absolute duration of an event might influence pleasures. First, let's discuss how we perceive short durations, which as I have argued are the timescales for many initial encounters with works of art.

There are two short timescales that many neuroscientists, as well as philosophers who engage with neuroscience, think are crucial to experience of the present. The first goes up to about two seconds and is measured in a variety of ways. For example, our eyes do not always move continuously. Vision is partially composed of quick sweeping motions known as saccades. As the eyes move from one part of a scene to another (or one part of a page to another), human visual systems create a discontinuous set of percepts that are generally experienced as continuous. These take about twenty milliseconds. At other times the eyes move smoothly. But even then the information received from vision to create a seamless perception is processed at varying speeds, not just in the brain but by the nerves that connect the eyes to visual cortex: the most active neurons process visual data more quickly, and that information can be slowed.[9] Some of this systematic slowing down of visual processing is cyclical and based on the physiology of neurons—how fast they can fire and how long it takes to recover and produce a new action potential. Some of it comes down to attention.[10] Think of it this way: some things catch the eye—a flash of color, movement in the trees, a zooming bicycle—and the speed of pertinent perceptions adapts to what we see so that we zoom along with the foreground and the background fades away.[11]

The fact that we sew together discrete moments in experience is not new to philosophy: David Hume made this argument in the eighteenth century, and Henri Bergson, influenced in 1911 by cinematographic technology, also argued that individuals sum discontinuous moments.[12] What is new is the ability to estimate more precisely the scale of these units of time. It appears that multiple mechanisms of time processing are at work, and a window of up to about two seconds appears to be "now." For longer periods, the "continuous [perception of conscious] flow . . . requires working memory" and spans around a rolling twelve seconds.[13] Individual differences in working memory and attentional or cognitive demands can widen or shorten this duration.[14]

Aesthetic Judgment, Pleasure, and Emotion in Present Time

Most experimental evaluations of pleasure take place over these shorter durations of a few seconds; in addition, when we come to investigate the relationships between pleasure and time we must also think about other kinds of affect, especially emotion. There are at least two routes to approaching aesthetic pleasure. One route involves understanding pleasure as a multimodal, integrated set of signals, with neurophysiological, behavioral, somatic, hedonic, and phenomenological elements. The other centers around emotion. The idea that there isn't an easy word for aesthetic pleasure, or an easy way to sum up what drives those pleasures, makes good sense in terms of much of the psychology of emotion. Definitions of emotions as complex responses range far: it is generally granted that emotional experience has somatic components (a set of canonical bodily feelings); neurological components both in the brain and the wider nervous system; a set of cognitive and action tendencies or outcomes (flight, reassessment, tears, hugs, cautious progress down a path); positive or negative valence; high or low arousal (alertness/engagement); a role in homeostasis (how we maintain steady-state processes); and semantic, social, or discursive elements, which involve how humans name our emotions, separate them from one another, and speak of, interpret, and seek to regulate our own emotions and those of others.[15] There are particular time courses attributable to each of these elements, and we have the beginnings of understanding them. What we know so far may lead us to revise the psychological models that have been useful for framing aesthetic experiences.

For many centuries of inquiry, the operative question was whether or not emotional responses to aesthetic objects like stories or paintings were truly emotions.[16] That question has been largely displaced by considerations of whether (and how) aesthetic responses might be related to a broader class of emotions, or if they belong to a unique class of emotional response. For example, in some cases the emotions a reader, viewer, or listener might experience in response to an artwork may have much of the clarity and specificity of everyday emotional experience: one might feel the elevated heart rate of suspense or fear, the gushing tears of sorrow, or the elation of joy in reading a book or discussing it with others. In this way, emotions elicited by art may be very much like other emotions.

However, there are emotional responses to art that seem more particular to an aesthetic realm, especially in that they involve particular kinds of evaluations or appraisals, and may have different relationships to pleasure than do other, garden-variety emotions. Fingerhut and Prinz identify several such emotions (e.g., interest, intrigue, amazement, wonder, awe, or admiration).[17] Work across multiple languages has also identified networks and clusters of words or emotion terms that are prominent in aesthetic life, like "horror," "melancholy," and so on.[18] In these views the puzzles surrounding emotion and aesthetics involve several layers of complexity. First, emotions evoked in aesthetic experience may have different kinds of action outcomes than do prototypical, everyday emotions (if those are the proper models): for example, most viewers don't run from a movie theater when a bomb explodes on-screen. If humans aren't preparing for action, we don't require the (sometimes long) latencies taken up with observation and assessment, nor do we need exquisite temporal precision. In addition, aesthetic emotions often involve contradictions, too, and in particular, since they often don't require action, they may be lower in arousal.[19] As high-arousal, negative-valence emotions (like frustrated waiting) can make time seem to stretch out, one might expect anticipation to slow aesthetic time—this is probably true to the experience of many of us.[20]

Given that aesthetic emotions generally do not harness the systems that consummate motor responses (with some exceptions, such as when one is dancing or performing, for example), I suspect that pleasure plays a somewhat peculiar role. Dopaminergic structures in the basal ganglia that are involved in aesthetic responses also play an important role in motor control, enabling rapid responses to salient information as part of routine, generally unconscious, self-monitoring.[21] It is not yet clear how human beings encode and process features of the environment that might require motion but on which we do not act. It is possible, however, that such *potential* for action may become particularly pleasurable, as when a viewer enjoys a film that presents terrifying content without physical consequences (e.g., horror movies). Nico Frijda and Louise Sundararajan have argued for aesthetic emotions being "refined" and subject to savoring across longer time periods, as opposed to the more discrete, sharp, and transient emotions of daily life.[22]

There are a variety of mechanisms by which this might take place; one involves attention and action. Freeing attentional resources from the demands of planning a novel or urgent action probably enables enhanced attention to bodily sensations—say tingles along the spine—or to cognitive complexity, when we might self-consciously examine our own motives for enjoyment or perhaps dwell on the ethical quandaries of pleasure. We also might simply revel in the social joys of excitement. Indeed, structures in the basal ganglia enable a trade-off between immediate motor action and an accompanying reward, in contrast with an expected reward that requires inhibiting a motor response. Such a delay allows information from frontal cortical regions concerning the value of an object or action to be integrated into motor planning.[23] It is also possible that the subjective slowdown of time as increasing amounts of salient information emerge (strong affect, increased pleasure) itself promotes savoring.

On Being Moved: Intensity, Pleasure, and Feeling

Given their complexity, aesthetic emotions may best be described by a complex rather than individual term like joy or beauty. Winfried Menninghaus and colleagues have proposed "being moved" as a prototypical complex phenomenon that could encapsulate aesthetic experience; this, they posit, is the signature contribution of emotion to powerful aesthetic experience.[24] The idea that certain situations and artwork are "moving" has a long history, stretching out to classical rhetoric, and it offers at the very least a useful portmanteau term for bringing together differing yet powerful experiences.[25] Unfortunately, the idea of a moving emotion is not readily or easily specifiable: for example, in English the etymology of the very word "emotion" involves the shared movement of a crowd of people. Menninghaus et al. start off their investigations by looking at both everyday and art-related experiences, finding that being moved may involve both joy and sadness, and that it often emerges in response to life-changing events like weddings or funerals, or to moments (say, heroism in warfare) that defy simple classification (combining, for example, victory and death). These moments generally involve dynamics over which an individual has little control (one is overcome or overpowered by circumstance); they strongly violate or validate ethical norms; and they often invoke a pro-social mindset. Scenes of injustice, for example, may move us to tears; scenes of restoration of right do so, too, with a differing valence.[26] Somewhat paradoxically, some researchers argue that these emotions are low arousal but high intensity.[27]

The mixed emotion that Menninghaus et al. describe comports well with other findings. In some of our early research on visual art, Ed Vessel, Nava Rubin, and I asked volunteers to measure the strength of their own aesthetic responses.[28] Participants described their affective experience using a seven-point scale for each of nine different terms: beauty, pleasure, joy, awe, the sublime, confusion, sadness, disgust, and fear. For highly moving artworks, these emotional and aesthetic categories resolved into two factors (using principal components analysis and rotated using the direct oblimin method). The first factor more heavily loaded on positive affects, and the second on negative ones, but both contained awe (figure 1.1a, panels A and B); both factors correlated with similar activations in key neural regions linked to reward (the left striatum) and the DMN (left anterior medial prefrontal cortex; figure 1.1a, panel C); and the two factors differentially activated other brain areas involved with emotion processing (factor one, the left inferior frontal gyrus, pars triangularis; factor two, the left substantia nigra—figure 1.1a, panel C).

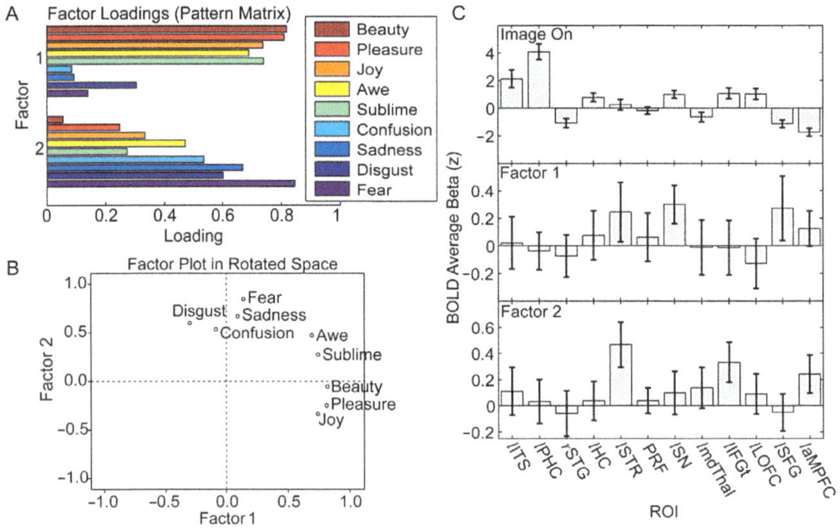

Figure 1.1

Emotion factors and associated brain regions. Reproduced from Vessel, Starr, and Rubin, "This Is Your Brain on Art," *Frontiers in Human Neuroscience* (2012).

Given this and other brain and behavioral evidence of responses to artworks, one might suspect that Menninghaus et al.'s specification of mixed-valence responses as central to aesthetics might be correct. However, the concept of being moved has challenges too.

The intensity of feeling that comes with reading a powerful novel like Toni Morrison's *Beloved*—with its harrowing depictions of slavery, infanticide, and the impossibility of human freedom from suffering—raises at least three questions in this context. First, is there an ethical problem in defining aesthetic experience by proposing a single core emotion, when it might unify art objects and life experiences that are seemingly incommensurable: the prima facie disjunction of a fiction of slavery and the reality of life as an enslaved person? Second, is there a problem in conflating genres? One might worry that this broad emotional/aesthetic category blends radically different kinds of artworks, say, Toni Morrison with John Coltrane or Jasper Johns, any of which might strike one as aesthetically powerful, yet in very different ways. Third, does privileging being moved skew the definition of aesthetic experience? It might be hard to believe that a static, abstract image that evokes powerful emotions shares a great deal with prototypical experiences of being moved like those described by Menninghaus and colleagues—say, birth or death—unless we accept that the unifying principle isn't thematic, ethical, or even an underlying admixture of sadness with joy. And as much as people describe experiences with artworks as "moving," they are also describable as "funny," "lovable," or "purely joyous." Perhaps what matters is a kind of *intensity*, a variable Menninghaus et al. find strongly correlated with being moved (more strongly so than the two most cited behavioral dimensions of emotion—valence and arousal).[29] As I will discuss shortly, intensity may have to do with an acceleration of affect over time. Part of resolving these considerations means exploring not just emotion but also the more basic effects of pleasure and displeasure.

I stated above that pleasure is an outcome; it is also not a unitary outcome. Pleasure of whatever kind allows for observation of and engagement with environments in important ways. It is straightforward to understand that pleasure can emerge when you successfully reach a goal. And many scholars of motivation have argued that pleasure doesn't only signal success; it also tends to increase as we get closer and closer to what we desire. If you imagine an archer aiming an arrow at a target, feelings of pleasure or displeasure help her both direct the angle at which she shoots as well as how much effort she puts into pulling back the string on each successive try. The further off she is in one direction, the more narrowly she adjusts her angle of approach; the further off in another, the more or less effort she uses to shoot. The highest pleasure should come when she hits the target at perfect center: without too much effort or too little, she goes straight to the heart of the bull's-eye. Pleasure thus can be a sign that we got it just right, or that we need to correct course.

Pleasures may in this way change our focus in apparently conflicting ways. They can narrow our vision to a single point of attainment; or they can broaden our reach to multiple maxima, enabling us to catch a breath and attend to more than a single set of aims. Fredrickson first described this as the ability of pleasure to enable one to "broaden and build."[30] Charles Carver goes on to argue that this works because pleasure allows us to repurpose attentional and emotional resources: "A pattern in which positive feelings lead to . . . an openness to shifting focus [may] minimize . . . adverse consequences" (e.g., being so lost in pleasure that you ignore the world around you).[31] In other words, avoidance signals also need to be overridden: pleasure helps balance both goals and anti-goals. Exploratory pleasures, in this same vein, require frequent self-checks to determine relevance for aims that may not be fully conscious (say, just walking about, looking for something interesting to do).

Temporal effects are important: pleasure that, in consummation, focuses attention should lead to a slowing down of external events because these pleasures are frequently involved with changes in the environment (hitting the target, for example). As described above, Craig argues that multiple, salient events in a small timeframe leads to a perceived slowing of time, as the "buffer" used to process information becomes overwhelmed and the internal speed of processing doesn't match the speed of external events. Under these conditions, there is a mismatch of scale when one attempts to integrate interoception (monitoring of one's bodily state) with exteroception (monitoring of external information presented to perception). Crucially, this mismatch alters temporal perception because humans measure time by the frequency of events, and there is a maximum frequency beyond which it is as if time does a stutter step:

> Recent functional connectivity analyses indicate that the mid-insula is also modulated directly by the ventral striatum (the nucleus accumbens), which provides an important incentive, or hedonic, signal for the integration of salience. Thus, this posterior to anterior progression—which is consistent with the general processing gradient for increasing complexity in the frontal cortex and with the enormous expansion of the anterior insula across hominoid primates—provides a substrate for the sequential integration of homeostatic conditions with the sensory environment and with motivational, hedonic and social conditions represented in other parts of the brain, and this substrate is constructed on the foundation provided by the feelings from the body.[32]

Importantly, both positive and negative affect involve a comparison between current circumstances and a reference value (usually understood as the goal). If the current circumstances don't match the reference value ("I hit it dead on!"), the brain computes an error signal ("Whoops, I missed!"); this signal could be positive or negative, and it may indicate the need to reduce the error signal or increase it. This second option—increasing one's distance from the reference value—is important because one may want to avoid, not obtain, an expected outcome. Imagine my ace archer once again. Missing center leads to an error signal that could push her to aim closer to the bull's-eye. However, she might not want to hit the target at all (maybe she's throwing the match!), and an error signal points toward the need to enlarge the distance between her arrow and the center of the target. In other words, there are both goals and anti-goals in the world, as well as goals that compete, or join together in an additive way. The end result is homeostatic balance, an evening out of extremes: our "system is organized in such a way that it 'wants' to seek neither negative nor positive affect. Either quality . . . would represent an 'error' and lead to a change in output that would eventually reduce it. . . . People who exceed the expected criterion rate of progress (and thus have positive feelings) will automatically tend to reduce subsequent effort. . . . They will coast a little—ease back."[33] Again in this case, exceeding a criterion rate can make time seem to slow down.

The picture of pleasure becomes more complex if one considers aiming at multiple goals at once—you want to hit all the targets you confront with effort that is just right, and adding subsidiary goals and pleasures may mean reprioritization.[34] For example, my mother often reminds me that you can't win at everything: succeeding at a greater goal can sometimes mean losing a little on something else. So, you might save strength for the bigger battle; be gracious about losing if your reputation or the rules of play are more important than winning; step out of the limelight to let a friend shine; or give up a pleasure that's solely for yourself so that someone else gets something they always wanted. Thus, pleasures may lead us to approach or back away from goals both actively and passively.

There is a difference, of course, between an error signal computed by feedback between brain regions and a *feeling* of pleasure. One way of understanding how feeling arises is by first noting the importance of context in goal seeking (my archer, again!). The magnitude of the error signal or even its direction may be less important than its rate of change. How quickly are you getting closer to or away from the target? Charles Carver and Michael Scheier contend that this *actual* rate of change is compared to an *expected* rate, which is "the acceptable . . . rate of behavioral discrepancy reduction. . . . [The] error signal in this loop is manifest subjectively as affect, whether positive or negative."[35] In this view, feeling—the subjective sensations that go along with affect and emotion—emerges along with the velocity of change in the error signal: time and direction work together. When you feel pleasure, what registers is a (negative) difference between how you felt *before* and how you feel *now*, and the steeper the difference the more intense the feeling.[36] In this calculus, we predict or anticipate either homeostatic constancy or a rate of change that matches past experience. But with intense pleasures, the sudden and steep nature of the change is what matters. If we're integrating multiple goals, achieving them in a brief time span could make a for a steeper, faster shift in pleasure; or a mismatch in goals might deflate the signal and reduce or remove pleasure from awareness. If my archer, for example, had previously missed repeatedly, a steeper pleasure curve might ensue; if hitting the bull's-eye is her norm, she probably feels flatter affect as the rate of change is steadier and the comparison value is closer to the outcome. Now, let's leave the archer behind and focus on aesthetic pleasures.

Goal Time and Aesthetic Time

If the rate of change is what makes us consciously aware of affect, what I call "goal time" is very important to aesthetic time. Goal time is the varying *subjective perception* of the passage of time as we posit, work for, or adjust our tactics, and succeed or fail at reaching our goals. For aesthetics, at a very simple level (following Prinz and others) we don't know an aesthetic judgment until we feel it, and this implies a variety of corollaries. First, the temporal dimension of pleasure might help us understand a bit better the finding I discussed in the introduction, whereby the perceived tempo of birdsong was influenced by experiencing pleasure—a learned, subjective modification of temporal perception.[37] Pleasure influences pattern extraction, one of the key elements of human cognitive capacity, by enhancing the detection of elements as relevant to or fitting within a predictable sequence. The rate of change of pleasure may influence conscious awareness, but in this case a threshold of pleasure influences perception of time, and this regulation is *below* conscious awareness. If perception of pleasure and perception of time are thus interrelated, hitting a pleasure threshold would set a temporal regulator. Exceeding the expected pleasure would lead to a change of conscious state, which would have the potential to change how we manage chunks of information that signal the flow of time. Put another way, pleasure sets a metronome. Changes in the external world that violate that metronome have hedonic implications. In turn, changes in pleasure can reset our metronome by altering the patterns that allow us to regulate how we extract a temporal signature from data.

If this view is correct, in music, for example, pleasure functions as a link between what are commonly understood to be top-down and bottom-up elements of listening. One of the most visible ways in which this could be measured is via the phenomena of entrainment, which stretch from the level of neural patterning to gross motor activity, and even group communication and action.[38] Entrainment facilitates a kind of learning. At a basic level, synchronization with a rhythm establishes what Mari Riess Jones has called a "referent time level."[39] Being able to keep a beat in this way is pleasurable and can be linked to two additional pleasures: the pleasures both of social interaction (being in time with others brings the reinforcement of community) and of satisfactory prediction. Keeping the beat is one thing; staying with it is another. From a behavioral standpoint, pleasure enhances our ability to follow the beat of others. From a neural standpoint, pleasure designates or directs a basic temporal window—the unit we use to establish a pattern—and regulates the firing of neurons that match temporal pattern extraction.[40]

This kind of interaction between pleasure and time is probably not be unique to audition. As I have discussed, reward probability can extend the subjective duration of a visual perception, effectively helping target individuals' actions to obtain a goal and enabling us to make resources readily available.[41] When subjective time "slows down" awareness of discrete separate moments in the external environment, it allows us to free resources to accelerate or integrate necessary calculations.[42] In fact, neuroscientists often talk about two key ways of understanding measurements of time: the subjectively perceived duration of an event (e.g., "How long did he take to walk from the car to the store?"), and the speed of one's experience of time during an event ("Wow, this day went really fast"). While what is often measured in laboratories are very short durations, in everyday experience these scales can be brief or can track to months or even years, and we usually make judgments about their duration that are retrospective or anticipatory. The amount and kind of information we must digest in any of these situations may change one's judgments of how fast time seems to run: "A higher information-processing load [makes] retrospective elements longer, but . . . prospective ones shorter. In contrast, passage of time judgments . . . are not affected by [whether or not the judgment is prospective or retrospective], but [are] significantly faster [with greater] . . . [information-processing] requirements."[43] This suggests multiple mechanisms across different timescales.

For aesthetics, Tuomas Eerola and colleagues posit different ways in which short, medium, or long durations mark a shift in emotion and pleasure that changes how we experience aesthetic objects. They call it "hedonic shift," and it comes down to how pleasures adjust to meet changing demands and contexts. They use this concept to reconcile the kind of concerns I raised around Morrison's *Beloved*. In their view, felt sadness interacts with individuals' multiple feelings and goals to produce positive aesthetic experiences. They generally describe a positive shift in affect as emerging from "cultural context," which interacts with goals to alter hedonic tone. For example: "Listening to sad music seems to fulfill the criteria for mood regulation. . . . [It s]eems to provide a sort of social connection, a *social surrogacy*, where the listeners enjoy the mere presence of a virtual person represented by the music."[44] Taken altogether, "sad music seems to be associated with different goals of mood regulation. . . . [Varying] mood regulation strategies describe a clear hedonic shift from negative to positive."[45] Eerola and colleagues argue that a hedonic shift integrates over three scales of intensity. One is biological, of weakest intensity, and happens most quickly. They call the second level "psycho-social" (e.g., sympathy); it involves longer timescales and greater shifts in positivity. At the most expansive level, cultural norms—like valorizing self-sacrifice—can make sorrowful events take on flavors of honor, or rules of genre help something like dramatic catharsis occur. In this model the starting point (the degree of negative affect) combines with conditions (set by social occasion or cultural norms) to determine the magnitude of a change of intensity and its direction. Pain thus may be turned into comfort.

Let's translate this to Morrison's novel. *Beloved* is the story of Sethe, a formerly enslaved woman who has murdered her infant, a daughter who is barely walking, rather than see her live in bondage. Sethe and her surviving children are haunted by this act: Was it mercy? Was it sin? Can there be forgiveness? None of these questions is pretty. None is morally simple. Each can bring pain, sadness, fear, or anger so deep it could leave you breathless: "Stamp looked into Paul D's eyes and the sweet conviction in them almost made him wonder if it happened at all, eighteen years ago, that while he and Baby Suggs were looking the wrong way, a pretty little slavegirl had recognized a hat, and split to the woodshed to kill her children."[46] I've never found any kind of catharsis in reading this tragedy. But I won't forget *Beloved*, and I feel with all my being its power as art.

In the Eerola framework the acuteness of this pain might be overcome or eased over time. I am more inclined to believe that I shift goals—to learning something (understanding the depths of pain humans can plumb and still survive) rather than loving it. I might find love in the idea of survival, in the sense that we can overcome. Still, the pain is there, too, and I don't love humanity the more for it. Indeed, the final lines of the book are comfortless for me, as I think they should be: "The rest is weather. Not the breath of the disremembered and unaccounted for, but wind in the eaves, or spring ice thawing too quickly. Just weather. Certainly no clamor for a kiss."[47] In this grave context, I'm not sure the idea of hedonic shift quite meets the mark.

It is not that I ever feel better about Morrison's depiction of infanticide, or that I ever leave the fear, disgust, and heartache behind. I do not reclassify the particular circumstances of this novel as good or even neutral. I don't reclassify infanticide in general as bearing more than poison as fruit. It is not even that I experience what eighteenth-century British philosopher Edmund Burke called "delight"—a relief that comes with the removal of pain.[48] As a reader, I arrive at the deepest horror, the opening in the tunnel to which the book has been guiding us inexorably, when men come to take Sethe and her children back into slavery. It is a fiction, yes, but its power comes not by the specific, imagined details particular to Morrison's characters and her story. The schoolteacher muses that one has to stand back when apprehending a fugitive slave:

> sometimes, you could never tell, you'd find them folded up tight somewhere: beneath floorboards—in a pantry, once in a chimney. Even then care was taken, because the quietest ones, the ones you pulled from a press, a hayloft, or, that once from a chimney, would go along nicely for two or three seconds. Caught red handed, so to speak, they would seem to recognize the futility of outsmarting a white-man and the hopelessness about running a rifle. Smile even, like a child caught dead with his hand in the jelly jar, and when you reached for the rope to tie him, well, even then you couldn't tell. The very nigger with his head hanging and a little jelly-jar smile on his face could all of a sudden roar, like a bull or some such, and commence to do dis-believable things. Grab the rifle at its mouth; throw himself at the one holding it—anything. So you had to keep back a pace, leave the tying to another period otherwise you ended up killing what you were paid to bring back alive. Unlike a snake or a bear, a dead nigger could not be skinned for profit and was not worth his own deadweight in coin.[49]

The passive voice here ("care was taken") points toward the numbers of human souls returned to bondage—nameless chattel no less real for their lack of name, the particularity of individual reference. The words are not in this sense fictional. So if I am to cry at this moment, it is not that I would have wasted my tears. And the fact that this is a fiction doesn't make the use of the N-word less grotesque or foul. My ability to move past anger, tears, and disgust, or to mix them with something else, comes from elsewhere: not because this is "merely" an imaginary undertaking, nor that I myself and my children are somehow "safe." There is irony here, when Morrison uses free indirect discourse (matter-of-factly narrating thoughts as if they were no more grotesque than scenery) to mock the slaveholder's idea that there's no use trying to outwit a white man. I don't think this is ironic distance. What I find, what I feel, what I respond to is the evidence of survival. What burns in my heart is recognizing the power it gives Morrison to be able to write this story, with its dread words and vicious sin. Her ancestors outlived them all. Her words are proof of valor. My heart sings to read it, to hear it, to see it. What I recognize is the power of craft. Horror becomes an artifact, a creation of human hands, not the perpetration of human depravity, and no longer only destruction. There is a cost to be paid when we face horror. Morrison has paid it, and I reap her strength.

In this case, I would argue that instead of the tempo of reading being set by pleasure, it is set by fear. Readers know what is coming. The novel has already told us that. What remains to be seen—if we can stand the looking—are the final, obscene moments. The mother's hands, ready to strike. The baby drinking in spattered blood with her milk. Thus, as Morrison drives her narrative forward, every word and every moment in this passage stretches out, drawn tight with the dreadful anticipation of Sethe's attack on her children. The metronome is set. Yet, over this temporal signature (watchful, tense waiting), Morrison weaves another. If you are going to get through this story—if you are going to keep reading—it is because you recognize that horror isn't the ending point. The story—the book—is only half over. And so by the final pages, what we confront is a different drumbeat; it is almost a lullaby, yet it has a haunting refrain, "It was not a story to pass on":

> Everybody knew what she was called, but no-body anywhere knew her name. Disremembered and unaccounted for, she cannot be lost because no one is looking for her, and even if they were, how can they call her if they don't know her name. Although she has claim, she is not claimed. In the place where long grass opens, the girl who waited to be loved and cry shame erupts into her separate parts, to make it easy for the chewing laughter to swallow her all away.

> It was not a story to pass on.
>
> They forgot her like a bad dream. . . .
>
> It was not a story to pass on.
>
> So they forgot her. Like an unpleasant dream during a troubling sleep. . . .
>
> This is not a story to pass on.
>
> . . .
>
> By and by all trace is gone, and what is forgotten is not only the footprints but the water too and what it is down there. The rest is weather. Not the breath of the disremembered and unaccounted for, but wind in the eaves, or spring ice thawing too quickly. Just weather. Certainly no clamor for a kiss.[50]

The idea of hedonic shift, then, doesn't get at the heart of the fabric of time Morrison weaves for her reader, where past and present, destruction and creation, coexist. And I don't think it fully gets at the heart of the kind of problems that the portmanteau phrase "being moved" poses for aesthetic thought and for a book like *Beloved*: the ethical quandaries that come with the sense of unmitigated evil I feel in my bones in reading, nor with juxtaposing the kind of situations that Menninghaus et al. argue elicit feelings of being strongly moved. While one might confirm experientially that a novel can move one to tears, it can still be worrisome that these feelings may be all too close to the kinds of responses we have to real historical atrocities (the Holocaust is one of the examples Menninghaus et al. adduce).[51] The proximity of real tragedy to fictive or artistic representation is not newly observed. Accounts of the sublime, from Longinus (the first century CE) to Edmund Burke, Immanuel Kant, Voltaire, and others (the eighteenth century), point out the same disturbing consideration. The traditional response is to argue that extreme experiences—destruction, massacre, disaster—may be encountered aesthetically from the standpoint of a viewer's own distance or safety.[52] The idea is that what would overcome us in reality may stir ethical analysis and lead to an assertion of our humanity once we have room for contemplation, rather than just being transfixed by the immediate swell of fear or loathing. Indeed, while it is hard to deny that such a phenomenon exists, it remains hard to accept its ethical permissibility, far less the idea that these moments give us a sign of the simultaneous physical weakness yet moral and rational strength of humanity: we can understand even what could destroy us.[53] While we may be transfixed by scenes of destruction, or the wreckage of humanity (I cannot *understand* slavery in any way that exceeds bare facts and figures), it is hard to imagine that in the milliseconds in which we begin to feel such emotion, we have adequately assessed our own circumstances to reach such profound ethical conclusions.

Part of the answer to this conundrum has to do with the multiple temporal scales over which we sum experience, how we learn, and what the scale of our need to respond must be. Art did not appear until relatively late in human history: the earliest musical instruments, for example, date back approximately sixty-seven thousand years, and visual representations to around forty-five thousand years ago, while humans appear nearly three hundred thousand years ago.[54] In this timeline, it would be quite surprising if evolution had produced separate, distinct emotional systems for responses to art, especially given that art forms emerge at a very rapid pace in comparison to species time. For example, if instruments emerged more than sixty thousand years ago, think about how quickly music changes: baroque music is four hundred years old and opera is a little bit older, while bluegrass, jazz, or rap are relative infants.

It is thus that artworks use ancient human physiology to create effects in the here and now.[55] The chills are an excellent example from both poetry and music (the phenomenon with music has been studied more thoroughly so far). There are various conscious and unconscious physiological mechanisms and phenomena that accompany the chills as a form of peak aesthetic pleasure. These peaks involve a buildup of arousal and tension; the resolution is the shudder, goosebumps, and prickly hairs we think of as the chills themselves. I discuss this phenomenon further later, but here I want to note that piloerection—when hairs stand up on the skin—is phylogenetically old. Goosebumps are a vestigial mammalian response that serves in other, more hirsute animals to insulate an organism against other autonomic nervous responses that could depress body temperature (dilation of blood vessels, for example).

The ancient nature of the chills in fact suggests that aesthetic responses are not a spandrel of evolution, a leftover piece of something once useful, or a piece of cheesecake humans opportunistically created to top off a meal.[56] If artworks engage long-formed physiology of reward and emotion networks, it is because those networks respond to goals that are universal across human populations. Many of these goals involve pro-sociality; I will explore part of the range of the pro-social aims that art may serve shortly, but let me lay out how this begins to unpack the dilemma of being moved by what might seem insignificant—an artwork—in comparison with what ethically signifies above all else, like human life. Pro-social goals also have implications for the timescales of aesthetic processes.

The first consideration involves computational complexity. As Philip Johnson-Laird and Keith Oatley argue, "almost all problems that fall within the purview of logic, probability, or decision theory are computationally intractable"; emotions can serve as a shortcut. Indeed, "many situations trigger emotions that direct attention, coordinate plans, prepare appropriate behaviors, and signal to communities."[57] The fact that those emotions appear in an aesthetic frame points out that we aren't evolved to distinguish clearly or easily between what is fiction and what isn't.[58] If emotions facilitate fast cognition, being moved by difficult and painful representations may clarify what violates ethical standards and what doesn't. However, ethical reckoning should follow perceptual or emotional dissonance, requiring that we examine the reason for our tears, our sense of being called to watch even what pains us, or our willingness to return to painful narratives that may help differentiate right from wrong.[59]

Feelings and emotions themselves are alerts: they signal a rapid change in experience, a problem, or a challenge to the way we perceive the world. But to meet these challenges, we need more than emotion. When, as with *Beloved*, a pro-social frame accompanies or initiates the feeling of being moved—in the sense that it places our focus on what brings us together or separates us as humans—then "being moved" might dispose us not just to feel but to talk. Feeling moved opens us to something else—the social uses of art I adumbrated in the introduction, and the calls to community circulation and community evaluation that are at the heart of humanist discourses. More simply, perhaps, pleasure can be a proxy that amplifies the need for analyses, without resolving conflicts between them.

It's thus not a simple correspondence with danger or safety that makes the contradictions of aesthetic and ethical life significant. Individuals confront a risk or a reward where the baseline of expected return is not clear. In other words, a swift access of pleasure in an aesthetic context employs the structure of pleasure that underpins human motivation, but with a twist. The so-called common currency of pleasure may become unmoored from the system of value it usually requires—the baseline representation, the expected value of right or wrong, the apparent success or failure—to point toward something new.[60] Pleasure speeds up time in this way, and we sit up and take notice. Our archer has put down her bow and is playing new music; as she hears a complex and changing beat, she finds that her newly intense pleasure makes time fly faster than her arrows. I read *Beloved* and weep, but the speed of my emotions challenges and even changes my internal landscape of value.

Pleasure in Time

Aesthetic pleasure takes a variety of shapes, each of which is context dependent. However, as Fingerhut and Prinz argue:

> There are . . . forms of pleasure that go beyond mere form and track content. Formal beauty can be assessed in abstract and representational art, but representations bring in something else: one can assess whether a given representation looks like a good exemplar of its kind. Depending on the kind in question, different forms of pleasure may result. A well rendered bowl of fruit may look delicious, a lavish interior may look inviting, and an attractive person might look enticing.[61]

While one person might separate these pleasures categorically or intellectually, however, it is not clear that they are fully differentiable in terms of brain activity or other physiological responses. This points to a crucial consideration in an expanded understanding of aesthetics. Pleasure, once again, is an outcome; it is most likely summative, and summative of numerous goals, numerous types of pleasures, and numerous kinds of signals (success, avoiding failure, intensity). I take it as fundamental that pleasure works to orient human beings, pointing us toward key elements of objects or our experiences of them: compositional elements of the objects, a sense of social belonging, individual outpourings of strength, and so on. However, it is now increasingly possible to propose differential models of aesthetic response that understand the orienting effects of pleasure differently based on the genres with which one engages. As an example, let's take visual pleasure and its time course in experimental conditions.

Colleagues and I have shown that even over brief time periods, the *use* of time means something very different, depending on whether an individual is powerfully moved by a work of visual art or not. We presented twenty-five volunteers with images of artworks for one, five, or fifteen seconds, followed by a fourteen-second period of contemplation. All images were seen once by each participant, to enable us to capture initial responses. We also obtained a summative rating on a sliding scale of total pleasure in looking.[62] As other studies have demonstrated, initial ratings of beauty or pleasure can happen very quickly, even within a single second.[63]

We learned something key about pleasure. First, grouping low (red), medium (blue), and high (green) responses together (normalized for each individual, as we assumed that individuals would have their own scales of strength of response), we found that increased time spent with a preferred painting increased the peak pleasure viewers enjoyed, and the overall shape of the curves suggests that, given the long tail, pleasure continues after an image has disappeared, and it only slowly decays.[64] If we think that the steep curve of felt pleasure carries with it spikes of salient information, once again the rate of change matters. The decline from the peak is greatest for the highest pleasure and longest exposure to a work of art, as shown in figure 1.2. Based on Craig's theory, this makes sense for the highest pleasure because it accompanies a spike of salient information. The decline from peak is greatest in the longest exposure for the highest pleasure, and lower

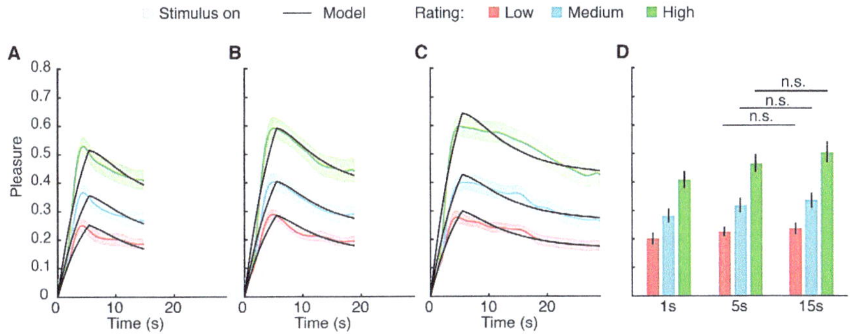

Figure 1.2

Continuous pleasure responses. (A–C) Average pleasure over time for high (green), medium (blue), and low (red) rated trials; colored shaded areas represent ±1 standard error of the mean (SEM). Black lines represent model fits. Gray-shaded areas represent time windows during which the stimulus was present. Each panel shows data for one duration: 1s (a), 5s (b), and 15s (c). (D) Average pleasure amplitude r_{steady} per condition. Error bars represent ±1 SEM. All differences between ratings or durations are at least marginally significant, $p < 0.066$, unless otherwise indicated. Adapted from Belfi et al., "Dynamics of Aesthetic Experience Are Reflected in the Default-Mode Network," *NeuroImage* (2019).

for the least. We would expect that for the longest time period, attention to an external object would lag, and the subjective experience of duration would be longer. In this sense pleasure from looking has a typical time course, reaching a high relatively quickly and giving prolonged pleasure. The fast peak suggests, in line with Carver and Scheier's view, that the rate of change of affect is what matters to conscious awareness. More than this, based on Craig's theory that peak amplitude should be compared to a slowing of felt duration, the slow decay of pleasure might make time speed up.

Intriguingly, while in laboratory experiments individuals report that the course of pleasure is relatively similar across durations of viewing, there is a divergent time course, in neurological terms, for both reward and DMN regions. For images that gave little pleasure, the disappearance of the image led to a rebound of activity in the basal ganglia, perhaps a reward signal akin to relief ("Great, that's gone"). This is apparent in the caudate, for example, at all viewing times (figure 1.3).

For five- and ten-second views, the caudate also shows at least one significant peak with pleasurable experiences. Significantly, it is not easy to fit neural activity (figure 1.3) to the behavioral curve (figure 1.2), whether in reward regions or anywhere else, suggesting that the scales of measurement (perhaps driven by rate of change) differ in the biological patterns underlying them.

The DMN findings are significant. First, note that continuous self-monitoring—the inspection of one's own pleasure—is not driving the differing responses between experiences giving low and high levels of pleasure. If that were the case, we would have found similar DMN activation in all trials. Moreover, while we ratified earlier findings about the DMN and intense aesthetic experience, we also learned something new: after initially and predictably dipping below baseline, for viewers who took little pleasure in an image there was a *later* rebound in DMN activity.

In interpreting this neural response, my colleagues and I argued that viewers disengaged from an image and began to think of other things—for example, the mind-wandering and kinds of spontaneous thought the DMN generally supports. Measuring from the start of viewing, we saw that powerfully moving images were interpretable using networks designed to integrate information that is self-relevant. However, when measuring from the opposite end—from the close of a visual encounter—we noted that viewers appeared to disengage over varied times and faster from art for which they have little taste. They returned to an inner world that seems, perhaps, more interesting than what they see outside of it.

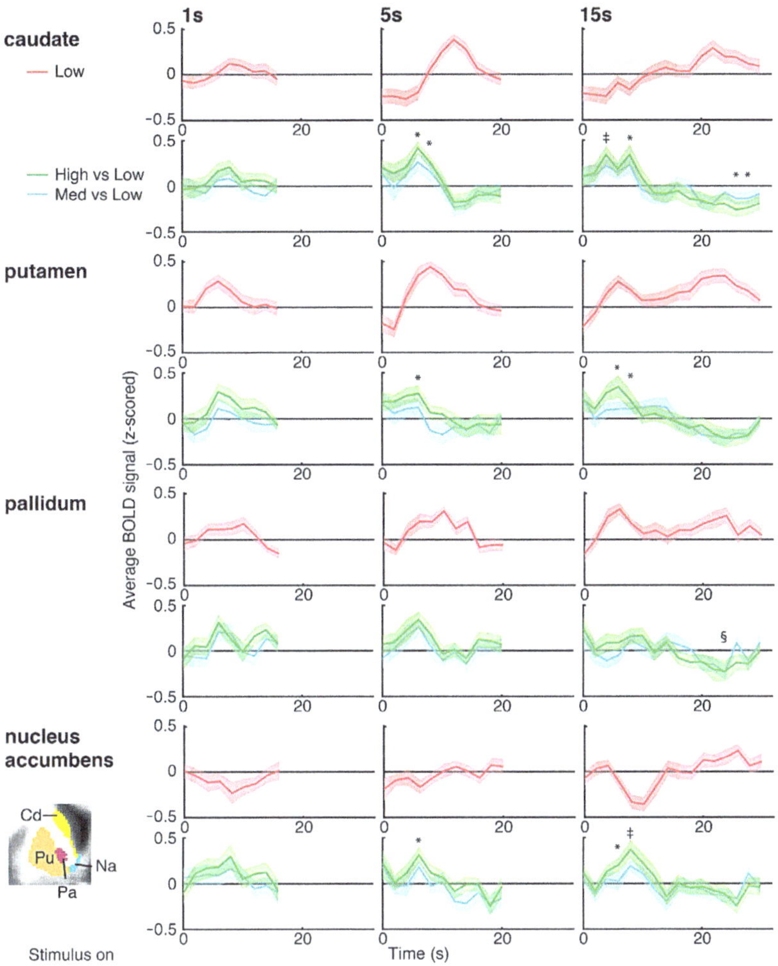

Figure 1.3
Differential sensitivity of basal-ganglia subregions to aesthetic appreciation. For each brain region shown in the inset at left, the first row illustrates the response to trials individuals rated as low (red), and the second row illustrates the *difference* between responses to high vs. low (green) and medium vs. low (blue) trials. Gray shading indicates image presentation (duration of 1s, 5s, or 15s). Anatomical regions of interest were created from an automatic volumetric segmentation of individual participants' high-resolution T1 scans (FreeSurfer aseg). Color-shaded areas indicate ±1 standard errors of the mean. *Indicates significant differences between high and low trials. †Indicates significant differences between high trials vs. medium and low trials. ‡Indicates significant differences between low vs. high and medium trials. §Indicates significant differences between low and medium trials. Adapted from Belfi et al., "Dynamics of Aesthetic Experience Are Reflected in the Default-Mode Network," *NeuroImage* (2019).

As I wrote above, the kind and amount of salient information looks different within the framework of pleasure, and in turn this should influence how time speeds up or drags on with individual perception. In this context salience is goal dependent. For example, discordant sounds should fill the buffer quickly, drawing on the idea that they signal potentially actionable events, like the need for fast movement in response to a sound that appears out of place. Anticipating salient events like rhythmic beats or other expected elements of an artwork could slow down subjective time (and might make reaction times slower; all of these possibilities can be tested experimentally). In the final chapter, I will elaborate on how goal salience affects aesthetic time.

Very little has been written to date about how aesthetic responses may change the perception of time. We have seen that pleasure can affect pattern extraction and thus change the experience of rhythm in the birdsong experiment cited previously. In general, high-arousal conditions tend to make time appear to speed up. As I've discussed, the theory advanced by Craig is something like this: the anterior insula keeps track of salient information and has a fixed amount of information it can hold in "memory"—like the buffer on a computer. If that information window is fixed and generally correlates to the experience of "now," the faster it fills with salient information, the more time seems to pass, and the more slowly we experience it. For any quantum of time, high-arousal moments deliver more salient information. However, as I have shown, aesthetic responses tend to bias toward lower-arousal states. This might imply that we should not expect alterations in the perception of time during aesthetic experience, yet many of us have felt that time seems to speed up or slow down in both powerful and weak aesthetic circumstances.

Understanding this discrepancy is important. Regardless of whether or not we are experiencing higher arousal, what is salient in aesthetic terms generally doesn't demand high-stakes physical movements, whether evasion or approach, and this points toward a key to how aesthetic time unfolds. The features of the world (or our ideas or imaginings) that matter aesthetically require complex cognitive assessments, many of which can only happen retrospectively, as we remember experiences and dwell on them; those that happen in the now may be triggered by confusion, not curiosity. In effect, I propose that the speed of information processing should be regulated by the goals that come to govern aesthetics. In the next chapter, I will describe how pleasure might direct these processes and thus influence the unfolding of aesthetic experience.

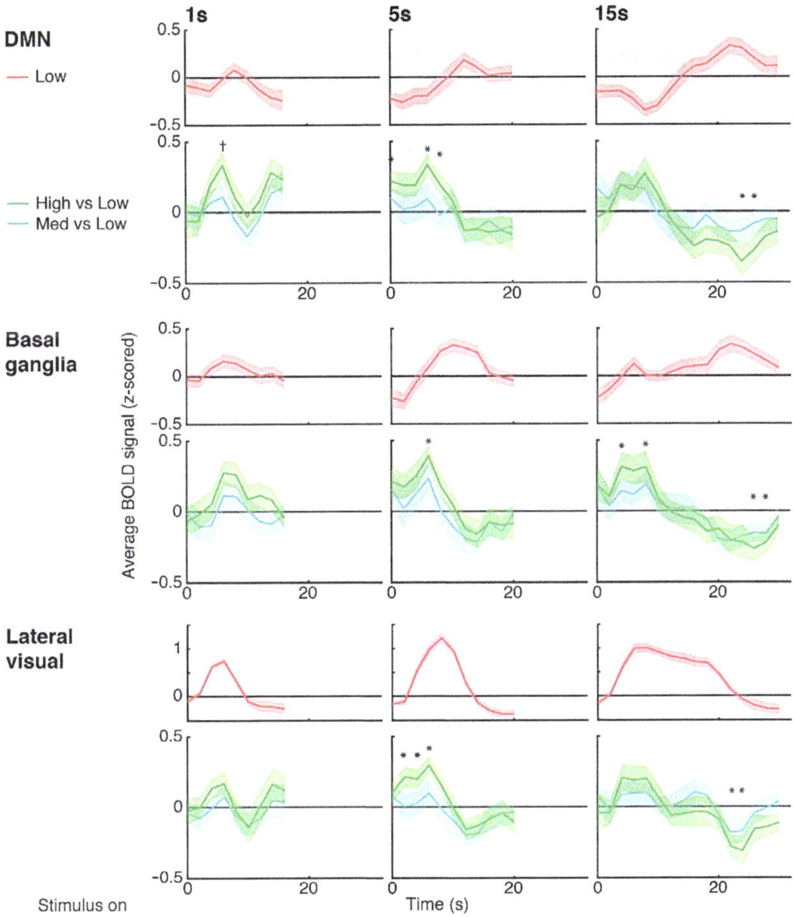

Figure 1.4

Effects of aesthetic appreciation in large-scale brain networks. Trial-triggered average blood oxygen level dependent (BOLD) signal extracted from three large-scale brain networks: The DMN, the basal ganglia, and a lateral visual network (consisting of lateral occipitotemporal, ventral occipitotemporal, and parietal visual regions). For each network, the first row illustrates the response to low-rated trials (red), and the second row illustrates the *difference* between responses to high vs. low (green) and medium vs. low (blue) trials. Gray shading indicates image presentation (duration of 1s, 5s, or 15s). The DMN and lateral visual networks were identified by correlating individual-participant independent component analysis (ICA) maps derived from a rest scan with network maps in Smith et al., "Correspondence of the Brain's Functional Architecture During Activation and Rest," *PNAS* (2009). Color-shaded areas indicate ±1 SEM. *Indicates significant differences between high and low trials. †Indicates significant differences between high trials vs. medium and low trials. Adapted from Belfi et al., "Dynamics of Aesthetic Experience Are Reflected in the Default-Mode Network," *Neuroimage* (2019).

2 Goals, Genres, and Orders

Aesthetic pleasures orient individuals to the world in a variety of ways, some of which are genre specific. Take music: it can be socially orienting, calling listeners to shared action or emotion (a funeral dirge, say, or a national anthem or protest song). One way this occurs is through entrainment, whereby groups of people synchronize their actions with one another. We also may use the exhilaration of music as a "prosthesis" whereby we can achieve more with its inspiration than we might on our own.[1] Music may help us feel stronger, faster, more competent or capable ("Chariots of Fire," anyone?). Music may also help shift attention to screen out elements of the world we can't control or don't wish to engage—to aid concentration, for example, or to close out sounds that are unpleasant or that we wish to ignore. However, aesthetic pleasure across the arts can orient attention by establishing a baseline positive affect that seems to put the world in one's control. It also points toward features, some new, some expected, that create orderly fictions or useful heuristics—like Tartt's, or Kant's—indicating that this world is made for our perception. Pleasure and displeasure order artworks, too, enabling viewers to find meaningful patterns. The variety of these pleasures is an outcome of the ways that humans learn. This chapter opens with the general case for aesthetics as an important factor in how humans extract meaning from the world, and moves on to describe how pleasure orders works of art too.

Aesthetic Artifacts and Learning

Pleasure as a motivator is part of the backbone of the accumulation of experience, enabling us to test views about the world and to understand—by feeling—when our predictions are verified. In theory, pleasures governed by evolutionary demands are relatively uniform and require little room for experiential learning, while differential experience generates differential pleasures, like those one might take in sonnets or sonatas. Indeed, a range of behavioral experiments has shown that we may usefully differentiate kinds of art by measuring how much people agree in the amount of pleasure they take in engaging with them. Individuals agree most about the pleasures of human faces and landscapes, followed by architecture, painting, and then poetry.[2] The lens of motivation can illuminate this phenomenon. Primary reinforcers such as food are unlearned, act relatively uniformly across individuals, and theoretically drive high degrees of shared pleasure in natural objects. When, however, we talk about the difference between artifacts and nature, and chalk up the individual variations in pleasure to experience, we are discussing not only primary motivations but secondary reinforcers and learned outcomes. Indeed, even the basic evolutionary drives that help shape pleasures in landscapes (e.g., safety, fertility) or faces (e.g., inside/outside groups, health) involve individual variations, and these are components of learning. On an elevated level, the contribution of experience might be understood by thinking about, say, learning to appreciate the complexity of late novels by Henry James like *The Golden Bowl* (as opposed to the relative simplicity of earlier works like *The Turn of the Screw*).

What if humans' ability to survive and adapt comes because we can learn so many pleasures? We are primed to explore the world, whether it is a world constituted by landscapes, people, or other animals. As humans navigate the world around us, encountering too many punishments would depress our exploratory impulses. Indeed, we often excel when we can work beyond our dictated environment, exploiting what we have learned to make room for discovery. Our potential for success increases as we learn new ways to satisfy our needs. Pleasure shows the way. Unexpected pleasures, those which go outside prior experience, are so important to exploration and learning that they are generally more powerful than those we expect, lighting up objects, people, places, and events for notice and reinforcement. Beyond these high-profile, unexpected pleasures, variations in pleasure (even in primary motivators) are useful to the human knowledge economy, because they help us learn new strategies for attaining what we need or want, as well as identifying new goals. Differences in pleasure even point out differences in the goals we understand ourselves to satisfy. For example, a distinctive cast to the everyday pleasures of socialization may be the first signal of sexual attraction . . . or so many Jane Austen novels have taught me. As goals multiply, ways of satisfying them do, too, and it is thus that aesthetic joys may open new gateways that can help human beings thrive.

Before I show how this might work, let's take a rather unorthodox contrast. Compared to the three-hundred-thousand-year history of *Homo sapiens*, the horseshoe crab has survived largely unchanged for more than three hundred million years. The crab, *limulus polyphemus*, remains morphologically similar over these millennia, and neurologically similar too. Neurons enervate their eyes and run along the spines in their shells, enabling them to move and adapt to changes in conditions around them, like light, temperature, availability of nutrients, and so on.[3] These responses are relatively automatic; their conservation across millennia and around the world relies on a high degree of shared genetic coding. A well-defined range of potential error (and a corresponding range of rewarding outcomes) enables these animals to be efficient at survival, and it appears they haven't needed a tune-up for a long time.[4] By contrast, humans and our primate ancestors have inhabited evolutionary windows dwarfed by that of the horseshoe crab. Ardipthecus for example (our earliest-known primate relatives), flourished around four and a half to five and a half million years ago. Humans shift our survival parameters a lot—by migration, for example—so we must master or mitigate a broad range of circumstances within a single lifetime. The wide range of problems to which humans can adapt suggests that we should have access to an *excess* of novel pleasures as rewards for learning. An excess of potential pleasures means that learning can be open-ended: we do not learn only what can fit snugly into a box.

One theory of the origin of aesthetics is that humans began to develop the arts as we escaped many of the evolutionary pressures that made the basic struggles for survival so exigent.[5] Perhaps, as well, the explosion in cortical folding that shortly predated the emergence of *homo sapiens* gave rise to new abilities around introspection, and in turn sparked artistic creativity.[6] There may be another explanation, however. To put it slightly differently, humans are distinguished (alongside a few other organisms) for our capacity to learn novel patterns; that is, our systems for motivation enable us to find new paths of discovery and even change the world in which we live, altering some of the evolutionary constraints that marked our most recent origins (through, say, medication, improvements in shelter, or feats of engineering). Reasoning inferentially, given that we learn through motivational systems and that aesthetic pleasures are poorly conserved across humans, perhaps those pleasures are the sine qua non of human learning: *variance in our pleasures implies variance in our goals*. As we multiply goals and find different ways to satisfy them, it is possible that we do so because our wide decision space yields a widened solution set.

A simple example of this principle can be found in the progressive complexity of games with increasing dimensions of play. Winning at tic-tac-toe is one thing; checkers another; chess increases the set of optimal outcomes (at the start of the game); Go increases them even more. A wider decision space produces a wider preference space, as defined by available "successful" moves. We learn as successful predictions multiply. As possibilities for winning increase, most of us need more room to explore them before we commit to a fork in the road. Similarly, in human learning the result of numerous potentially rewarding paths can be mapped onto the wide preference space of aesthetics. Divergence in potential paths, when there is low risk in deciding which to take, multiplies possible pleasures. Divergent aesthetic pleasures, then, can be read as the equivalent of low-stakes, exploratory possibilities.

Let's take a rudimentary aesthetic example, involving landscapes. Discrimination of shades of green can be useful in judging the age of foliage and timing the harvest or planting of crops. The ability to make such fine discriminations isn't just dependent on having visual acuity suited to detecting these differences and the computational capacity to compare, label, and distinguish a particular shade. Being able to perceive and categorize matters when pleasure is deployed in successfully matching a perception to a reference shade ("Aha! This is *just* right!") or in assessing the overall composition of a scene ("This is a beautiful vista; it's perfect. . . ." or not). A simple aesthetic assessment of this kind can be understood as a generalized affective response that encapsulates other judgments and prioritizes elements of and objects in our environment, as well as our own needs. In this way, aesthetic pleasure teaches us what is good, useful, productive. As eighteenth-century philosopher Francis Hutcheson suggested, aesthetic pleasure exists because nature takes an interest in our motivations.[7]

While the shorthand that a judgment of a landscape may represent is thus reasonably clear, the equivalent shorthand for a judgment about a haiku is not. Indeed, the number of judgments possible about sound, imagery, and social or personal meaning is far greater than the number of distinctions one could make about shades of green. As those dimensions of analysis increase, the configurations that can generate pleasures grow exponentially. This breadth is not "noise" to the "signal"; indeed, there are so many possible signals that could matter it is mind-boggling: what do I love about you? Everything Shakespeare could describe in all of his sonnets. And more. It is not that the ability to describe our pleasures in the beloved is candy on the evolutionary tree. It is rather that the ability to describe them, and the ability to take pleasure in those descriptions, are an outcome of the plentiful aspects of the world that are available to human perception and human comprehension. The wider the window of knowledge, the greater the potential for pleasure. We can learn to extract pleasure from novel circumstances, and with little in the way of a predetermined pattern. Aesthetic pleasure is thus an emergent property, appearing like a kaleidoscope in motion over a glittering field.

The connection between aesthetic experience and learning is deep. Let's return to music and entrainment. As I noted in chapter 1, entrainment to a beat facilitates prediction: it allows a listener, a dancer, or a musician the ability to predict what comes next and to adjust to it. Importantly, adjusting to changes in rhythm does not require very precise timescales or estimates. Indeed, as Martin Clayton, Rebecca Sager, and Udo Will note, many everyday events change their tempo in surprising ways, whether it is the movement of a bird on the wing or the speech patterns of another person: "the disparities between actual event onsets and the expected onset first cause a 'time estimation response' in which the new time relationship is evaluated. Next, the disparity triggers an adaptive response. Adjustments in expectations and the focus of attention are made in an effort to accommodate the unexpected, new time relationships."[8] The unexpected here is not necessarily unpleasant—that is, it is not experienced as a failure to predict—because humans' ability to keep time is meant to help us catch up: "the ease with which an oscillator phase adjusts in comparison to the stability of the oscillator's period may explain why many temporary changes in musical timing, such as . . . breaths taken between phrases, do not disrupt the underlying sense of rhythmic structure or tempo of a piece of music."[9] The ability to adapt to minute changes comes in part because keeping a master beat—an overall referent time—allows one to attend to multiple, distinct sub-rhythms (like the relationship between an eighth note and a sixteenth note).[10] Altering the frame of attention allows "anticipatory behaviors like those you might expect between musicians desiring to play in time with each other."[11] Humans can thus adapt to and predict extremely complicated behaviors, whether throughout an entire orchestra, across a dance floor, or—in a more evolutionarily constrained example—among a group of people closing in on their prey. Aesthetic pleasure can be a multipurpose learning mechanism, enabling individuals to adapt quickly to novel circumstances that disrupt a prior pattern.

My view of the central connection between aesthetics and learning carries three important corollaries. First, our ability to extract pleasure in an encounter is in part determined by the goals we take to it. Finding pleasure in a human face might look different when the goal is safety, rather than reproduction. Finding pleasure in a still life should look different if we are seeking to learn something about style, or to discover and share a new compositional pleasure. With music, we can shift goals, too, like "keeping track of the unfolding formal structures [like melody], or . . . noting fine subtleties and timbre or pitch."[12] Pleasure and motivation are shaped by goals, and the objects of our pleasures are shaped accordingly. Second, aesthetic form coalesces from the myriad, differing ways that we can extract pleasure from an artifact. Third, the temporal experience of aesthetic life depends on how we navigate and prioritize our goals, as well as the intensity with which they are satisfied and our ability to identify new goals over time.

Pleasure and Perception of Order and Form

The idea that aesthetic pleasure is goal oriented is contested in some philosophical and psychological arenas (they are often understood as autotelic—pleasurable for their own sake). Given that the arts emerged relatively late in human evolution, it would be difficult to argue that artworks or pleasure in engaging them meets goals defined by evolutionary requirements. Yet reward systems that seem designed to regulate basic needs (food, sex, hunger, social engagement) also serve aesthetic pleasures. Some researchers make a distinction between liking (preference and pleasure) and wanting (anticipation of pleasure), suggesting that aesthetic responses have largely to do with liking, not the anticipation and desire that go along with the consummatory pleasures of satisfaction. Still, some physiological aesthetic responses, like chills in listening to music, reading poems or novels, and watching films, are consummatory pleasures, with buildup, heightening of anticipation, and satisfaction.[13]

However they come into being, by learning as well as inheritance, there are goals that may be satisfied through aesthetic engagement and that lead to aesthetic pleasure—specifically, pleasure that comes by virtue of engaging with an artwork or natural object, but cannot come simply by hearing about it second- or thirdhand. For works of art, these goals vary by genre; as human creations, they imply a range of social goals, even if they achieve none or few at a time.[14] Take for example the goal of emotion regulation. Music is often approached in this regard as we seek to calm ourselves, to set a mood, or even just to indulge in pleasure itself. Decorative arts may serve goals of environmental or social ordering or mood regulation (though that is not all they do). Art may also offer vicarious experience at relatively low cost; to learn from the adventures of, say, *Tom Jones* or *Tom Sawyer*, without incurring the price of direct knowledge.[15] Art may further goals of mastery, too; for example, take one's ability to understand or appreciate complex, difficult, or initially strange artworks. The *Target* series with which I began offers one such possibility. What, at first glance, is artistically significant about a bunch of painted targets? This is a question with little in the way of an obvious answer, outside of a viewer's training in art history or a work's placement in a gallery or museum: why would a viewer spend enough time with such a piece to find out its worth? We have one answer from an expert viewer with surrealist Alain Robbe-Grillet, who transformed the *Targets* and *Numbers* into a short fiction that takes place in a darkened room.[16] Is there a more fulsome way to assert aesthetic mastery than by placing another artist's abstract visual work inside a blindingly dark prison cell at the heart of your own detective mystery? In this vein, a variety of knowledge-based goals may lead to aesthetic experiences, and while mastery may be one of them, as with Robbe-Grillet's novella, I'd also add self-knowledge, the quest for information, and the search for or imposition of order.[17]

So, aesthetic pleasures are diverse, and while some serve to meet goals, others participate in the reward, risk, and error analyses that define pleasure and goal seeking in ways that other kinds of pleasures do not. When a sudden shift in affect—the kind of shift that produces *conscious* pleasure—occurs in confronting a work of art, it alerts us to a change; it's not necessarily that we have reached a goal we might immediately describe, but we've learned that we need to pay attention. One might be struck in a rush by a splash of color, an oddity of composition, an alteration in meter or rhythm, a wrenchingly new perspective. When we suddenly change registers, there can be ambiguity about why we feel so strongly so quickly, why attention has shifted, why affect has suddenly moved from its baseline. This acceleration of feeling can have many correlating elements in a work of art, from the formal to the thematic. Equally, when one is reading tragedy or witnessing truths that are painful to hear, the swift approach of feeling might signal a pro-social concern: What have I done? What has this done to me?

Earlier I noted that one way we can distinguish artifacts of culture from natural objects is the degree to which individuals vary in the pleasure they take in these objects. A distinguishing feature that may account for the comparative uniformity of pleasure taken in natural scenes and the disagreement over a painted version of them comes down to form or style.[18] Formalist critics like Viktor Shklovsky sought to define form by focusing on features that slow down perception. For literature, this includes elements like meter, rhythm, line breaks, stress, and imagery:

> the general purpose of imagery . . . is to transfer the usual perception of an object into the sphere of new perception. . . . A work is created "artistically" so that its perception is impeded and the greatest possible effect is produced through the slowness of the perception. As a result of this lingering, the object is perceived not in its extension in space, but, so to speak, in its continuity.[19]

Slowing down perception through features like these (often called foregrounding) can have the paradoxical effect of creating an aesthetic whole: it is intuitively strange (even if accurate) to suggest that a complete perception may depend on breaking what we see into parts, and yet stranger to suggest that the intentional fracturing of an experience might make it more whole.

While it has proven difficult to define specifically poetic language as opposed to the language of prose or everyday speech, formalist poetics has proven quite useful for helping to identify features that tax readers in special ways.[20] For example, take parallelistic diction, a common feature of ancient poetry from Homer to the Hebrew Bible or *Beowulf*, in which half lines of a poem repeat content or sound.[21] Such features slow a reader's pace and may put a heavier load on resources used for attention.[22] Thus, these features might draw us out of an immersive state (or our own inner wanderings) by bringing us back to the surface features of a text (this possibility will become important as I comb through models of aesthetic experience in the next chapter). These artistic features, highly crafted indices of technique, can also have hedonic value.

The idea that pleasure might be a marker of creativity makes particular sense in the context of cognitive psychology.[23] Amy Belfi and I have argued that pleasure in reading can enable one to widen one's focus to see the broader shape that is the formal presence of a poem.[24] While some elements of poetic form emerge by definition (for example, the fourteen lines that make a sonnet), or by content (as with the shepherd/ess of pastoral poetry), others emerge not by definition but through subjective experience. Form, style, and other markers of technique are actively perceived in part because their component elements are painted with the bright colors pleasure brings (what Kent Berridge and Morten Kringelbach call the gloss of hedonic experience) or because they are strikingly discordant.[25] Form is, in this sense, something like Samuel Taylor Coleridge's "organic" form: the totality of marks that make up the aesthetic stamp of an artwork.[26] Coleridge argues that the reader must be drawn on by pleasure, but it is puzzling that this is a fundamental principle of engagement, because pleasures in the written word—or in the arts more broadly—are not universal. If pleasure is to be a standard of poetic achievement, it makes for a risky bet.

One way in which formal features emerge as sources of attention and pleasure is via expectation mismatch: we first register them as disruptive and then as we learn more, pleasure may follow. Animals thrive in an environment where they have some reasonable ability to extrapolate about what the future holds. We have expectations about what will happen next in life, on a walk, in a relationship, or in stories, music, and poems. When we predict correctly, we are rewarded by the outcome in the world as well as by means of neural signals that correlate with felt pleasure or displeasure. A mismatched expectation is generally not associated with positive outcomes, but humans, like other animals, learn from those mistakes, both through negative outcomes and the pains or displeasures that emerge. Sometimes a seeming mistake is not a mistake at all; it is a discovery.

In aesthetic terms, a simple way to conceive of the power of violated expectations is a wrong note; indeed, as American poet Wallace Stevens wrote, "Personally, I like words to sound wrong."[27] If in a piece of music, the sound you expect to come next doesn't appear—you yourself played the wrong note, or maybe the composer is playing a game with your expectations—something happens. It is probably not pleasurable on the first go (I will discuss an important exception in the next chapter). If it is truly a mistake—you hit the wrong key, or your fingers just didn't do what you needed—it probably never produces a positive experience. But if, say, you begin to understand what John Coltrane is doing or why Wallace Stevens just won't satisfy your expectations about rhythm in a particular line, word, or poem, pleasures may emerge. In and of itself, the missed expectation produces a disruption that might become pleasurable, but it ain't necessarily so.

Nicholas Myklebust describes disruption of expectations around metrical violations in Stevens's "The Comedian as the Letter C," where the poet schools readers over many lines to expect iambic pentameter; suddenly, Stevens changes his tune: "Inscrutable hair in an inscrutable world."[28] The line sounds wrong to the inner ear—or the outer one—if only because there are eleven syllables where there should be no more than ten. Ultimately, in whatever way any particular reader assigns stresses in this line, "what . . . matter[s] is the *felt* need to repair the line, to make it fit prior expectations."[29] Something has to give when the pattern has been violated, and (following the work of Reuven Tsur) Myklebust argues that the poem "exploits this . . . by turning interference into pleasure."[30] Mending the line, figuring out what the deviation from the poem's past patterns might mean, generates a kind of satisfaction for readers who solve the metrical puzzle in a way that makes sense to them. This is not to say there is only one solution: there are different ways to "hear" the stress of the line (Myklebust suggests using two anapests or syncope to elide one syllable), but finding the poem pleasurable in part means finding a pleasurable solution. Pleasure here is a revision of surprise or even disinterest.

If recognizing literary form partially depends on the signs of craft (the word "poetry" comes from the Greek *poeisis*, or "making"), it is worthwhile to honor the time course of reading so as not to assume the reader knows a poem's form outright. In that way we can think both about how form comes into being and about the roles of pleasure in perceiving form over time. Take Stevens's "Bouquet of Roses in Sunlight," where he utilizes a characteristic richness of patterns and sound to violate a different kind of expectation. The stress pattern in this poem is not so much governed by a regular rhythm as guided by rhetorical precision, a sense of linguistic propriety that seems to belong more to emphasizing an argument than to effecting the beat of a poem. Here, it is possible that under certain conditions, elements of a poem that might defy normative concepts of poetic form emerge as salient formal features because they take on the weight given by pleasure. This mode of aesthetic experience relies on possibilities of redefinition, sketching out new versions of form by freighting experience with sensation that has been given a value—not just sensation but pleasurable sensation:

> Sáy that ít is a crúde effect, bláck réds,
> Pínk yéllows, órange whítes, tóo múch as they áre
> To be ánything élse in the súnlight of the róom,
> . . .
> And yét this effect is a cónsequénce of the wáy
> We féel and, thérefore, is not réal, excépt
> In our sénse of it, our sénse of the fértilest réd.[31]

The stress sweeps across the line to emphasize points of argument, the key elements of contention in a philosophical and phenomenological statement about perception and reality. Thus, from the very beginning, Stevens uses sound to unsettle the poem's status as poetry, an irony made clear in the final lines, where he writes that the very sensual nature of the "roses" (roses readers can never see) makes them resistant to "the rhetorician's touch."[32] However, the sensory frame of the poem—the sounds of metrical stress—emphasize the rhetorician's skill at argument, using aesthetic power to blend genres of speech (poetry and rhetoric), to disrupt generic expectations, and to render poetry's effect as—often retrospectively—evoking conviction as well as piquing imagination. Still, effects proper to poetry at times explode onto the page, as with the sudden shift from everyday argument and rhetorical emphasis to a changed beat that comes with florid color: "fertilest red." An explosion of poetry paradoxically interrupts the poem, cascading visual brilliance into a fluid background of sound. As Stevens jots down in his "Adagia," "The poet comes to words as nature comes to dry sticks": poetry refreshes language, and as language is made new, we might find startling pleasure in a sudden vividness, when one rose, even against a riotous background of others, stands out with sharp virility.[33]

In reading the poem, one might find the intimacy of (imagined) shared sight to be intense. What is "real" in this poem is perception, and perceptions change with us as we settle in together with the poem's speaker "in a completing of . . . truth."[34] However, this kind of readerly intimacy is threatened in the final stanza. Throughout the earlier lines, the speaker of the poem has emphasized the strength of sensation: those percepts generated by the roses are "too actual, things that in being real / Make any imaginings of them lesser things."[35] Reality is sensual.

The paradox is obvious. Glaring, even. So what? Well, take the final lines: "We are two that use these roses as we are, / In seeing them. This is what makes them seem / So far beyond the rhetorician's touch."[36] The challenge is that the scene the poem plots can be seen in two ways: an actual room in which two people look at the bouquet and "use these roses" as paradigms of sensation and aesthetic pleasure; and alternatively, a space marked out by the reader's and poet's imaginations, in which the reader is part of the "we" and is the addressee of Stevens's first lines.

The double scene of the poem is thus at the end made disorienting—who gets to use the roses? And which "roses" are they: the real ones, which are "too much as they are," or the imagined ones, which also are "too much as they are"? This disorientation distinguishes a feature of literary form—the instability of the genre called colloquy. Who is really listening to the conversation the poem evokes or implies? And how is the intimacy of conversation constructed? The discomfort of attending to the split perspective ultimately calls attention to the poem as a formal object. Yet, because the "use" of the roses is to revel in sensation, pleasure here is the marker of aesthetic form. "Wait: did I feel it?" A reader might ask. "Was I supposed to?" Thus, the end of the poem enables subverted or altered expectations to lead to a shift in how a reader might interpret the formal structure that is genre.

Aesthetic Minima

The evocation of the lush vibrancy of Stevens's roses might imply that aesthetic response in my view can only take you by storm, flowering full-force within and around you. Powerful aesthetic experience, however, doesn't necessarily require powerful emotion, or even vivid imagination. Stevens is well aware of the power in even a breath of air, or a wisp of night. One important kind of aesthetic experience—what I call an aesthetic minimum—is a moment of interaction between an artwork and its audience in which an individual registers that art has subtly changed their world in some material, embodied way. Poetry is a good place to look for such moments (though not an exclusive one) because the initial percepts on which reading relies do not map neatly onto the experience of reading. With visual art, by comparison, such a minimal moment must be carefully constructed, as it always exists in competition with the confrontational engagement vision produces.

The blackboard images of American artist Cy Twombly here come to mind. The large-scale masterpiece *Untitled* (1970)—roughly thirteen- by twenty-one-feet—is covered in nonsense versions of traces of lines of text.[37] The chalk marks are made by hand, but they are not writing and convey no denotative meaning. They suggest a hidden or occluded message, perhaps even words that have been erased. The monumental impact of the piece, however, makes the absence of meaning seem insistent, and viewers may find themselves transfixed, in search of a message that will never come. Vision does not serve its putative purpose—showing us what we need to

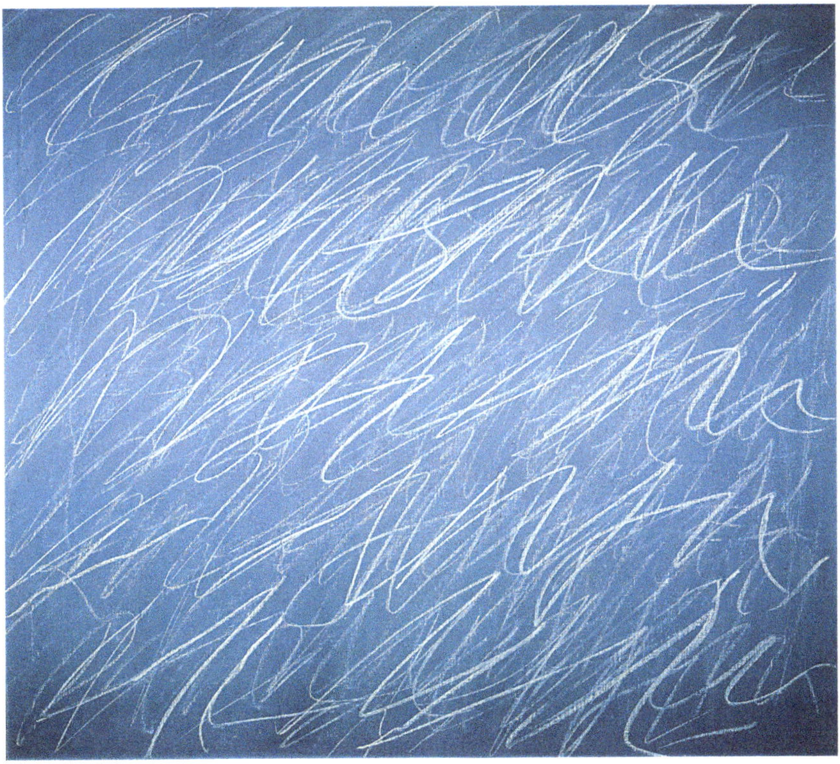

Figure 2.1
Cy Twombly, *Untitled*, 1970. MOMA.

know. Thus, the disruption of the everyday that marks aesthetic experience elevates the work of art not as vibrant reality but as marking a hazy border between what we sense in the world and what we feel on the inside.

With literature, on the other hand, sensory competition plays out differently. Imagery is one feature that clearly distances perception from aesthetic experience; it is highly individual and metabolically costly to produce, but it may generate experiences that are otherwise impossible to encounter. Stevens is a master of imagery that transforms sense data attributable to one form of perception and makes it available to another. Take "An Ordinary Evening in New Haven," where Stevens suggests that his reader imagine a scene:

> Suppose these houses are composed of ourselves,
> So that they become an impalpable town, full of
> Impalpable bells, transparencies of sound,
>
> Sounding in transparent dwellings of the self,
> Impalpable habitations that seem to move
> In the movement of the colors of the mind.[38]

No house in the world is truly made of dreams, of course; only the houses poetry built are made of transparent sound, unavailable to touch. That is the fundamental paradox of poetry, as well as one of its fundamental qualities: words can be felt by some other means than hands alone, and sound becomes "movement of the colors of the mind" as well as breath across the lips. The whisper-thin nature of the figures poetry draws is on display in the opening two stanzas of "The Stars at Tallapoosa":

> The lines are straight and swift between the stars.
> The night is not the cradle that they cry,
> The criers, undulating the deep-oceaned phrase.
> The lines are much too dark and much too sharp.
>
> The mind herein attains simplicity.
> There is no moon, on single, silvered leaf.
> The body is no body to be seen
> But is an eye that studies its black lid.[39]

The first stanza sketches an "image" of something invisible to the eye: the lines that transform pinpricks of light into constellations. More importantly, it's not that these imaginary lines have the kind of clarity one can find on a map, for they are "much too dark and much too sharp," but poetry brings to life things that are all around us but forever at the edges of consciousness. These undiscovered places are "simplicity" itself, but they require that we decenter the body as we experience it every day, in favor of trying to sense the inside of our skin, becoming "an eye that studies its [own] black lid." I draw attention to these moments in Stevens to emphasize that while beauty functions within daily life as the most recognizable aspect of aesthetic experience for many (if not most) people, beauty isn't the end of all art. Equally, while the power of an emotional response is one sign of the most powerful aesthetic experiences, it is not sufficient on its own, and aesthetic minima as well as aesthetic failures are part of how we make sense of aesthetic value.

Duration, Pleasure, and Form

The view of form I offer centers affect: you know form when you feel it. Like Caroline Levine, I argue that forms emerge through affordances—the ways that you grasp them. But unlike Levine, I argue that these forms are necessarily dynamic, and not necessarily stable. She claims that "once we have agreed to look for principles of organization . . . [in works of art, form involves] configurations and arrangements [that] organize materials in distinct and stable ways, no matter their context or audience."[40] Certain particular forms (those that emerge by definition, like the fourteen lines that make up a sonnet) do what Levine describes. Aesthetic form in general, however, is different, actively constructed by a reader, viewer, or listener as their attention is drawn to features of an artwork. The emergence of form as one reads, listens, or views is one aspect of the temporal shape of aesthetic experience. Form, as Dewey notes, "is dynamic organization. . . . It takes time to complete because it is a growth."[41]

Pleasure thus marks aesthetic time in a variety of ways. One is the pleasurable unrolling of form itself, as one reads from line to line. However, sometimes form emerges only retrospectively. Indeed, many critics assign a particular canonical value to an aesthetic whole, granting the entirety of the object a different weight than any particular part might have. This raises an important methodological question for experimental aesthetics. In general, one may assume a contrast between freely engaging, for as long or as little as one would like, with a painting, poem, or song (as well as returning as often as one might like). In experimental conditions, however, music or poems may be presented to a reader as an excerpt, or given line by line, and visual art will often be shown for just a few seconds. Such manipulations are important, for they allow researchers to connect components of the artwork with behavioral or neural events (e.g., x occurred at t_5). They also enable enough artworks or excerpts to be presented in a time frame that is manageable for a participant—to reduce the chances for fatigue, yet to acquire enough data for adequate statistical power in analysis.

These conditions have been a problem for some critics of neuroaesthetics.[42] However, it is not fully clear how the temporal constraints of controlled experimental conditions (often described as being without "ecological validity") influence or alter aesthetic experience. For example, while experimenters may show artworks to research participants in a lab setting for only a few seconds, studies undertaken in museums have shown that the average time an individual spends with a painting ranges from twenty-seven seconds to as few as eleven.[43] Moreover, these kinds of timescales are longer than those many neuroscientists and some philosophers who study temporality argue make up the "now" of present experience.[44]

To begin, we should not expect aesthetic experience to be simply present-facing, that is, about the here and now. Indeed, there are layers and cycles of engagement that underpin any conscious moment. Think of it this way: Human beings need our timing to be precise to its finest point over very short timescales because these are crucial to action preparation and execution. Longer timescales matter, too, but we need not be terribly precise ("it was, say, eleven or twelve years ago" is usually close enough for most estimations in daily life). However, Usain Bolt is the reigning fastest man alive not because of a matter of seconds but a matter of tenths of seconds (his reaction time was 16.5 tenths of a second off the starting blocks in 2009 at the Olympics). Even for those of us who aren't elite athletes, split-second intervals are a routine part of daily life, from the 20–250 millisecond sweep of the eyes that comprises a saccade, to what is, by some estimates, the minimum quantum of human consciousness—from 150–200 milliseconds.[45] A saccade is a good proxy for a minimum extended experience that appears seamless to consciousness; we regularly sum over saccades without noticing any gaps in what we see, and that suggests we build up such minimum durations to create a whole.[46] For aesthetic experiences, like any others, the coherence of subjective time comes from layering (what kind exactly—summation, integration, retrospective or prospective filling-in—will vary).

Aesthetic experiences must stack, one way or another, influenced by continually changing conditions, comparisons to the past, and extrapolations to the future.

There may be many ways that laboratory settings can influence aesthetic experience. For example, individuals tend to enjoy artworks in museum settings more than laboratory ones; this makes sense given conditions of free viewing (rather than a defined window of time) or the ability to move and change perspective (not to exclude other elements of context like individual expectations, reputations of artworks or spaces, crowds, size and scale of artworks, and so on).[47] In experimental conditions there seems to be a flattening out of positive affect over time, as well as few changes in judgment of many aesthetic qualities as time progresses (e.g., "impressiveness," "specialness," and "beauty").[48] Work on music has also shown plateaus in response over time, and that a set of "accurate" judgments (meaning consistent and durable for an individual) may be made quite quickly—within three seconds with a sixty-second clip and in under a second for excerpts up to ten seconds.[49] The timescale of brain responses is rapid indeed. So, what do we learn in studying such truncated experiences?

On a psychological and neurophysiological level, there may be important mechanisms that enable us to stack truncated experiences into wholes (we needn't go that far just yet, but we will in the next chapter). It is also possible that excerpts have aesthetic integrity. In fact, older ideas of literary form that privilege "beauties"—that is, passages circulated in letters, conversations, commonplace books, anthologies, and so on—as complete, and even paradigmatic, gave way historically in nineteenth-century Europe to Samuel Taylor Coleridge's view of organic form.[50] This view went on to be contested by twentieth-century formalist criticism, in which a work declares its aesthetic shape quite early on.

In research at New York University, Amy Belfi and I selected two subjective features of reading poetry that we thought particularly likely to involve temporality: vivid imagery, which may be constructed over several lines or across stanzas, and an individual's emotional response, which may change or build over the course of the poem. We designed an experiment to test the relationship between the strength of emotional reaction, emotional valence, the perceived vividness of imagery, and overall aesthetic pleasure in reading the whole of a poem or increasingly longer parts.[51] As a highly regularized genre that is easily subdividable, sestinas seemed a good test case: they require six six-line stanzas, in which the end words are repeated in differing order in each stanza, followed by a three-line grouping that uses all of the preceding end words in any order.

We divided volunteers into three groups: those who read short (*n*=48), medium (*n*=47), and complete (*n*=46) versions of the sestina. Each participant read one version of each of the twelve poems, and after each, they rated the poetry in four dimensions: vividness of imagery; valence of emotions experienced while reading; strength of their emotional arousal; and aesthetic pleasure derived from reading the work. Length had no significant effect on any of these ratings (see figure 2.2).

Based on individual subject regressions, on average, strength of emotional arousal was the best predictor of aesthetic pleasure, followed by the valence of felt emotions, and vividness of imagery (see figure 2.3).[52]

Using intraclass correlation coefficients (ICCs) from single measures for each characteristic, we determined that participants showed similar patterns of agreement for short, medium, and complete conditions. For all lengths, the highest agreement was for valence, followed by vividness, then arousal and aesthetic pleasure. Overall, agreement was quite low for each rating scale (see figure 2.4).

One might think that reading a poem in its entirety, or even increasing the length of engagement—and with it increasing the amount of available

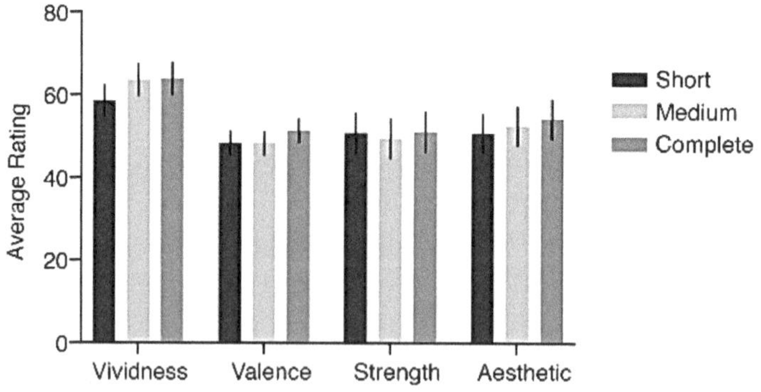

Figure 2.2
Mean ratings for short, medium, and complete (full-length versions of sestinas). Error bars depict 95 percent confidence intervals; overlapping error bars show length has no effect on any of the four ratings. Reproduced from Starr and Belfi, "Pleasure," in *Further Reading* (2020).

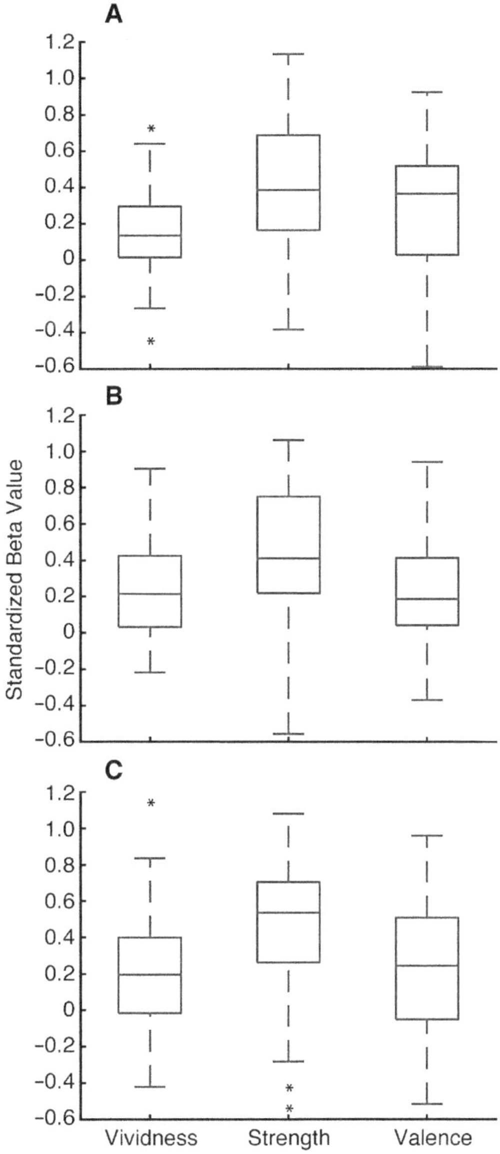

Figure 2.3
Summary statistics for individual regressions for short (A), medium (B), and full-length (C) versions of sestinas. Boxes show 25th percentiles above and below the mean (center line). Extended lines ("whiskers") show 75th percentiles, with asterisks representing outliers. Reproduced from Starr and Belfi, "Pleasure," in *Further Reading* (2020).

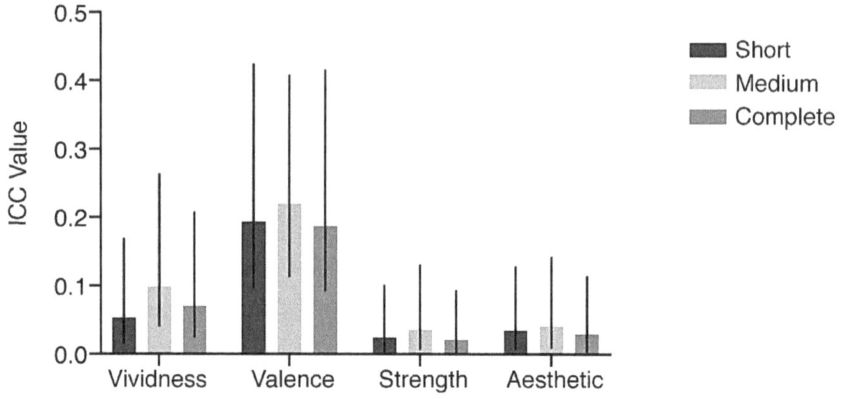

Figure 2.4
ICC values for short, medium, and full-length versions of sestinas show low agreement across individuals for each assessment. Error bars depict 95 percent confidence intervals. Reproduced from Starr and Belfi, "Pleasure," in *Further Reading* (2020).

information and detail—might promote the ability of readers to engage emotionally or to imagine vividly. However, we found that reading both parts and wholes elicited similar levels of pleasure, as well as similar vividness of imagery and strength of feeling. We speculated that part of this finding may be linked to the internal cohesion of individual stanzas. While sestinas are generally unrhymed, the formal repetition of end words from stanza to stanza establishes a pattern that may promote readers' sense that even a pair of stanzas is a complete entity. Importantly, we also found that aesthetic pleasures seem to be constituted in similar ways across both the excerpts and the complete poems: the relative contribution to aesthetic pleasure (as measured by individual subject regressions) of vivid imagery, strength of pleasure, or affective valence was unchanged either by length or by reading a part rather than a whole.

These findings contrast slightly with a version of aesthetic formalism that suggests poems have internal signals of closure, but which has held that the final lines of a poem as a whole have particular resonance in signaling aesthetic completion.[53] Perhaps individual stanzas carry such signals as well. Indeed, in studying readers' experiences of chills in response to poems, researchers found words and phrases eliciting chills clustered toward the ends of stanzas, or single lines.[54] Further support for this hypothesis can be found in Kraxenberger and Menninghaus, who studied formal devices like alliteration, assonance, and stress, and explored interactions between them as they influence perceptions of sadness and joy. Importantly for my argument here, they found that interaction between position in a single line and these formal features was positive and significant (meaning they often came later in a line); but it was significant and negative in terms of their position in the poem as a whole.[55] Additionally, in our study, because both medium and complete versions contained the short one (the first two stanzas), it is also possible that early components of poems have an important influence in determining the degree of aesthetic pleasure overall, consistent with Kenneth Burke's argument that in their opening lines, literary objects train readers in how to read them.[56] In other words, emotion perception—as some part of aesthetic response—depends on formal features, but the formal features in the ending of the poem are not key players in that perception. We have to find an explanation elsewhere.

How we find it involves the varying time courses established by the affordances of an object we encounter as aesthetic, and part has to do with our own sense of timing. Film, music, and poetry have a range of time courses that are largely objective, and they seemingly run on their own clocks. A musical piece has a tempo and, played properly, lasts a reasonably precise amount of clock time.[57] The time of literature varies somewhat more, as readers stop and start, slow down in our engagements or speed up. We read excerpts all the time as we engage with longer works, setting our own tempo to either what are natural stopping points (e.g., ends of chapters, pages, sentences, or episodes) or based on what our environment allows. These variations in time can have to do with features of the text (complexity, recursiveness, difficulty, foregrounding), characteristics of the reader (associations, expertise, susceptibility to distraction, desire to savor), and characteristics of the environment and our ability to meet them (my roommate gets in the way of my reading for pleasure; I enjoy things more when I'm in a quiet space; my goals are in reach of my abilities to attain them, and so on).

So, one important distinction is between clock time—which might be measured in seconds, by rhythm (say, a metronome that divides segments of time reliably), the "inherent" time of the object (its duration of play, the sequencing of notes, its size and comprehensibility)—and what I will call goal time: the amount of time it takes to satisfy a goal in engaging an artwork and, failing that satisfaction, to move on or to discover a new goal and to explore it.

Beyond Pleasure: Deploying Form

The different profile of the pleasures humans find with artifacts (compared to natural objects) suggest other processes besides pleasure at work. What else does beauty require other than pleasure? Unlike simpler gustatory or tactile pleasures, the pleasures of beauty can be selectively disrupted or diminished by adding cognitively taxing tasks. Aenne Brielmann and Denis Pelli asked individual participants in one study to bring six "movingly beautiful" images into the lab, where they were also shown images with highly positive valence (from the International Affective Picture Scale [IAPS] picture set, one long studied and tested in psychology research), plain images (medium valence IAPS and what Brielmann and Pelli identified as plain IKEA furniture), and given two different sensory pleasures (candy and a plush stuffed toy).[58] They found that a two-back task (which requires working memory and the ability to control attention—an individual must remember whether an item in a sequence is repeated two steps back in a sequence) had no effect on the pleasure individuals took in the IAPS pictures (highly valenced or not), photos of IKEA furniture, candy, or plush object. However, the task radically diminished the pleasure individuals took in what they had previously found beautiful.

The pleasures of beauty thus are distinctive in that they require additional, and varied, cognitive acts: remembering, imagining, comparing, projecting, evaluating, feeling. This is not somehow to verify a Kantian formulation that "free play" of particular cognitive faculties is essential in aesthetic response. Rather, it is to say that there may be ways of more fully understanding the varieties of cognitive processes that are particular to the pleasures of reading, viewing, or listening to works of art, and to affirm that these cognitive processes are in fact essential to the pleasure, not ancillary to it.

Part of the answer lies in how aesthetic experiences change the way we think. If aesthetic pleasures open the world around us by enhancing our ability to detect new things that give us pleasure, they feed the need for exploration and thus change perceptions of temporality and risk (as risk tolerance is necessarily linked to a willingness to range into what is unknown, and maybe even dangerous). Aesthetic experience thus might modulate tolerances for risk or ambiguity by making the world seem more or less orderly and coordinated. Tia DeNora, for example, points out how music may help in crowd control, say on boarding a plane and before take-off.[59] She also notes how the apparent order created by aesthetic responses may increase confidence in systematic power, whether it is the classical architecture of a bank as it whispers ideas of permanence, or the meticulous details of municipal design in, say, Georges-Eugène Haussmann's Parisian boulevards or those of Benjamin Banneker's Washington, DC. The admiration and awe one might feel in these surroundings may translate to the systems they represent. The effects of aesthetic pleasure in changing evaluations of the world around us may not just have ramifications for objects, situations, and institutions that are not themselves essentially aesthetic (banks or government), but elsewhere. It is reasonable to ask what the risks of art might be: exposure (to discomfiting ideas); incomprehension (frustration, feeling left behind); sorrow; moral violation; revision of belief; even self-doubt and fury. In this sense art may involve anti-goals, and they, too, evoke hedonic responses.

Before I close this chapter, let me offer an example of how form can be learned through pleasure and, once learned, how it can be manipulated. Henry James's final novel, *The Golden Bowl,* is a fit culmination of a career built first as a serialist. Most of James's fiction was published in installments, in popular magazines, and he took seriously the ways in which he needed to train his readers in the rhythms of his writing, drawing them back for more. His late fiction is notoriously complex; not only does each scene carry the layered, invisible complexities of secrets, illicit relationships, and unspoken passions, but each sentence pushes the boundaries of semantic cohesion by complicated syntax and lushly impressionist description.

The bowl of the title haunts the two volumes of the novel. It first appears as former lovers Charlotte and the Prince search for a gift for his intended. They are bidding goodbye to their past as he prepares to marry Maggie Verver, and Charlotte prepares to marry Maggie's father, Adam. The bowl is "a drinking-vessel larger than a common cup, yet not of exorbitant size, and formed, to appearance, either of fine gold or of some material once richly gilt."[60] It comes to represent the threat that both unions are marred before they even begin, tainted by the amorous history of the pair of former lovers. Charlotte asks the shopkeeper: "'Does one make a present . . . of an object that contains to one's knowledge a flaw?' . . . 'But he wouldn't find [it].' She kept her eyes on him as if, though unsatisfied, mystified, she yet had a fancy for the bowl. 'Not even if the thing should come to pieces? . . . Not even if he should have to say to me 'The Golden Bowl is Broken'?'"[61] There's a flaw alright, and the Prince sees what Charlotte can't: "'Then,' she asked, 'what *is* the matter?' 'Why it has a crack. . . . I saw the object itself. It told its story. No wonder it's cheap.' 'But it's exquisite,' Charlotte . . . found herself moved to insist. 'Of course it's exquisite. That's the danger.'"[62]

The bowl is not just filled with two flawed marriages; it comes to overflow with the erotic energy of the two lovers. The storekeeper looks at Charlotte and the Prince as if they were artifacts too: "'Didn't you see'—she was to ask it with an insistence—'the way he looked at us and took us in? I doubt if either of us have ever been so well looked at before. Yes, he'll remember us'—she was to profess herself convinced of that almost to uneasiness. . . . 'because, given his taste, he was pleased with us, he was struck—he had ideas about us. Well I should think people might; we're beautiful—aren't we?—and he knows.'"[63] Charlotte leaves the store without purchasing the bowl, but she and the Prince are indelibly linked to the vessel and its beauty. The former lovers rekindle their affair one wet afternoon, and their re-consummation places them firmly in the shadow cast by the beautiful object.

Maggie eventually discovers their intimacy; she wanders into the same shop and purchases the bowl. When the shopkeeper delivers it, he sees a photograph of the Prince and Charlotte: he remembers them alright. Maggie's process of discovery is both erotic and aesthetic. In a grand confrontation, Charlotte twists the knife, gloating about taking both Maggie's father and husband and taunting her, by asking if she knows of anything Charlotte has done to hurt her. Maggie knows too much: "it was only the golden bowl as Maggie herself knew it that had been broken. The breakage stood not for any wrought discomposure among the triumphant three—it stood merely for the dire deformity of her attitude toward them."[64] Yet she refuses to be cowed: "'You must take it from me that I've never at any moment fancied I could suffer by you.' And marvelously she kept it up—not only kept it up but improved on it."[65] Maggie embraces the power a social fiction can confer—the smooth patina of composure in crisis.

By the end of the novel, the bowl no longer figuratively holds others or their power over Maggie's life and her story. It becomes more the shape

Maggie gives herself. Ultimately, Maggie turns the putatively flawed crystal back into a thing of beauty. Even as she conceals her own knowledge of her husband's affair from Charlotte, she lets him know she is no fool, and at the same time engineers Charlotte's departure for America with her father: "'[Charlotte] won't let you take her for unhappy,' [the Prince] says. Maggie retorts, 'Oh I know better than any one else what she won't let me take her for! . . . You spoke just now of Charlotte's not having learned from you that I 'know.' Am I to take from you then that you accept and recognize my knowledge?'"[66] As the question hangs in the air, it—some yet unapprehended, shapeless "it" happens: "For that then when it had had time somewhat to settle like some handful of gold-dust thrown into the air, for that then Maggie showed herself as deeply and strangely taking it. 'I see.' And she even wished this form to be as complete as she could make it. 'I see.' The completeness had clearly after an instant struck him as divine. 'Ah my dear, my dear, my dear—!' It was all he could say."[67] Maggie has become the artist of her own fate. The bowl is her(s). The ending is her(s). The beauty is her(s). Her rival, Charlotte may possess a "mastery of the greater style."[68] But the closing scene leaves only Maggie herself beautifully framed, as Charlotte fades into the distance, bound for America: "'Isn't she too splendid?' She simply said, offering it to explain and to finish. . . . He tried, too clearly, to please her—to meet her in her own way; but with the result only that, close to her, her face kept before him, his hands holding her shoulders, his whole act enclosing her, he presently echoed: '"See"? I see nothing but *you*.' And the truth of it had with this force after a moment so strangely lighted his eyes that as for pity and dread of them she buried her own in his breast."[69] Maggie has learned to create beauty and temptation of her own.

It is thus that goals—what we desire—and anti-goals—what we seek to avoid—like shame, error, social exclusion, even futile love ("the expense of spirit in a waste of shame," to quote Shakespeare)—unite in aesthetic experience, even as each may have a different time course of resolution. In the world of intimacy created in *The Golden Bowl*, the social cohesion that accompanies shared pleasure is the ultimate value. As the curtain drops on the final scene, Maggie and her Prince face a life of implied bliss. Time is not measured now by clocks or individual satisfaction, but by interaction. As she takes the golden bowl for herself, she fills it with what she wishes. James's novel—as perhaps all of his late work—seems dedicated to the proposition that art (as life) will not meet one's first expectations; it is thus, by linking pleasures to risks, that art may have its most far-reaching effects.

As I have argued in this chapter, pleasure helps readers, viewers, or listeners create a kind of salience map of a work of art. This dynamic understanding of the shape of aesthetic experience emerges from features of the artwork; together, these features make up aesthetic form. The ability to engage thus with artworks is not an accidental capacity that artists are able to exploit—it is a necessary outcome of the vast parameters of human learning. Because we are drawn on by pleasure in exploring the world around us, and because human goals and the means of satisfying them multiply with experience, our ability to take pleasure in novel circumstances leads to a dizzying array of possible configurations of features or elements that we may find pleasing. The divergence of pleasures commonly understood as "taste," then, reflects the kinds of diverse salience maps that humans create, and is reflected in the objects we build to conform to them. In the next chapter, I will lay out a behavioral and neural model of aesthetic experience that can help us understand the unfolding of these experiences in time.

3 Goal Time: Varying Maxima and Aesthetic Experiences

Researchers have generally distinguished among aesthetic experiences, both behaviorally and neurologically, by focusing on perceptual modality, and in turn have centered on higher-order cognitive activities as a place of broad unification.[1] After all, one could argue that the experience of a piece of art depends necessarily and hierarchically on how it comes to awareness: what sense or sensations does the work first address? This approach has proven productive in identifying core systems contributing to aesthetic experience across the arts; it may even help clarify why it is normal in most cultures to classify objects and cultural practices across many sensory domains as artistic (when they are made by humans) and aesthetic (whatever their origin).

Ultimately however, neither origin (whether objects are natural or artifacts) nor modality (vision, hearing) gives the clearest picture of the arts, because artworks aren't only objects that our senses detect; artworks and our engagements with them include their surrounding practices and contexts.[2] To understand and model different kinds of aesthetic flourishing, we need to understand why humans turn to the arts. This chapter lays out an argument for why the goals we bring are primary determinants of the overall temporal shape of aesthetic experience, and provides a starting point for a phenomenological and neural model that can function across the arts.

The discovery that the canonical DMN is important to visual aesthetics seemed to point toward something special about intense aesthetic experience, potentially serving as a physiological indication that art can touch deeply upon one's sense of self. However, even if the DMN is not primarily involved through its role in self-relevant cognition, there are other reasons the DMN might matter for visual aesthetics. As Randy Buckner and Lauren

DiNicola point out, the DMN overlaps significantly with areas where information across sensory modes is integrated: they argue the DMN is "the apex transmodal association network."[3] Indeed, given the crucial role of visual input in the human cortex, and that vision in sighted individuals becomes the basis for a multisensory representation of the world, the usual anticorrelation of visual and DMN networks makes perfect sense. Because visual aesthetics integrates a range of sensory data, association processes should be fundamental: visual arts may evoke the imagery of motion, for example, as well as providing clues to sensations of texture, or may pique the desire to touch, grasp, and manipulate.[4] On the one hand, pleasure seems to serve a gating function; intense pleasure is required for intense aesthetic response.[5] At the same time, pleasure has to be integrated into other complex functions: in Brielmann and Pelli's beauty "knockout" experiment, taxing working memory (via a two-back auditory task), but not short-term memory (recalling a string of digits), disrupted ("knocked out") subjective pleasure and beauty ratings. As they put it, "updating and manipulating working memory seems likely to demand much the same resources as binding dynamic sensory input together with higher-level cognition."[6] They argue that "limiting a cognitive resource" limits the experience of beauty—or at least the reporting of it. So a key question for aesthetics involves the conditions under which global, energy-demanding hubs can work together.

One of the puzzling features of the neural picture of aesthetic responses is that areas of the DMN so important to integrating varieties of sensory, emotional, and cognitive data in visual aesthetics seem to play little role in many responses to music and poetry. Indeed, several studies of music and literature have shown task-related suppression of regions of the DMN that are otherwise implicated in visual aesthetics. Take poetry: while reading networks and the canonical DMN overlap, it appears that at least one element of reading poems is incompatible with networked DMN activation—reevaluation.[7] Frequently, poetry revises an initial impression or first take so that the aesthetic power comes in reimagining or newly understanding what we read. Moving backward along the arc of an artwork can be mentally taxing, as it often involves confronting contradictions. Shakespeare's sonnets are an excellent example, where the final couplet or even the end of a line is often a counterpose to what has gone before. Take sonnet 73:

That time of year thou mayst in me behold,
When yellow leaves, or none, or few, do hang
Upon those boughs which shake against the cold,
Bare ruined choirs, where late the sweet birds sang.

In me thou seest the twilight of such day,
As after sunset fadeth in the west,
Which by and by black night doth take away,
Death's second self, that seals up all in rest.

In me thou seest the glowing of such fire,
That on the ashes of his youth doth lie,
As the death-bed whereon it must expire,
Consumed with that which it was nourished by.

This thou perceive'st, which makes thy love more strong,
To love that well, which thou must leave ere long.[8]

In the second line of the sonnet, time seems to run backward. The poet evokes first a bough in fall—with yellowed leaves; then comes winter, and no leaves; at the end of the line, with the unwillingness of the poet to accept his own passage through life, a "few" leaves somehow return. Logically, it should be yellow leaves, or few or none; but it isn't. Later, in the final couplet, again, logic is replaced by desire, so it is not that the lover will pass away and hence must abandon the beloved addressee; it is that the beloved will abandon the one they love.[9]

Readers, listeners, or viewers may pleasurably revise their expectations in other ways, particularly when it comes to laughter. Satire thrives on this kind of mismatch. Take Jonathan Swift's "The Lady's Dressing Room," which manipulates the conventions of extravagant praise in love poetry to display, far from the beauty of a young maiden, Celia, the detritus of vanity and deceit. Even Celia's dog, Tripsy, is in for it:

Five hours, (and who can do it less in?)
By haughty Celia spent in dressing;
The goddess from her chamber issues,
Arrayed in lace, brocades and tissues.
Strephon, who found the room was void,
And Betty otherwise employed,
Stole in, and took a strict survey,
Of all the litter as it lay;
Whereof, to make the matter clear,

An inventory follows here.
. . .
There night gloves made of Tripsy's hide,
Bequeathed by Tripsy when she died
With puppy water, beauty's help
Distilled from Tripsy's darling whelp.[10]

The puppies end up in Celia's face wash, but Swift has more in store for Strephon. Watch that last step! It's a doozy:

Thus finishing his grand survey,
Disgusted Strephon stole away
Repeating in his amorous fits,
Oh! Celia, Celia, Celia, shits!

Swift can generate laughter (and a grimace) by asking readers to revise each image, whether that of a cute puppy or the perfumes on a dressing table.

In general (and outside the narrow context of laughter), the call to revise an image or an idea is not the only thing working against the recruitment of the DMN in reading poetry or engaging with other arts. For another key element of poetic artistry, while imagery networks overlap with regions of the DMN, creating imagery may be a costly strategy for many readers, even as it can enhance aesthetic pleasure.[11] For music, in another example, areas in the posterior cingulate cortex may be engaged by processing tonal brightness, a far cry from many postulated functions of the posterior cingulate cortex when networked with other regions of the DMN, where it seems to be engaged with imagining other minds.[12]

These examples point to a crucial reality about brain resources: total metabolism is nearly constant, and one part of our neural architecture generally increases activity at the cost of decreasing activity in another. Indeed, the quest to understand this competition for resources helped lead to the discovery of the canonical default-mode network as interconnected regions that tend to be anti-correlated with many task-based activations in other brain areas.[13] While there may be regional activation, Buckner and DiNicola have suggested one reason the DMN may not be recruited across seemingly similar tasks. They argue that the hubs in the canonical network have close anatomical doubles, so that very tightly adjacent brain tissue creates two similarly connected networks (hence their shift in terminology from one DMN to two).[14]

In actuality, the brain boasts numerous resting-state networks—baseline connectivity that enables responsiveness to varying demands. Such baseline connectivity is a necessary corollary of the principle of metabolic conservation that governs trade-offs in neural networks. Sensory networks have resting states, as do reward networks. But action requires both homeostatic balance and a set of alternative conditions to facilitate changes in actions, needs, thoughts, and feelings. Generally, the DMN is primarily in productive competition with two other networks, one that directs attention (the central executive network, or CEN), and another that detects emotional, somatic, and environmental changes that matter to an individual (the salience network, or SN). The SN (as will be important later in this book) also processes information from the enteric nervous system—the vast majority of neurons throughout the body, including in the heart, blood vessels, and the digestive system—as well as striated muscle and the fascia.

The connectivity that exists between the three apex transmodal networks is central to brain architecture as part of a "rich-club" connectome: a subset of brain regions (by one estimation, from nine to twelve) with rapid and strong connections that mediate higher-order brain functions and also connect to lower-order ones.[15] Essentially, it makes more sense to expend high amounts of energy broadcasting some signals from a set of central relays than to use cheap (lower-energy), local routes. One might understand this by thinking about communication not within the brain, but across another roughly spherical space: earth. We frequently send low-energy/low-bandwidth messages, say, from our phones: texts. Higher-energy messages like those including video require more power and more cell tower strength to relay them without signal loss. But if you have an information-rich message that needs to go around the world in the blink of an eye, cell towers won't cut it; you need a network of satellites. The human brain also uses high-power signals and high-power networks for key messages. The folds of cortex help neurons navigate problems of the curvature of terrain (the problem on earth known as line of sight); as with folding, neurons can communicate from one peak of the landscape to another. But being able to leapfrog across a valley isn't enough for some essential signals. There you need insulated and protected (myelinated) channels, with strong and consistent ability to transmit, so a high-cost, high-power communication strategy makes great sense for valuable information.

The rich-club nodes of human brain connectivity thus create a kind of superhighway, enabling switching between differing neural systems and functions. The DMN overlaps with these nodes in part; Martijn P. van den Heuvel and Olaf Sporns hypothesized that "the rich club [connectome] may serve to link different functional modules in the brain, through partial overlap with several [resting-state networks] possibly including the default-mode network, the salience network, the executive network, and primary motor, visual, and auditory networks."[16] More specifically, and crucial to the models of neuroaesthetics I will advance here, while the DMN, SN, and CEN directly influence one another, the SN holds a keystone position (see figure 3.1).[17] The anterior insula, as part of the SN, acts as a superhub for the three networks, placing the SN in the unique position of being able to modulate the other networks directly, as well as to modulate the crosstalk of the CEN and DMN, and thus to regulate their ability to mutually influence distribution of resources in the central nervous system (as well as throughout the body in the autonomic nervous system). The anterior insula would thus effectively enable shifts between, for example, focus on the world beyond the body, awareness of bodily state and changes, and internal thought processes like daydreaming or mind-wandering.[18]

This configuration is important for aesthetics. As Marcos Nadal and Anjan Chatterjee point out, "encounters with art can differ because the information that is combined to produce the experience of art varies. Many of the brain regions identified by neuroimaging studies of art appreciation play a key role in integrating information derived from the diverse transient functional networks . . . , including the default mode network, the salience network, the executive network, and motor and sensory networks."[19] Resource competition among these different networks is useful, as switching between them enables us to focus attention, move from task to task, and prioritize among competing goods. Indeed, prioritizing where to put attention at a particular time is one of the most important things human beings do, and one clear component of that prioritization involves understanding our goals: what do we want? Of course, what we want may not be what is most important, and at any given point we may need to have spare attentional resources for new demands. For example, I may be entranced by a book, but if one of my children calls for me, I need to hear. In everyday life, there is in general no single goal that overrides all others (except perhaps the goal to survive, and even that can be demoted). We

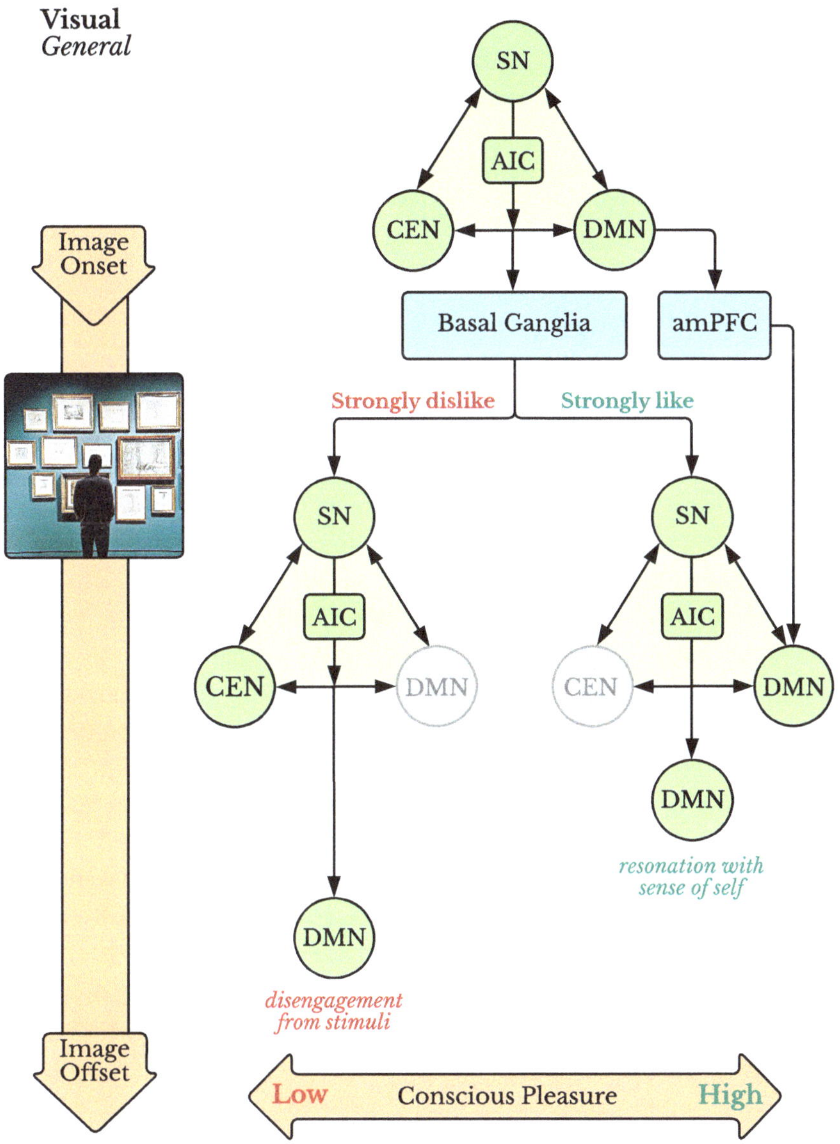

Figure 3.1

Apex transmodal networks. The SN can modulate and be modulated by both the central executive network and the DMN. The CEN and the DMN interact directly. The SN can modulate their interaction by way of the anterior insula cortex (AIC). Image credit: Marilyn Perkins, adapted from Goulden et al., "The Salience Network is Responsible for Switching between the Default Mode Network and the Central Executive Network: Replication from DCM," *NeuroImage* (2014).

constantly juggle what we need and want with what we can achieve, what is possible at a given moment, and what is most urgent.

Prioritization of goals is important for aesthetic experience, yet it raises a problem too: aesthetic experiences may not always have a clearly defined set of goals. Indeed, in many ways aesthetic life doesn't respond in the way of a basic appetite, whether it is a primary, unlearned reinforcer at play (like the need for food, water, safety, rest, sex, or social contact), or a secondary, learned reinforcer (like money). We see this clearly, as I indicated previously, in the ways in which individuals diverge in the pleasures they take from artifacts of culture compared with natural objects: the comparative similarity of taste across cultures for natural objects suggests highly evolutionarily conserved mechanisms underpinning pleasure and reward.[20] However, even with the creations of nature (rather than those of the people in it), pleasure and reward mechanisms may diverge: Itzhak Aharon and colleagues demonstrated a separation between reward value—wanting—for beautiful faces (how much viewers would work to continue to see them) and liking—how much male subjects found pleasure in looking at them (based on subjective ratings).[21] There is a different pattern for other aesthetic responses: experimental evidence has shown anatomical distinctions in the caudate and striatum that generally map onto these two components of reward may be absent in visual aesthetics; on the other hand, chills show classic patterns that map to a clear buildup of reward expectation.[22]

That the arts and aesthetic responses in general engage reward systems makes sense given the "common-currency" idea of reward representation, which holds that the orbitofrontal cortex maps a variety of rewards within a condensed area.[23] It's understandable, then, that cognitive models of aesthetic experience that prioritize an aesthetic judgment as the "output" of complex systems and analyses generally focus on the affective and reward components of this judgment—components that lead to conscious liking or positive, prolonged, and sometimes repeated engagement. But what goals activate or inform aesthetic pleasure? How do these goals compare to others we prioritize? And how do we decide to pursue experiences or encounters that feed these goals? Aesthetic experience ought to be understandable within a framework of goal-oriented behavior, if only because pleasure is one of the key outcomes of our pursuit of beauty and its kin.

Even though aesthetic experiences may involve unusual reward activity, given the omnipresence of aesthetic pleasures in human life, it is very difficult to argue that they should primarily be understood outside goal attainment. Thus, researchers have proposed that aesthetic experiences may be self-rewarding or may feed into a more general human need for information.[24] Alternatively, aesthetic experience may primarily concern the pleasures of perception without any further goal or measure. As Louise Kirsch and colleagues argue:

> modulation of neural activity in reward, perceptual and motor areas during aesthetic experience and positive attitudes to stimuli may not so much be segregated in their neuroanatomical organization, but rather in their temporal dynamics and ultimate outcome. For example, while the ultimate consequence of an affective appraisal of a stimulus may be to approach positive stimuli and avoid negative ones . . . , the ultimate product of aesthetic experience may be stimulus perception itself, as reflected by greater activation for pleasant than neutral and unpleasant stimuli in areas involved in perceptual processing and embodiment.[25]

That the pleasures of aesthetics might resolve to perception (or imagination, especially in the case of literature) is not a new idea: when Alexander Baumgarten coined the term "aesthetics" in the eighteenth century, it was to identify pleasures of sensation. But that does not mean that the pleasures die with sensation, or that their end goal is exclusively something like pleasure for its own good, much less art for art's sake.[26] In fact, many of the early Western philosophers of aesthetics associated aesthetic pleasures with social ends.[27] As I have argued, there are a variety of aesthetic experiences that involve pro-social goals (though, of course, not all aesthetic experiences do so). Depending on these goals and on the genre engaged, we should have recourse to differing modes and outcomes of aesthetic response.

Modeling Aesthetic Experience

There are multiple ways of modeling how aesthetic experiences emerge, as well as of defining and modeling what counts as aesthetic experience. Alva Noë contends that aesthetic experience extends well beyond the sensory presence of a work, both because art can only be evaluated within the framework of culture, and because art is an object of contemplation, not merely sensation.[28] This is certainly true, and true not just about the tail end of the encounter (as described above). The beginning of an aesthetic encounter can reveal much about the ways that an aesthetic experience might unfold over time. Processes that seem instantaneous help form the foundation from which what might be understood as descriptive layers (e.g., those accessible to memory and interpretation) or contextual layers (like museums, autobiographical circumstance, expertise, and so on) emerge.

Crucially, understanding aesthetic experiences through the goals that mediate them implies that the conditions for an aesthetic encounter are often set *before the encounter begins*, before you walk into a concert hall or open a book. Historically, this context has been analyzed and understood through the idea of an aesthetic attitude. At the birth of modern European aesthetics (as philosophy and criticism), this attitude was often framed as a kind of connoisseurship—not necessarily the taste of an expert, but that of a cultivated gentleman (with the myriad implications of class, race, education, gender, and Eurocentrism that the phrase carries).[29] However, from the moment writers like Anthony Cooper, Earl of Shaftesbury, lauded an ideal of tasteful savoring, counterviews emerged, as with William Hogarth, who mocked Shaftesbury's aesthetic detachment in favor of the position of a craftsman, an artist who taps into the perceptual, appetitive, and cognitive underpinnings of beauty.[30] These debates flourished for more than two hundred years, with the idea of a calm, disinterested, and passion-free appreciation of the arts in fundamental opposition to an emotionally charged, physical, and passionate enjoyment persisting through at least the work of George Dickie in the twentieth century.[31]

Alternatively, a historicist view contends that art and our attitudes toward it are conditioned by institutions. This view of art takes many forms, but an institutional theory of art generally argues that from galleries to museums, schools, universities, religious establishments, and so on, we know art by the authorities who label it. The material conditions (e.g., white walls, silence, classrooms, impressive architecture, crowds) of our encounters inside these institutions shape aesthetic experiences. Indeed, some critics argue that art is a closed and self-defining system, where the only institution that can define art is the artworld itself. The "system of art," as Luhmann calls it, exists to "concede to the perceiving consciousness [reader, viewer, audience] its own unique adventure in observing artworks—and yet it makes available . . . the formal selection that triggers the adventure."[32] Artworlds present the results of their curation to us for consumption in prescribed, culturally specific, and local ways.

However, none of these frameworks frees aesthetic experiences from goals. Indeed, one might still posit pleasure as a goal, or learning, attaining cultural capital, or challenging oneself to appreciate and understand something new or complex. Simple curiosity might also be the point. Indeed, individuals come to aesthetic experiences with multiple goals; or an aesthetic experience might come upon you without your pursuit of it.[33] Such an unexpected experience, in keeping with the literature on reward, should be particularly powerful.[34] It is also important to keep in mind that goals may vary by genre. So, for example, Andrei Miu and colleagues note that self-education is more frequently identified as a goal for viewing visual art than for listening to music, while music often is pursued for "keeping company" or mood regulation.[35]

Cognitivist models of aesthetics have included some of these notions of attitude and institutions as framing elements for aesthetic experience.[36] One of the most important of these models was that developed by Helmut Leder and colleagues and subsequently revised as the Vienna Integrated Model of Art Perception (VIMAP).[37] The VIMAP synthesizes some of the more promising routes cognitive science has taken toward understanding the role of aesthetic pleasures in our daily lives, deconstructing functional systems, as well as brain structures, in order to understand large-scale patterns in aesthetic responses. This focus on systems has elucidated a range of significant components of aesthetic experience, including fast and slow emotional and hedonic responses, as well as brain systems and regions involved in complex integrations of information.

The VIMAP suggests candidate information-processing relationships, is grounded in visual art and accounts for much of the available behavioral evidence. Notably, it enables identification of a variety of timescales for the processes it lays out. For example, it is clear that not only is the gross, high-level depictive content (the "gist") of an artwork perceived within ten milliseconds; but style (as mode of depiction or historical movements like impressionism) is recognized within fifty milliseconds. This fits nicely with the model and within the window generally understood as the "now" in much neuroscience.[38] Other findings fit nicely as well: for example, one study showed that very small timescales could enable recognition and evaluation: "beauty" and "specialness" were evaluated (steady evaluations, given unlimited viewing time) in as little as ten milliseconds. Intriguingly, "impressiveness," a measure of something perhaps more like awe or monumentalism, took slightly longer, but still within a narrow temporal window. In addition to establishing a framework for quick, putatively bottom-up analysis, the VIMAP raises three important considerations: first, there may be multiple feedback loops between supposedly top-down and bottom-up processes; second, some top-down processes like meaning making may occur over extended periods of time; and third, aesthetic experiences refer back to goals about who we want to be as well as what we want to do.

While deep, engaged aesthetic experience may depend on prolonged contemplation over minutes, hours, or years, our aesthetic temperature—the warmth of response to an object we may come to deeply love—may be set quite early. As much as some of us might wish it were not true, a variety of studies have shown that on average, individuals spend very little time looking at art in museums (though they may take longer in contemplation—they may return in memory, in photographs, in imagination, or in person): the maximum time in one study was thirteen minutes.[39] As I argued earlier, this seems to hold true for poetry as well: artworks may direct their audiences in focusing attention, and in noticing and valuing the aesthetic stakes at play. In other words, as the critic Kenneth Burke argued, the beginning may offer keys to the middle and the end.[40] The VIMAP is one of the most complete models to date of aesthetic experience, yet some of its key elements depend on principles that require further analysis, beginning with considering how far it can be generalized to other, nonvisual, aesthetic modalities.

For music, one of the more advanced models has been proposed by Elvira Brattico and colleagues; it also, however, offers some guidance for a more domain-general model of aesthetics.[41] The Brattico model lays out sequential brain processes, beginning with sensory analysis, and it proposes five timepoints in processing that track relatively closely to the five internal stages (subjective/internal to the beholder) of the original Leder model and the VIMAP, with a few key revisions. Brattico includes early emotional reactions in the first stage; next comes rule-based cognitive processing of musical features; more complex emotion emerges at stage three; particularly aesthetic forms of affect and judgment come next; and finally, conscious liking follows. The model spans an expanded temporal range, from the vanishingly brief timescale of around 1,000 milliseconds to more open-ended processes and experiences of emotion and thought. However, as with many cognitivist models, the possibilities for longer-term engagement pose challenges; it is simply hard to address these processes experimentally. Indeed, only a few such approaches have been effectively shown to date—for example, looking at effects of expertise, evidence of brain plasticity or repeated exposure, and developmental processes or disorders.[42]

Bottom-Up versus Top-Down

Both the VIMAP and Brattico models begin their detailed analysis largely with sensation. However, some aesthetic experiences by their nature deemphasize sensation as origin, like the pleasures that may come with reading. Sensory input is not the start here in part because some of the sense data that undergirds reading has minimal importance for literary experience: the visual input of black ink on a white page generally fades quickly from conscious perception as we extract meaning and become engaged, contented, or simply bored.[43] Hence Arthur Jacobs's model of reading begins with the goals readers may bring to a text, and divides literary experiences into two paths, rather than integrating them into a single, hierarchical sequence. One route leads to aesthetic pleasure and is driven by formal features of the text; the other leads to immersion and occurs when formal features recede as the frame might around a window.[44]

For Jacobs, motivation for reading matters because it helps determine conditions for attracting attention. Reading for pleasure, for example, may make a transporting experience more likely—if you also pick the correct book (for instance, most readers are more likely to get lost in a novel than a refrigerator manual—though that's not a universal truth). Motivation (and training) are also important in whether or not a reader attends to formal features like rhyme or assonance; as I have argued, literary form is only present when known. It may be known declaratively (by, say, the rules of a sonnet or a sestina), but we can also learn about form through pleasure, as pleasure, too, directs attention.

All these models to some degree maintain the common distinction between higher- and lower-order or top-down and bottom-up processes. In general, researchers theorize that lower-order processes are relatively automatic and fast, while higher-order processes are slower, more subject to conscious control, and more fully involve judgment. Simon Lutterbie argues that this split shapes far too much cognitivist aesthetics.[45] To begin, the top-down/bottom-up distinction is not entirely clean, and integration can happen incredibly quickly, even within 200–300 milliseconds.[46] With music, for example, emotion regulation may be influenced by formal characteristics of the work itself, which may generate sensory pleasures without higher-order, integrative processes; but attentional direction can also influence emotion. Indeed, as we have seen, learned preferences and pleasure may influence very early, "lower-order" events, as with the temporal segmentation of birdsong by human listeners.[47]

There also is evidence that the common view of hierarchical, top-down/bottom-up processes may cloud accurate understanding of the ways percepts and visual features are integrated into complex aesthetic experiences. John O'Doherty and colleagues demonstrate how a simplified, linear model can integrate three relatively basic components of visual processing into a predictor of aesthetic pleasure. In their first analysis, they identified nine low-level visual features (like mean hue contrast) and four high-level ones (e.g., "concreteness" or "dynamism") that hierarchically contributed to a positive aesthetic judgment. But on a second pass, they discovered that not only did a linear feature summation predict pleasure, but a deep convolutional neural network model (DCNN) could do so as well.[48] In this analysis, some (though not all) higher-order features emerged spontaneously from lower-order ones. While, as these researchers note, their linear model may simplify multiple underlying, complex computational functions and neural systems, it does so with little loss of predictive value. This underlines the relative blind spots surrounding conventional wisdom on hierarchical processes, and while it may trouble the distinction between high and low, it still gives hope that we can model aesthetic judgments cleanly.

Modeling Motivation

Understanding the integration of sensation and cognition requires a look more at motivation than putative hierarchies of bottom or top because motivation has a significant impact on distribution of resources. There is a path-dependency in motivation that may be crucial in aesthetic responses: we may change goals; we may alter our tactics; we may adjust attention, and more. I start off by offering a model based in visual art, and with a relatively general goal, then move to domain-specific revisions, exploring ways particular goals may alter the basics and shape of aesthetic experience over time. In the first take, I contrast an aesthetic "miss" with a home run, incorporating some of the findings of an experiment described in chapter 2, in which my colleagues and I showed participants images of museum artworks for varying durations.[49] Notably, not only did the DMN rebound quickly during the most pleasing experiences, but it also rebounded—with a delay of a few seconds—for the least pleasurable ones too.

This raises a key question: what is the ultimate measure of artistic success? Is the correct measure transformative experience, as the authors of the VIMAP suggest (in their view, this emerges usually over a long time course: days, months, or years)? Or is it Menninghaus and colleagues' "being moved" (which may happen in a single encounter)? Certainly, reading through a poem once can be transformative, if you see, hear, or understand the world differently afterwards. Most analyses of aesthetic response are interested in elucidating particular aesthetic experiences or responses, whether positive, negative, or mixed. However, little attention is paid to aesthetic failures. An aesthetic failure in my terms wouldn't be, for example, a viewer's evaluation of something as not beautiful (say, ugly or challenging), or even a mistaken judgment (a viewer might have misunderstood the aesthetic aims of an artwork). We often withdraw from aesthetic experiences that we find to be *un*moving. We walk out of a film house, close a book, or turn away in a gallery. Up until the moment we pull away, many of the same analytic processes are most probably underway, especially if we take something like the Leder model as instructive, where evaluation is reserved for stage five; in the Brattico version, emotional responses emerge at early sensory processing stages, but conscious liking emerges only at the end. As we have seen, however, the findings of O'Doherty and colleagues place the idea of aesthetic evaluation as purely high-level analysis into question.

At least three possibilities exist. First, given that early sensory processes (e.g., auditory analysis) may generate pleasure or displeasure as well as emotional responses, perhaps a later process may kick in at a certain threshold when a powerful sense of aesthetic pleasure is produced. For example, peak pleasure in visual art selectively engages regions of the DMN (figure 3.2).

Another possibility is that such gating/thresholding works only within particular modalities and/or looks different in different modes. Thus, for example, peak pleasure in music and poetry may emerge through the phenomena of chills, which have their own (neuro)physiology that differs from most peak visual pleasure. Finally, retrospective assimilation of early moments may determine the *felt* outcome of aesthetic experience as pleasurable in sum. For example, the first notes of a fugue may become recognizable as variation on a theme that is only resolved when the listener

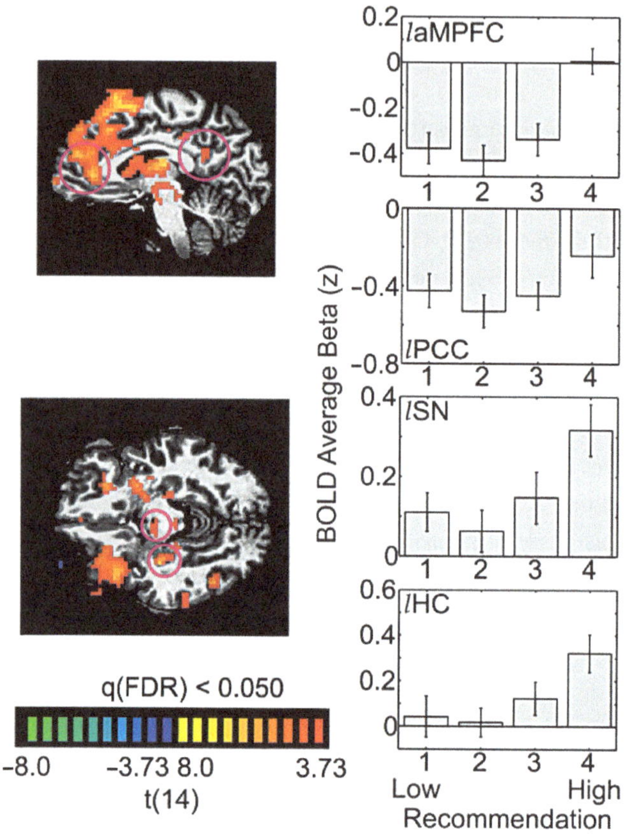

Figure 3.2

The default mode network and several subcortical regions show increased activation for only the most aesthetically pleasing images. The whole-brain images illustrate the *t*-statistic for the 4-vs.-321 contrast. Panels on the right illustrate the average beta weight (as a *z*-score) for each recommendation level, averaged across 15 observers (*l*aMPFC = left anterior medial prefrontal cortex; *l*PCC = left posterior cingulate cortex; *l*SN = left substantia nigra; *l*HC = left hippocampus). Error bars are standard errors of the mean across observers. Reproduced from Vessel, Starr, and Rubin, "The Brain on Art," *Frontiers in Human Neuroscience* (2012).

comes to the conclusion of the work. For some kinds or exemplars of the arts, this might be the behavioral equivalent of O'Doherty's linear integration to a summative judgment. Indeed, continuous measures of subjective pleasure exhibit some kinds of summation. For example, in comparing overall judgments of enjoyment of music to moment-to-moment sensations of pleasure, Belfi and colleagues show a relatively linear curve, wherein ratings, averaged across individuals, for strongly preferred trials increase asymptotically, while low trials decrease in a similar fashion (figure 3.3).

The second panel of figure 3.3 shows that the earliest judgments are farther from the final judgment than are later ones.[50] Again, such a summative curve might suggest that this kind of pleasure shares some features of processes involved in perceptual binding—how we put together disaggregated features to create a unified percept—or to the "hard problem" problem of how conscious aesthetic experiences emerge from a diverse range of inputs.[51]

But what are the "inputs"? Some of us object to a kind of reductionism that renders an artwork simply as "input." Indeed, if we think of an aesthetic experience as beginning with an encounter with an object, and extending sometime after the object is no longer physically or perceptually present, we should, conceivably, link multiple experiences (of the same or different objects) together in cycles over an indefinite period of time. Each aesthetic experience shapes taste, expectation, and learning. Yet we should also note that there is always a preexisting state that the aesthetic moment interrupts or builds upon. Those prior states may be influenced by other aesthetic experiences, via memory, expertise, or declarative knowledge, by current affect or mood, as well as by a variety of individual traits.[52] The model I put forward begins at what I call summative baseline states, which integrate conditions that vary for different individuals and at different times.

Finding a Baseline

From an experimental as well as a more everyday perspective, a summative baseline state should be capacious, but some aspects are difficult to isolate experimentally. Researchers frequently collect data about mood or affect, openness to aesthetic experience or genre, experience and expertise or knowledge, and so on.[53] Those measures are crucial for exploring potential confounds but also for gaining a broader knowledge about aesthetics. One also may attempt to constrain physiological baseline states in key systems, as when investigators use a fixation cross in visual experiments to indicate the start of a trial, or resting state scans to establish functional connectivity. However, I am less concerned with all the precise conditions at play for an individual than with a schematic and systemic perspective on baseline.

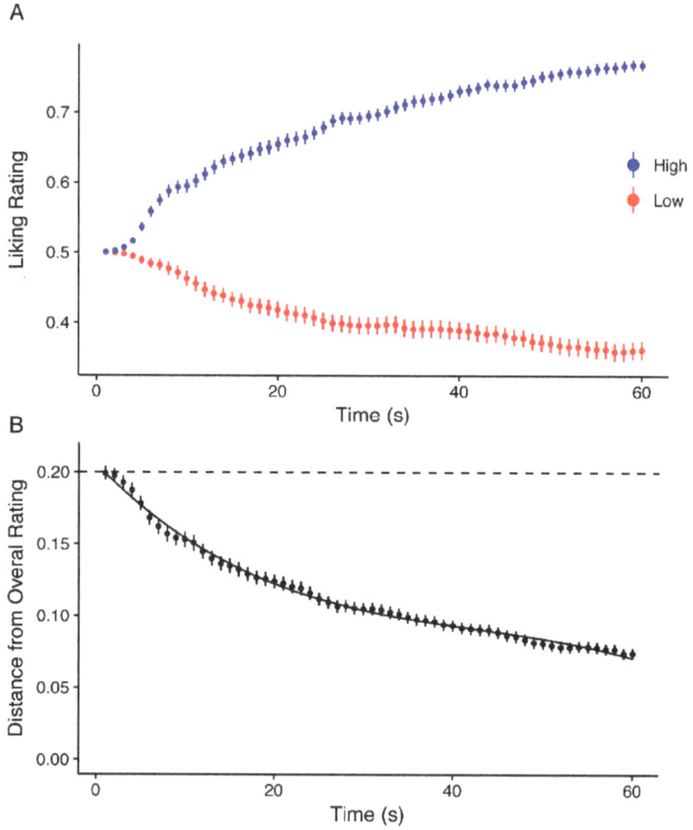

Figure 3.3
Continuous ratings over time for music. Panel A. Continuous ratings averaged over the most liked ("high," blue) and least liked ("low," red) trials. Error bars indicate standard error the mean. Panel B. Continuous ratings across all trials plotted as the distance from the overall rating. The solid black line represents the model fit. The dotted horizontal line indicates "chance" performance. The chance level was determined by calculating the mean difference between the final rating for each trial and the starting value of each trial (.50). Error bars indicate standard error of the mean. Reproduced from Belfi et al., "Rapid Timing of Musical Aesthetic Judgments," *Journal of Experimental Psychology: General* (2018).

Whether in a lab or in daily waking life, we are generally aware, to a greater or lesser degree, of our own surroundings and the status of our bodies and emotions.[54] It is notable that no single brain system would integrate all of this information; rather, it would require activation (simultaneously or sequentially, hierarchically or recursively) of several systems to fully engage these states. However, the SN carries out much of our centralized monitoring of exterior and interoceptive, salient data, with the posterior insula facilitating responses to changing conditions through connections to visual and sensory-motor regions. In particular, the anterior insula connects to middle and inferior frontal gyri, the basal ganglia, and the anterior and medial prefrontal cortex. Thus, the anterior insula has dynamic connections that allow switching between the DMN (via, for example, the amPFC) and the CEN (enabling, for example, motor planning). The input into the anterior insula and its involvement in overall tasks of self-monitoring enable the SN to support the integration of a somatic, sensory, and affective baseline.[55] As Steven Brown and colleagues argue, aesthetic evaluation involves "interaction between interoceptive and exteroceptive processing via recurrent connectivity between anterior insula and OFC."[56]

To see how this can work with aesthetics, let's reexamine the idea of a baseline state and how it could be represented parsimoniously. While no single network will be able to represent all of experience at a given point, this is in part because much more is happening around and within any individual than what can be captured in a snapshot or even over the unrolling of several moments in time. A variety of events are simply unavailable to consciousness or perception, including a wealth of physiological changes. Still more, there is much that *could be* available to conscious perception at a given moment, but lies outside perceptual focus, outside a current task, or is simply inactive (e.g., content stored in memory). However, to model a successful (enjoyable/moving/intriguing) visual aesthetic experience, in contrast with an unsuccessful one, let us assume a few things.

First, I posit there is generally a goal: one such might be simple enjoyment. Indeed, that is the instruction we have frequently given participants in the work I have carried out with colleagues. For example, we often ask individuals to go through a sequence of images, looking for those they find moving. That goal isn't achieved all that frequently—moderate or little pleasure is more common than intense experiences.[57] However, even when we don't have an explicit task before us, human beings nonetheless engage in goal-oriented behavior. Some of our persistent needs underlie daily activities, like seeking companionship, sustenance, comfort, or pleasure. Given the prevalence of aesthetic experience in daily life, I contend that we frequently scan our environments for what brings aesthetic joy or piques aesthetic interest.[58] Evidence for this exists in the repeated findings that even without making an explicit judgment of beauty, individuals exhibit neurological activity that indicates we have perceived something pleasurable.[59] So, let's assume that this scanning of the environment takes place consistently (unless other goals demand attentional resources or there's other interference—anhedonia or negative mood, for example, may lower our susceptibility to the experience of beauty.)[60]

I focus on a subset of structures and systems that are modulated with the success of an aesthetic experience (even as evidence is not clear at every level—with some exceptions—about the *necessity* for these systems to a given experience, they are certainly implicated by multiple layers of experimentation).[61] For example, the lateral visual network is modulated upward alongside increased pleasure in looking.[62] We know that more goes into aesthetic processes in the brain than can be accounted for by pleasure alone, but I focus on complex hedonic processes because aesthetic experience cannot exist without them. As Fingerhut and Prinz argue, there is no such thing as a cold aesthetic judgment. Calling something a "good" artwork is an evaluation and necessarily involves emotions; in turn, emotions have a hedonic tone.[63] My model seeks to elucidate the relationship between systems that integrate our somatic experiences with those that enable hedonic evaluation of aesthetic objects.

Figure 3.4 shows two potential short-term outcomes of an experiment like that described in chapter 2. Participants were instructed to inform the experimenters of how much pleasure they took in looking at images of museum artworks, which were displayed for one, five, or fifteen seconds. They used a squeeze ball to indicate their own levels of pleasure from moment to moment, and then made a summative judgment of pleasure at the end via sliding a trackball. I argue that in the baseline condition—at the start of an experimental trial—the SN would be engaged in monitoring the individual's immediate environment and the CEN directing attention; when an image is presented, a variety of systems begin analysis and synthesis of components of that environment, leading to several kinds of evaluation: emotional, semantic, mnemonic, and hedonic. Systems throughout the body register changes in feeling, features of coherence and meaning, and finally they help answer for at least a moment, if not longer, a key question: does this experience meet the bar that an individual recognizes as aesthetic pleasure?

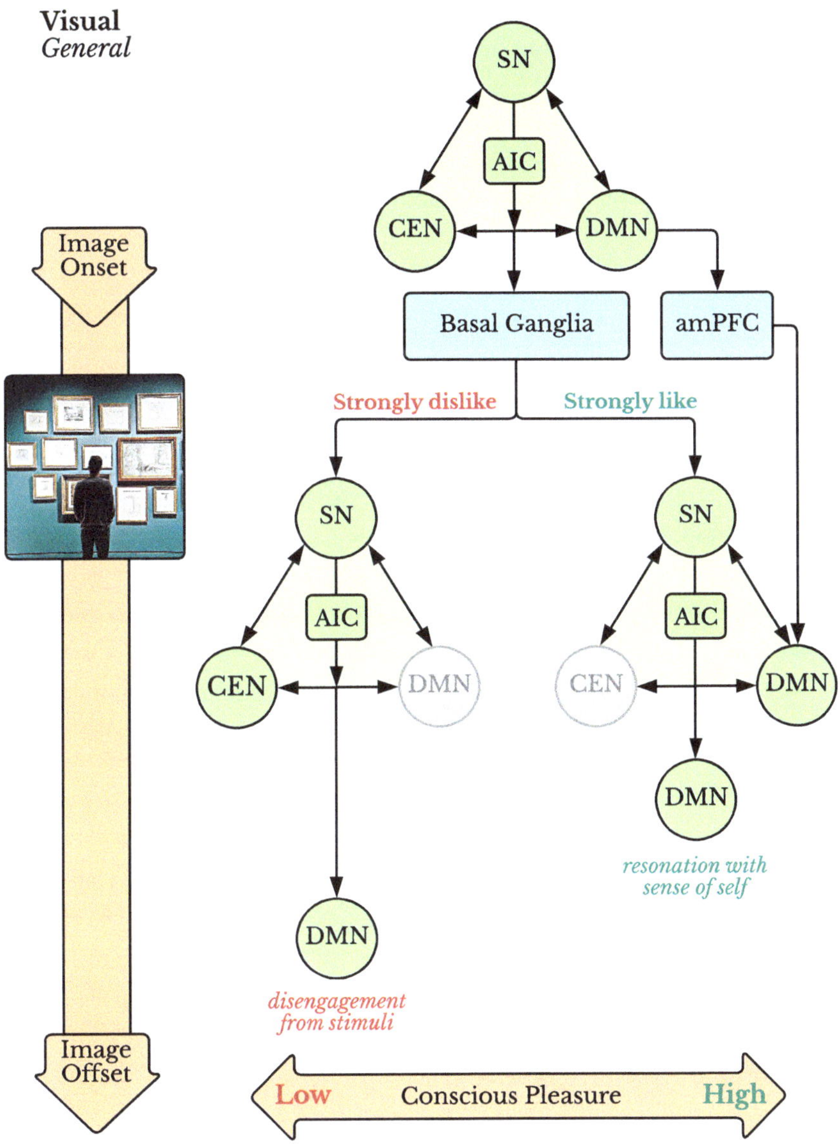

Figure 3.4
General visual model. Each triangle represents the dynamic balance between three apex transmodal networks: salience (SN), central executive (CEN), and default-mode (DMN). Areas in the basal ganglia and anterior medial prefrontal cortex carry out evaluations of reward and affective potential, respectively. The SN detects the outcome of these analyses and modulates the balance between the DMN and CEN. Image credit: Marilyn Perkins.

The leftmost panel of figure 3.4 tracks the presentation of the image. The right side shows a strong aesthetic success. While the SN is undertaking normal monitoring, the DMN and CEN should also be active in a baseline state. In an everyday context, one might imagine, for example, encountering an aesthetically powerful object while on a walk and daydreaming. Equally, it might be that you are concentrating on a task like framing a portrait; the CEN enables focused attention, while a stray glance takes you deeper into what you are seeing. The greater the immersion, the more engagement of the DMN, and less of the CEN. However, in a controlled experiment we can match neural and behavioral events to moments like when an image appears on-screen. The co-activation of the DMN alongside the SN or CEN reflects what Camilo Cela-Conde and colleagues have described as regulation of attention based on the relevance of "guid[ing] conduct [while engaging with] . . . stimuli of special importance."[64]

In the middle of figure 3.4 is an aesthetic failure. A variety of events may follow, depending on whether or not an individual identifies a new goal, and what that goal might be.[65] Ultimately, in the relatively brief time of an image presentation in an experiment like ours, we argued that the viewer gives up on artwork that doesn't generate profound response, and turns to a combination of rumination; I here add baseline monitoring.[66] The process starts again with a new trial and a new image (our intertrial interval ranged from two to twenty seconds, with a mean of 6.76 seconds).

A key question in systems neuroscience is particularly germane here: what counts as a neural system? This is especially important given that early work in neuroaesthetics identified brain regions (not connectivity among them) and that current research indicates that what had been understood as *the* DMN may in fact be two closely linked networks. Theoretically, almost every neuron in the brain can "speak" to another one given enough relays, as I have described. But neurons can be subdivided, classified, and connected in a variety of ways. Some of the earliest categorizations depended on visual characteristics of cells, grouping like ones together. More recently, techniques for studying gene expression enable scientists to detect other kinds of similarities. Cell types may also be identified by staining (as with the longtime near ubiquity of Korbinian Brodmann's anatomical map), by tracing uptake of radiation (e.g., through positron emission tomography or PET), by neurotransmitter selectivity (a neuron dopaminergic or

GABAergic, for example), or by something so basic as Hebb's Law: whatever fires together is wired together.

Understanding brain activity as localized in a region or part of a system for aesthetics begins with assessing underlying functional connectivity. My work with collaborators has involved the acquisition of resting-state scans for individual participants, and then comparing them to a set of reference maps.[67] This helps model connectivity for individuals. In addition to this kind of spatial analysis, one can also examine connectivity in small time windows. Using magnetoencephalography (MEG) to gain fine temporal resolution, Cela-Conde and colleagues were able to identify three brain states at work in aesthetic judgment. The first is something like my summative baseline: "Both recent experience and consolidated abilities leave memory traces that affect the resting-state networks" in the state they call TW_0—the beginning of an experimental trial.[68] Because individuals cannot know whether or not they will find an artwork beautiful before they see it, connectivity at TW_0 is similar for individuals across the entire experiment.

Their experiment also identified two separate time windows for aesthetic evaluation. In the first window (250ms–750ms after an image is presented), both "beautiful" and "not beautiful" judgments emerge, and they rely on analysis in the same brain regions (primarily in the OFC); this synchronization is linked to the examination of characteristics of an object in light of its reward value and the emotions an individual experiences or considers (emotion information need not necessarily involve online experience, but may involve consideration of potential emotional responses). However, "assessment of beauty seems to appear in the dynamic transit between" them, in a narrow window of about 250ms.[69] In the second time window (1,000–1,500ms), the DMN comes online, and intriguingly, the authors suggest that two other systems that focus attention are implicated. One "maintains endogenous signals based off expectation of seeing an object at a particular location, linking relevant stimuli to responses." The other, which they call "the ventro-parietal network, responds along with the dorsal network when behaviorally relevant objects or targets are detected."[70] Together these systems allow attention to be reoriented to different kinds of important events or objects: those that come from expectation and are important to preparations for action, and those that individuals identify as relevant in a particular context—in this case, it is the context of aesthetic pleasure. Both of these kinds of evaluations involve the match between an object or event and a goal; they argue that these merge when a viewer experiences beauty and diverge when they do not.[71] My model of apex transmodal systems in aesthetics is consistent with the authors' view in broad terms, yet proposes that goal identification or switching—rather than primarily switches in attention—would coordinate temporal sequencing that leads to an extended or truncated aesthetic experience.

It is important to note that not all the processes indexed in this model need take place as quickly as 1,500ms. While the three networks on which I focus are transient in nature, they are subject to reengagement and they reflect conscious processes. For example, changing goals when engaging an artwork may be quite common, especially on an extended encounter. If, say, an artwork conflicts with one's moral or ethical principles, that could activate a competing goal that matters to a viewer (like understanding why an artist would make the particular choices that lead to what one sees). At the end of the process, if a viewer feels pleasure, the final state might be something like calm relaxation.[72] If the goal is understanding complexity, the final state might be excitement or frustration, and so on.

Shifting Sensory Modes

This model can't work in the same way for listening to music, in part simply because the demands placed on some regions of the DMN by elements of musical analysis mean the network cannot be recruited for some works. Indeed, experiments to date have shown no coordinated DMN activity with most musical responses (I will discuss an important exception, familiar music, shortly). Yet more intriguingly, a key behavioral phenomenon that may be correlated with DMN activity for visual aesthetics has also *not* been demonstrated for song: the self-relevance effect. One possible explanation of DMN function in powerful visual aesthetic experience has to do with the idea of self-relevant cognition: an artwork activates a DMN response by generating thoughts and ideas that are internally relevant.[73] The self-relevance effect is well known around memory—we tend to remember things better that have some connection to our sense of self.[74] Intriguingly, a self-relevance effect has been found in relationship to visual aesthetics, where for novices (but not experts), undertaking a pleasurable aesthetic evaluation is enhanced by the presence of a strong memory of an artwork.[75] In addition, visual objects presented to individuals for aesthetic judgment are recognized at the same probability as items presented as part of a task in which individuals judge the degree of self-relevance, *but only* for items rated very high or low on an aesthetic pleasure scale.[76] In other words, powerful aesthetic experience seems to drive enhanced recollection. Thus, there is further evidence that the engagement of the DMN in visual aesthetics specifically involves concepts of self and self-knowledge, and is driven by powerful affect.[77]

Yet while visual aesthetic experience may be influenced by an assessment of self-relevance—this matters *to me*—similar self-relevance effects have not shown up with music, as Anna Kasdan and Amy Belfi have demonstrated: memory is not enhanced for self-relevant, aesthetically pleasing pieces.[78] This negative finding is surprising, given that music is full of possibilities for self-relevant thought: remembering a song from a summer's enjoyment, reliving past sorrow, or (perhaps worse) recalling one's teenage years are quite common musical experiences. Indeed, many people give an important place to music as part of autobiographical memory.[79]

The importance of the DMN to visual aesthetic experience, combined with the connection of memory to visual aesthetics *and* the ability to disrupt the experience of beauty by taxing working memory, raise at least two considerations.[80] First, is it necessary to have a functional and fully interconnected DMN to experience intense visual beauty? If so, that would exclude many non-neurotypical individuals and would also make it questionable as to whether young children could access intense visual beauty at all. Second, it raises the question of why visual beauty might recruit the DMN when other arts do not: is it simply a matter of competing demands on cognitive capacity as a whole or in some particular brain regions?

Let's take the first concern. Current knowledge about both neural plasticity and signal transmission suggests that if one path does not work, is damaged or busy, another route may be recruited.[81] This may occur on a network scale, rather than that of a single brain structure: for example, children do not have a fully myelinated and functionally connected DMN, compared to that of neurotypical adults. But this doesn't mean that children cannot perform many of the activities the DMN subserves, like thinking about the future or the past or daydreaming. They may not do so as cleanly as adults, at times confusing reality with dream, but they can do it. And while most children may not appreciate Cy Twombly's art as much as do some of their elders, that doesn't mean they can't appreciate it at all.

So how does the DMN matter in visual aesthetics? One possibility may be that the DMN and its regions function for aesthetic response differently at different developmental moments or for different genres and sensory modes. For example, to return to the metaphor of the information superhighway, if the interstate isn't yet connected, there still are networks of local roads that can get you from point A to E. If a hub of the DMN is unavailable for transmitting information, there are workarounds: the nine or more superhubs of the human brain connectome also link to medium- or low-power, and increasingly local, networks. Thus, it is arguable—and in fact testable—that we might be able to enhance visual aesthetic experiences in a young person by connecting an image to the child's future or past through discussion, even if the child might not do so on their own. Context and interaction thus might help shape an experience biology would not automatically support. Understanding and "getting" art is at some level a process of meaning making. As we as individual viewers learn more, we might more easily come to the kind of holistic view of an artwork that enables powerful aesthetic experiences.

Beyond questions of development, there are other considerations at play in whether or how the DMN might engage during intense aesthetic experience. One key element has to do with complexity. The DMN tends not to be task-negative (the way it was initially described), but to be sensitive to the demands of the tasks or experience at hand and to trade-offs around them. So, for example, the DMN has been shown to be active in listening to *familiar* music, pieces that would presumably involve less taxing analysis; moreover, as with visual art, both highly preferred ("favorite") and least preferred familiar music engaged the DMN.[82] In these cases, the ability to prioritize pleasure may be at stake, as well as the capacity to de-emphasize taxing sensory analysis.

Another key concern involves genre and the particular goals we bring to engagements with them. For example, the enjoyment of music often involves establishing different goals than does the enjoyment of visual art. As I described previously, with music, we might wish to regulate or enhance the relationship between our bodies and the world around us: thus, you might take advantage of entrainment to a beat to move faster or more precisely as you work on a technique that requires rhythmic, fine motor control. Alternatively, one might seek to screen out unwanted elements of your environment, like noise or silence, by producing soundscapes conducive to a desired activity. We may also bring a concern about regulating a social environment to an engagement with music: we might want to set a mood for a party or a dinner for two; we might wish to dance with others; or we might seek to share the emotions of a moment through, say, songs about faith, patriotism, or love.[83]

In all these cases, music facilitates a nonmusical task, and one that may require adjusting aims or tactics. One might wonder if these experiences are aesthetic. However, while they may not carry all the features we could associate with intense aesthetic experience, these encounters involve interactions with features proper to music, as well as pleasure or emotion evoked by music, and they rely on the experience of music rather than just a description of musical elements. Thus, these experiences *enable* aesthetic engagements, even as they may not match the view of aesthetic appreciation that has become canonical in the West (e.g., rapt attention in a concert hall). Indeed, because of the broad way that music moves our lives, models of aesthetic experience ought to be able to accommodate their rich variety.

So, let's begin with the idea that listeners establish goals for musical engagement: the *whys* we bring to listening. The next steps in one's experience, and the brain systems involved, should vary by goal. At the start, at least three elements influence early auditory processes. Pleasure can help determine the extraction of time and tempo, thus influencing the potential for reward by establishing conditions for expectation violation. Emotional responses may also be almost reflexive in the early moments.[84] Familiarity may matter, too, easing analysis of musical features and thus release of attention for other tasks.[85]

One way familiarity may shape neural responses is via adaptation and habituation.[86] With paintings and other static visual art, sensory features like light or color are relatively stable, and while initial semantic analysis may be complete relatively quickly, over extended viewing two things happen. First, the visual system quickly adapts to a stimulus after having encoded it: this happens at the level of cells in the retina, as well as with neurons in visual cortex, so that these cells no longer respond as strongly to visual input. At longer intervals, we tend to habituate, no longer paying as much attention to familiar elements of the environment as when they were fresh. Resources may be devoted to other kinds of analysis or engagement, whether that means mind-wandering, lingering over emotions, exploring content more deeply, or pursuing free association, all of which should promote DMN rebound. However, with unfamiliar music, listeners need to continue to engage with a changing auditory landscape, and neither habituation nor adaptation is as easy. Of course, particular elements of a composition might also promote disengagement from immediate sensory processes, like repetition of a thematic element, particular notes, or instruments.

Third, familiarity may also bring other possibilities, as it may carry the freight of past encounters. For many years, I could not bear to hear "Amazing Grace" without bursting into tears, as for weeks following September 11, 2001, a bagpiper played the hymn outside my window in New York City. Perhaps those moments point toward a classic example of music and its pro-social uses. Many of us who passed by or gathered in Washington Square Park and had seen the towers fall (or worse—we could still smell the smoke of the pyre, and buildings weren't all that fell that day) could not help but mourn, and to mourn together as that music accessed memories and feelings just underneath the surface. The sociality of listening to music was evident both in bringing people together in a public space and in the act of collective mourning. For strangers to experience these moments as both individual and collective, we needed to be aware not just of our own responses but the responses of those around us. In facilitating the shared experience of listening, the piper, I imagine, found some solace in making music for wanderers in a broken city.

While we are now able to understand many of the neurological processes that might be involved in elements of such an experience (say, those that lead to tears or goosebumps), more broadly significant in my view are those systems monitoring self and environment that help coordinate the experience as a whole.[87] Many of my fellow listeners in the park probably had not arrived with an aesthetic goal in mind (other than enjoying the bright sunshine in one of the few green spaces in lower Manhattan), and only the loosest of social goals (walking, perhaps in the company of others), but once the opening tones were played, it was hard—at least for me—to hear or think of much else. Much of my attention was drawn within, to reliving the original experiences, into a chain of memories. However, once collective mourning and remembrance began, a temporal arc accompanied the music. I won't say my mourning was complete at the close of the hymn, but a certain social experience was over once we dispersed. As an audience, many of us experienced a shared time of elevated sadness, a feeling of release and a return to our irrevocably changed daily lives.

To model this, again I begin with a baseline condition that balances the three high-level transmodal networks, and have modified it to consider how audition and different goals—especially a pro-social goal—might alter their interaction. As individuals listened to the piper play, I suspect the DMN and SN were relatively upregulated compared to the CEN, as the salient cues here involve internal registers of emotion and social cues about expressiveness and affect.

At the top of the model in figure 3.5 is goal identification. This can include more than a single specific goal, and the range of relevant goals that may be active as we move through our environments may also change.[88] Goals may increase in priority as needs, attention, or environments shift. Enter a party, and social goals may take pride of place; experience sadness, and mood regulation becomes important, should you wish to feel better; see or hear something unusual, and the desire for comprehension may be a priority, and so on. Goals lead to expectations for reward, which in turn influence evaluations of salience and task focus. A range of regions key to music analysis or more generally important in emotion and aesthetic processes may engage throughout listening. Reward signals emerge in the basal ganglia (as well as the OFC); depending on the reward outcome, the CEN-SN-DMN homeostatic wheel spins again.

In broad brushstrokes, cycles of listening and emotion such as I describe set a tempo for goal time. Goal time here encapsulates the serial and cyclical thoughts, feelings, and actions that accompany achievement or frustration of a reward; in this case, it also helps define our interactions with aesthetic objects. Such interactions need not be in the flesh, but can happen in memory, via a reproduction, or even conversation. They can dilate over an expansive period—years even—or narrow down to the briefest of encounters (say, an osprey's arcing across the sky).

A useful model of these experiences should, of course, make testable hypotheses. In spring 2021, I was teaching a course on time and aesthetics, and we closed out the semester by reviewing a broad range of cognitive models of aesthetic experience. We began our discussion with a question: how would you test these models? The answers my students gave were striking, ranging widely across multiple questions on sensory mode or genre. When they came back from their breakout groups, however, their skepticism was

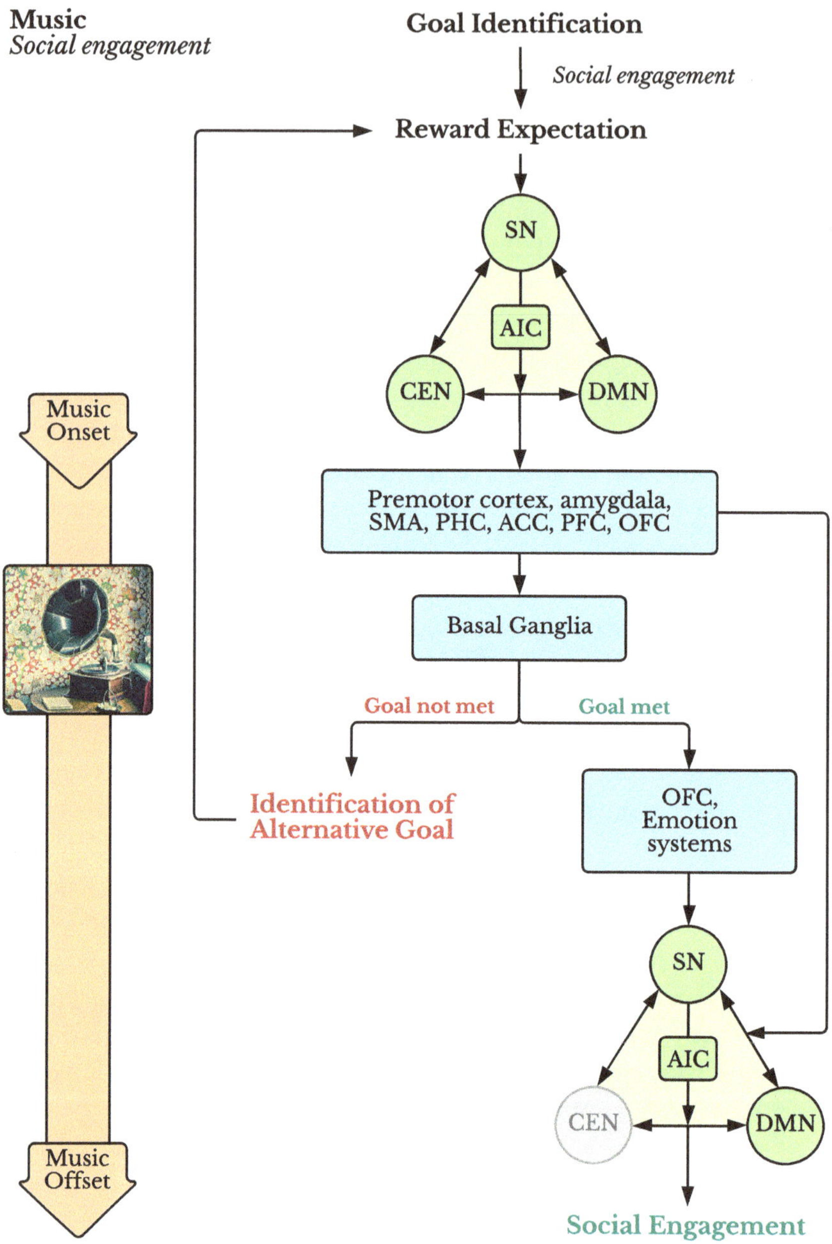

Figure 3.5

Music, social engagement. When the context is set by a desire for social engagement, the DMN should engage as part of a representation of emotional and behavioral analysis and imagination of others. Image credit: Marilyn Perkins.

bracing: how could you test the entirety of any of these models? I agreed with them; I didn't think any of these comprehensive approaches to date could be fully tested. For example, fMRI and EEG are designed for timescales of seconds; transcranial magnetic stimulation (TMS) has relatively poor spatial resolution; lesion studies tend to be better at confirming other methods as human lesions are necessarily uncontrolled; longitudinal studies on aging or development are hard to maintain in large populations, and so on.

A good model need not answer every question. Still, there are important principles worth discussing. William Seeley argues the dominant aesthetic models draw on a principle of biased competition, whereby "priming the firing rate with populations of neurons in sensory systems to the expectation of diagnostic features at a particular location" disposes attention to what fits the expected pattern.[89] These models (including those I discuss above) are largely hierarchical (as Seeley points out), and they rely on feedback loops that are not entirely well-understood. They do describe some processes well, yet what we still have to understand are longitudinal processes, both those that evolve in hours or days and those that spread over years or a lifetime.

Chatterjee and Vartanian suggest a large-scale view that places key cognitive systems in an integrated and nonhierarchical cycle, an "aesthetic triad," balancing systems for emotion/value, knowledge/meaning, and sensory-motor responses.[90] Among the virtues of Chatterjee and Vartanian's cyclical framework, it does not require strict separation of top-down and bottom-up processing, and it promotes understanding of the dilation of aesthetic experiences across time. However, it has limited predictive value regarding how neural systems interact or how they might change or be ordered differently depending on circumstance.

To think about how to model different kinds of aesthetic experiences in a way that helps explain the changing, cyclical interactions of neural processes, let's return to an elementary observation about the DMN and its role in visual aesthetics: DMN activation is important not for all positive or pleasurable visual aesthetic responses—but primarily for those that are the strongest—to what might be understood as peak pleasure. There is substantia nigra activation that increases in a similar pattern to the DMN with hedonic intensity, consistent with the idea that intense pleasure (via dopaminergic signals) might work as part of a gating or threshold mechanism in mutual engagement of the DMN and SN.[91] In other words, self- and situational monitoring might become more easily compatible at high levels of pleasure when motor planning is not required: at high, rather than low, levels of satisfaction there is little left to do.[92] In this context, the relative infrequency with which individuals experience intense visual pleasure is important: my collaborators and I found that "on average, observers used the highest ('4') rating significantly less than 25% of the time. . . . That . . . observers . . . did not calibrate their responses so as to give a rating of '4' to roughly a quarter of the stimuli suggests that they reserved this response for images which met a certain internal (and generally high) criterion."[93] Such relatively infrequent, unexpected pleasure would generally involve a dopamine kick.[94]

If we understand the DMN as engaging as part of peak visual pleasure, we might approach aesthetic failure and peak aesthetic success in varying ways for different genres. For example, many researchers identify the experience of the chills as an expression of peak pleasure for music (and for poetry and film). The musical version of this phenomenon has well-defined contours. A basic structure for musical chills passes through stages of increasing arousal, culminating with a final release of tension. David Huron lays out a clear cognitive view of the chills response (he uses the term "frisson"), arguing that it emerges when a musical feature indexes to or signals potential danger (e.g., biologically, sudden loudness indicates the possibility of imminent threat) so quickly that we cannot consciously label it and may not consciously apprehend it. This is because relatively automatic processes produce a physiological profile that matches to what we generally experience as fear. However, while we don't have a *conscious* sensation of fear, the theory goes, we are aware of a positive appraisal of context—enjoyment of the music itself and the ideas and emotions it raises. Fear anticipates something yet to come; the physiological sense of anticipation in listening to music, however, here takes on a positive valence, so that the prickling of the skin is exciting, even climactic.[95]

Neurologically, the chills include a clear element of reward expectancy, which is anatomically linked (by Salimpoor et al.) to regions in the caudate.[96] Caudate-insula connectivity is central in reward circuitry, and remarkably, in musicians, the anterior insula appears more closely connected to the salience network than in nonmusicians.[97] This might enable speedy affective responses as well as focus on a task like musical analysis. In such a

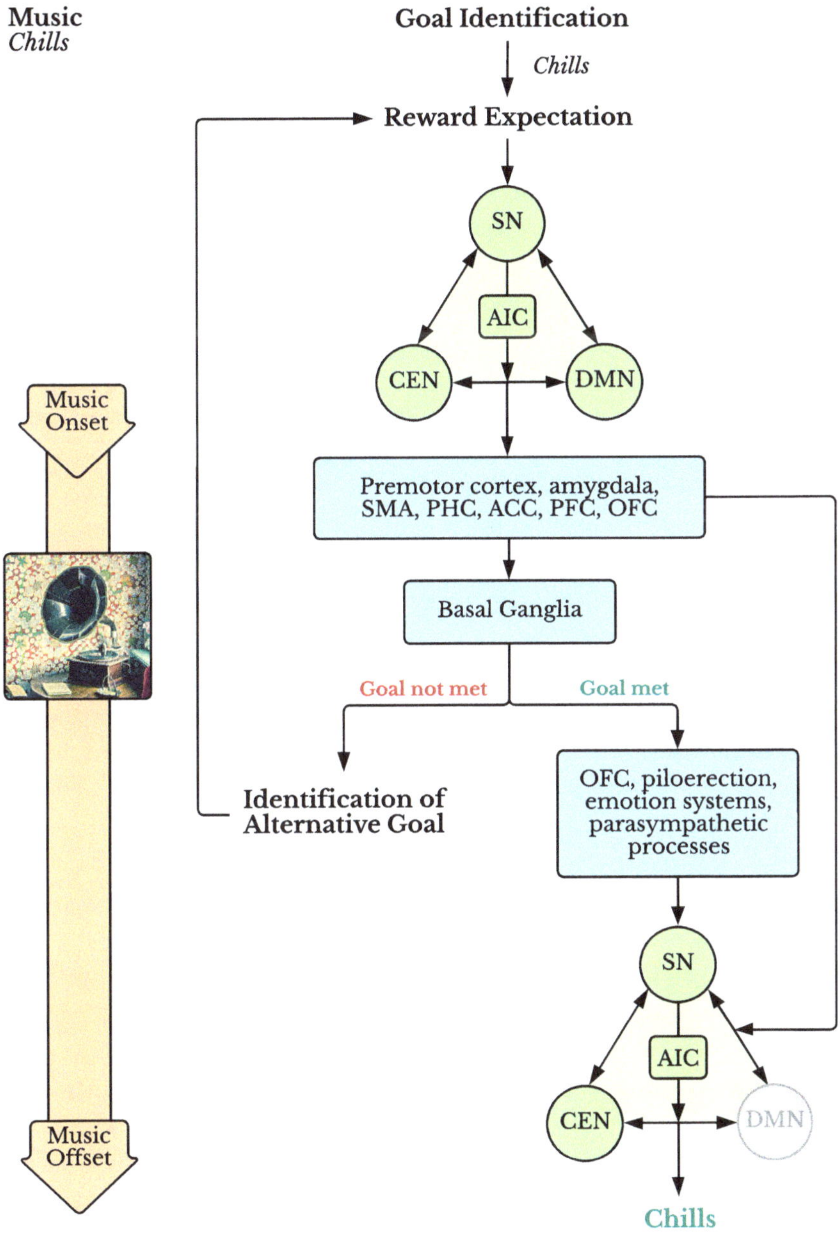

Figure 3.6
Music, chills. Arousal builds in expectation of a peak of pleasure. The SN is engaged in bodily and environmental monitoring, with input from the brain areas indicated in blue. Image credit: Marilyn Perkins.

case, in my model the CEN would be involved in tasks of tracking musical patterns, while the SN would monitor internal and external environment. Changes in musical patterns set the expectation of culmination—chills—that matches onto piloerection and the expected reward of a shudder of delight. Attainment of the goal is rooted in a set of physiological alterations, and one would expect the DMN to be downregulated.

While the temporal structure of music offers ample opportunity for chills, the relatively static nature of painting or photography might make chills more unlikely. While I have rarely encountered chills in looking at visual art, I have experienced them, and they are memorable. One such occasion involved a brief, haunting encounter of a sequence by American photographer Dawoud Bey, *In This Here Place*. The black-and-white photographs are large, the size of windows. Each pane reveals a different vista, remnants of a slave plantation.

Bey begins with the bare clapboards of slave cabins, bleakly textured, tonal: they are purely, simply, and forcibly impoverished, yet they miraculously still stand, and are now fixed in photographic gel. Pane after pane awaits Bey's viewers; the landscape opens up, leaving all structures behind. We depart a world slaves built, to see only the land they worked. Swamps. Grass. An irrigation ditch. Flat water unfit to drink. As I passed from one to the next, my skin broke out alive, moving as of its own accord. The photograph that pierced me so was *Light on the Swamp*.[98]

Out of the desolation, patches of sunlight strike still water; the surface seems to steam, exhaling wet, heavy mist toward the sky. To me it was the moment of escape, the fraught instance of grasping for freedom on the edge of discovery, capture, death . . . or life, everlasting. Nothing moved in my view, but everything moved in me. This moment marked an empathetic precipice, where I, too, entered a terrifying world, alone, with my companions long gone. What registered on my skin is that art altered the way my body exists in time. My imagination hovered over the swamp's exhalations. The treacherous surface of the water reflected sunlight so clearly as I looked into its depths, but somehow there was no face looking back at me. Indeed, it is the uncanny absence of human beings in all these images that haunts me, still. Bey's photographs reveal the ruins of lives as well as landscapes.

My shiver may have something in common with the way chills work in poetry. Eugen Wassiliwizky and colleagues argue that chills are social, most often emerging in response to moments of direct address to the reader, when

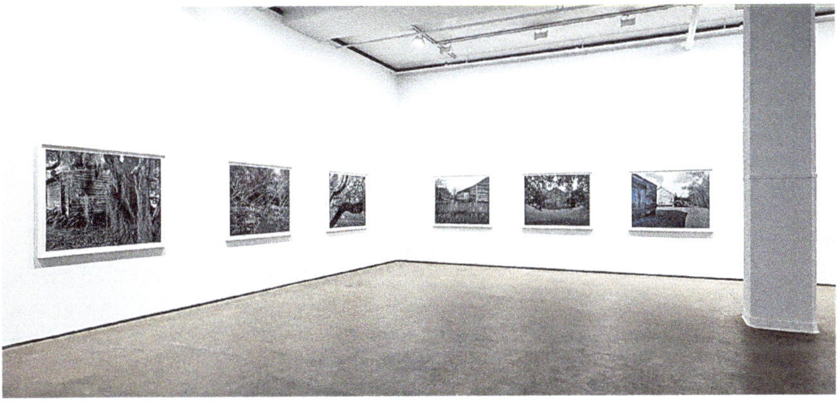

Figure 3.7
Dawoud Bey, *In This Here Place*, 2019. Installation at Sean Kelly Gallery, New York City, September 10–October 23, 2021.

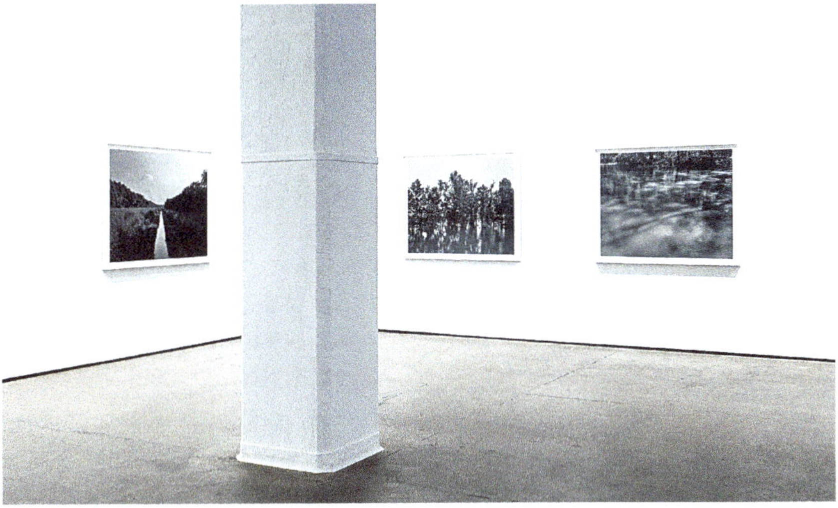

Figure 3.8
Dawoud Bey, *In This Here Place*, 2019. Installation at Sean Kelly Gallery, New York City, September 10–October 23, 2021. *Light on the Swamp* is the third photograph from the left.

a voice speaks out, greeting, commanding, calling out for an answer. Physiologically, the pattern of these responses is straightforward.[99] The authors separate poetic chills into a pre-chill, anticipation phase in which nucleus accumbens activation goes along with an increase in arousal, followed by a dip and a second peak in the chills phase itself; activity in the insula is here shifted posteriorly, compared to music. In order to understand what the authors mean by social address, it may be useful to think about poetry as a performance, because reading aloud, intonation, cadence, and speed are tools in the hands of the speaker to elicit select responses.

For me, Robert Frost's "Once by the Pacific" is like a script for inducing chills. The poem describes looking out over an ocean that seems not just tumultuous but ready to eat the world alive. This sonnet is divisible into three parts, each defined by a different form of voice or address and culminating in a final access of darkness. The three segments map, with some deviations, onto different literary traditions. Sonnets emerged in early modern Italy primarily in the form of love poems, often addressed to the beloved. In English, Edmund Spenser is perhaps the most famous sonneteer of this style. These poems are distinguished by an interlocking rhyme scheme and separate into two parts: octave (the first eight lines) and sestet (the remaining six). The two parts are divided by a "turn"—the volta—that signifies a change in idea, scene, or address.

The first part of "Once by the Pacific" is a variation on the Spenserian pattern, beginning not with a set of eight, but rather six distinct lines. The opening sestet lays out the motivating literary device for the poem—personification, a figure that carries possibilities for direct address, as it imputes social character to nature or an otherwise abstract concept. The second section takes a turn, enacting the volta with directly addressing the reader rather than the furious water. The final couplet makes a third significant shift, one reminiscent of the closing of the Shakespearean sonnet, in exploding the preceding order. I have the benefit of years of accumulated knowledge of the sonnet form in my own awareness that something is very much amiss in Frost's poem. But a good reader can signal to listeners (hence my suggestion that one imagine a performance) the poem's irregularity by emphasizing the two moments of changing address (indicated in bold, with pauses marked by a caesura, °) and lingering over the building darkness and swelling noise, with pauses and breaths shifting moment by moment and line to line. The central, anticipation-producing moment in "Once by the Pacific" comes with the final shift in poetic voice, where it is the *almost* finality of God's almighty words that frames what we might see or hear:

The sháttered wáter ° máde a místy dín.

Greát wáves ° lóoked óver óthers cóming ín,
And thóught of dóing sómething ° tó the shóre
That wáter ° néver díd to lànd befóre.
The clóuds ° were lów and háiry ín the skíes,
Like lócks ° blówn fórward in the gléam of eyés.
You cóuld not téll, ° and yét it loóked as íf
The shóre was lúcky ° in béing bácked by clíff,
The clíff ° in béing bácked by cóntinént;
It lóoked as íf a níght ° of dárk intént
Was cóming, ° and nót ónly a níght, ° an áge.
Sòmeone had bétter bé prepáred ° for ráge.
There wóuld be móre ° than ócean-wáter bróken
Befóre Gód's lást *Pút out the líght* was spóken.[100]

When I read or hear this poem, the shudder rumbles forth—it's not just the thunder of the waves, but the apocalyptic voice from the whirlwind. As with T. S. Eliot's *The Waste Land*, it's not just "What the Thunder said," but that it spoke at all.

Here, the aesthetic power of poetry can be found not primarily or solely in internally focused thought, but rather a social world of collective judgment—the annihilation of humanity. It is indeed noteworthy that moments of direct address frequently produce chills, one of the more intensely pleasurable aesthetic responses.The idea that art might hold a special place in learning social cues and social cohesion is not new, and a number of theorists who approach art via evolutionary psychology have placed this at the heart of the emergence of the arts in human history.[101] My central contention is different. I have argued that the high variability of aesthetic pleasure across individuals is a necessary outcome of the breadth and capaciousness of the decision space that underpins human learning, that pleasure is a signal that allows us to differentiate between outcomes, quickly and memorably, and to discover new goods that one did not anticipate, and that such surprise pleasures are generally particularly powerful. This has important implications in the context of sociality.

One of the key functions of the arts involves social engagement, social ordering, and communication; the peculiar importance of social address (the vocative "you" or "thee," for example) to poetic chills emphasizes the urgency with which aesthetic experience can strike us to the bone when the stakes are high. Frost pushes those stakes near their limit in invoking the moment of utter annihilation, of being damned or saved—which, we yet don't know. The power of poetry is to bring us to the edge of knowing, to the chills of anticipation, of knowledge we hope to find just on the other side of silence, once even God's voice goes beyond our hearing.

In neural terms, I would expect this plays out in part via activation of the posterior cingulate cortex (PCC) here as one might contemplate alterity and imputed thoughts, but not PCC activation as part of engagement of the DMN. Indeed, while elements of the DMN are important to reading, in general the network emerges when readers are engaged in mind-wandering that is closer to distraction from a text than engagement with it, at least with nonfiction.[102] Indeed, by contrast, with visual art the strongest DMN regional activation is in the amPFC, in areas known for self- (not other-) directed thought. The "decision" about whether or not the DMN is engaged is an important one (I put "decision" in quotation marks because individuals don't make conscious choices about brain function or connectivity). As a reader balances goals, textual features, affect (e.g., interest, pleasure), and salient cues in their environment (internal—like being alert or tired—and external—say, a looming deadline or a sudden noise) DMN recruitment reflects one kind of resolution to complicated analyses and choices. In this calculus, distraction is the sibling of immersion; they are two sides of the same neural coin.

As Paul Armstrong points out, one of the aspects of reading that is most important from a cognitive perspective is its extended temporality.[103] Thus, any encounter with literature may involve multiple demands, multiple kinds of response, as well as multiple, sometimes competing, neural systems. For reading, then, I would expect concatenated cycles of goal time, each shaped by changing conditions, pleasures, and desires. Readers can experience these cycles consciously, but awareness of a shift from cycle to cycle may come at varying points, and this, too, will shape the temporal arc. For example, I often find that I enter immersive states or become distracted without noticing. It is only retrospectively, once in the state of immersion or distraction, that I am conscious that I've crossed some mysterious threshold, where colors are extra bright, my own thoughts extra loud, and the page disappears in favor of an imagined scene prompted by words or by my utter disengagement from them. In one case, immersion, time seems to speed up; in the other case, distraction, time seems to slow down. In both, my mental activity seems no longer fully to match the unrolling of words on the page; my eyes move or I turn the page at a pace that doesn't correlate to changes in the richness or paucity of my inner experience. Salience and attention make the difference, as *what* I attend to and *how* I attend to it vary. This is certainly true when it comes to figurative language. Convergent evidence suggests that increased effort in deciding

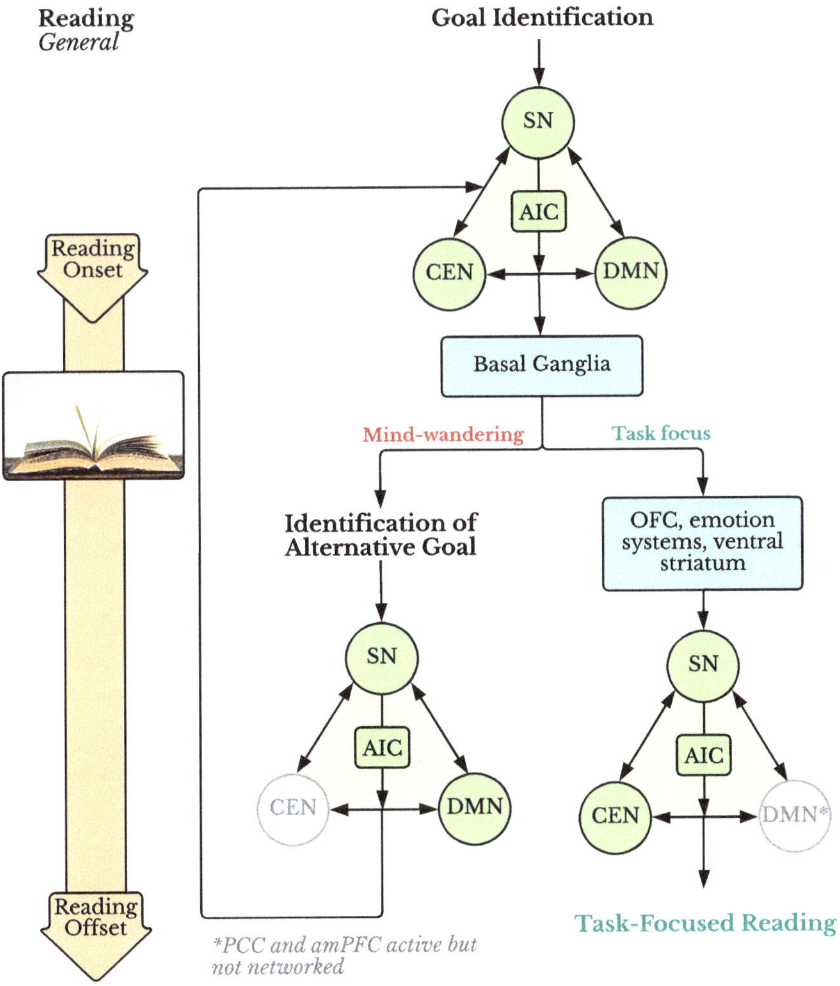

Figure 3.9

Reading, general. Reward regions detect and influence the ability to remain on task while reading by delivering positive or negative reinforcement. Image credit: Marilyn Perkins.

between alternative interpretations in decoding an idiom is correlated with increased emotional intensity, as on the right side of figure 3.9, where task focus and DMN suppression accompany emotional response.

Finally, immersive reading may involve a "flow" state—a state of seemingly effortless concentration, which individuals may experience during otherwise difficult or taxing activities, like playing an instrument, participating in a sport, composing music, writing a poem, or performing fine/dangerous work with the hands. In these circumstances, "attentional resources are fully invested in the task at hand, so that objects beyond the immediate interaction generally fail to enter awareness. . . . Without the required attentional resources, the self-reflective processes that often intrude into awareness and cause attention to be directed from what needs to be done are silenced."[104] In line with the conception of time in the attentional pacemaker I have described, time in this case would seem to fly as the magic of music or literature takes over. Then, like Eve wandering with Adam under the stars, "with thee conversing, I forget all time."[105]

Expanding and Quantifying the Model

The model I offer can be altered based on predictions about many different things: the level of demands in a given task (more cognitively demanding tasks will generally downregulate the DMN), the recruitment of areas within a given network for tasks that would impede network-level interactions, the relative demands on internal versus external monitoring, or even knowledge of altered connectivity in individuals based on age, neurotypicality, or illness. The model is only as good as the assumptions we make based on current evidence in each of these areas.

What should be clear, however, is that the time it takes to adapt to a new goal matters. Some goals will by nature require the buildup of expertise over time. Others—think social goals—may have long or short latencies, as we accumulate the information that helps us determine success or the need to readapt. For example, using music to aid seduction or social fluidity takes time and knowledge. Employing music to hone movement may take less. So as we explore the timescales of aesthetic perception and action, we need not just to separate the time course of an aesthetic object from that of responses to it, but to understand what our aims in aesthetic encounters may be, as well, for they will help predict key elements: how long we remain engaged, how and when we redirect attention or change goals, and the neural systems that underpin goal attainment or reset (which can help us think through potential temporal latencies in redirection).

In a final set of examples to elucidate these dimensions, let's consider some common ways of listening to music. In the case of free listening to familiar music, I would expect DMN activation, as there would be decreased demands for musical analysis, and the possibility of mind-wandering would be enhanced. (Active mental rehearsal of a familiar piece might, however, get in the way of networked DMN activity, as motor preparation might recruit both the CEN and SN.)[106]

On the other hand, if we wish to change our soundscape, it is (a common goal) to facilitate task focus, one would expect downregulation of the DMN in favor of enhancement of task-focused networks and the CEN: we don't want our minds wandering too much while trying to remember a set of chemical syntheses.

For a goal like shared movement, I would expect the CEN and SN to be most active, as one plans and prepares for motion and monitors the environment. Pleasure in this case could set a positive baseline, freeing attentional resources to devote to attaining rhythmic motion as well as engaging with others' emotional responses and expressions. For shared aesthetic experience (say, joining in the experience of a concert), my model would predict that the SN and DMN would upregulate, if a listener wishes to shut out extraneous cues, and focus on internal responses while also watching those of others. However, for novel or complex music, the challenges of analyses could downregulate the DMN strongly.

Overall, this model of aesthetic time is based on the idea that with the achievement of a particular aesthetic goal, the competition between three brain states will be resolved in favor of two of them at a particular time point. The result is a probabilistic view of what brain state an individual might occupy at a given point. Essentially, while a number of brain states are possible with any aesthetic encounter, an individual will move through only a few of them—we've got one brain after all. I have simplified the picture to leave out other important states (and brain systems)—visual or auditory systems, for example, and focus, as I have indicated, on a summative baseline state involving transmodal networks. I also assume that reward is a central element driving the maintenance or transition from state to state. While the flow charts explore possibilities, this model overall depends on

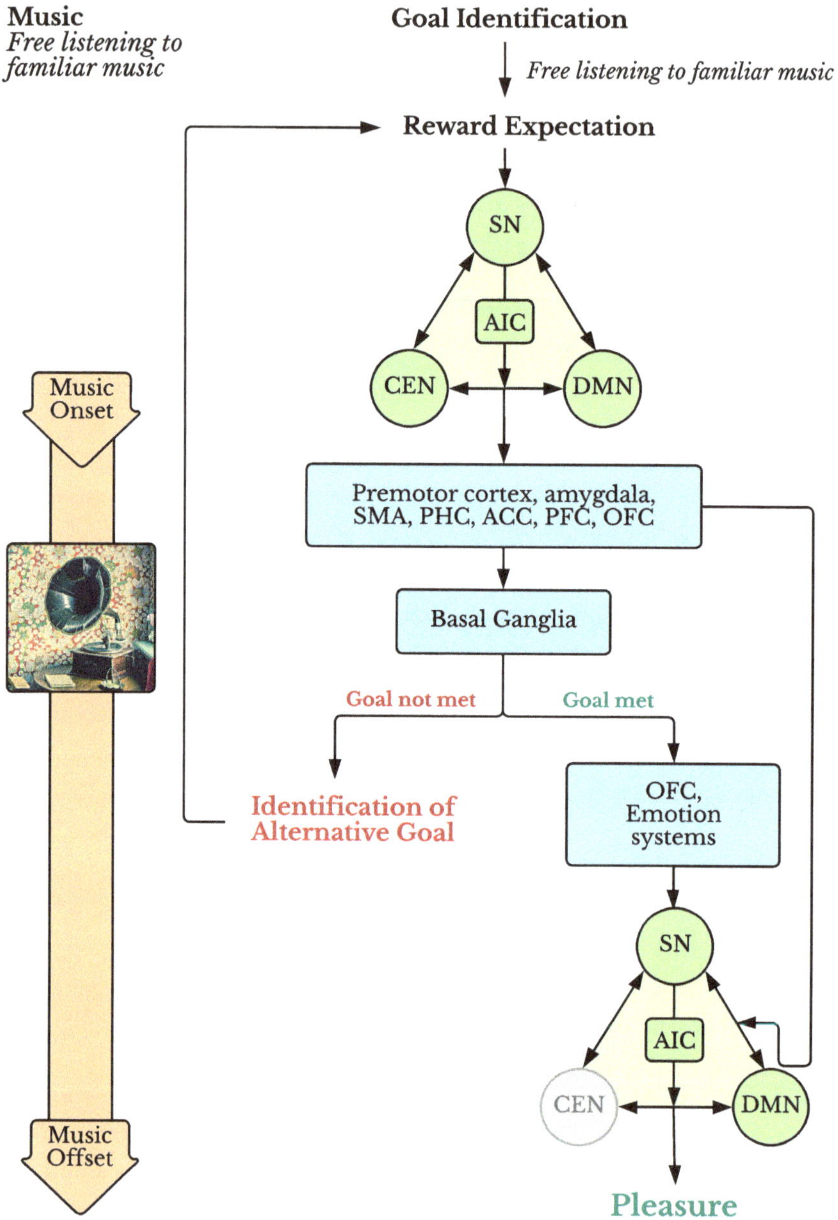

Figure 3.10

Music, free listening to familiar music. The ease of following familiar music enables the rebound of the default-mode network with pleasurable (and perhaps neutral) experience. Image credit: Marilyn Perkins.

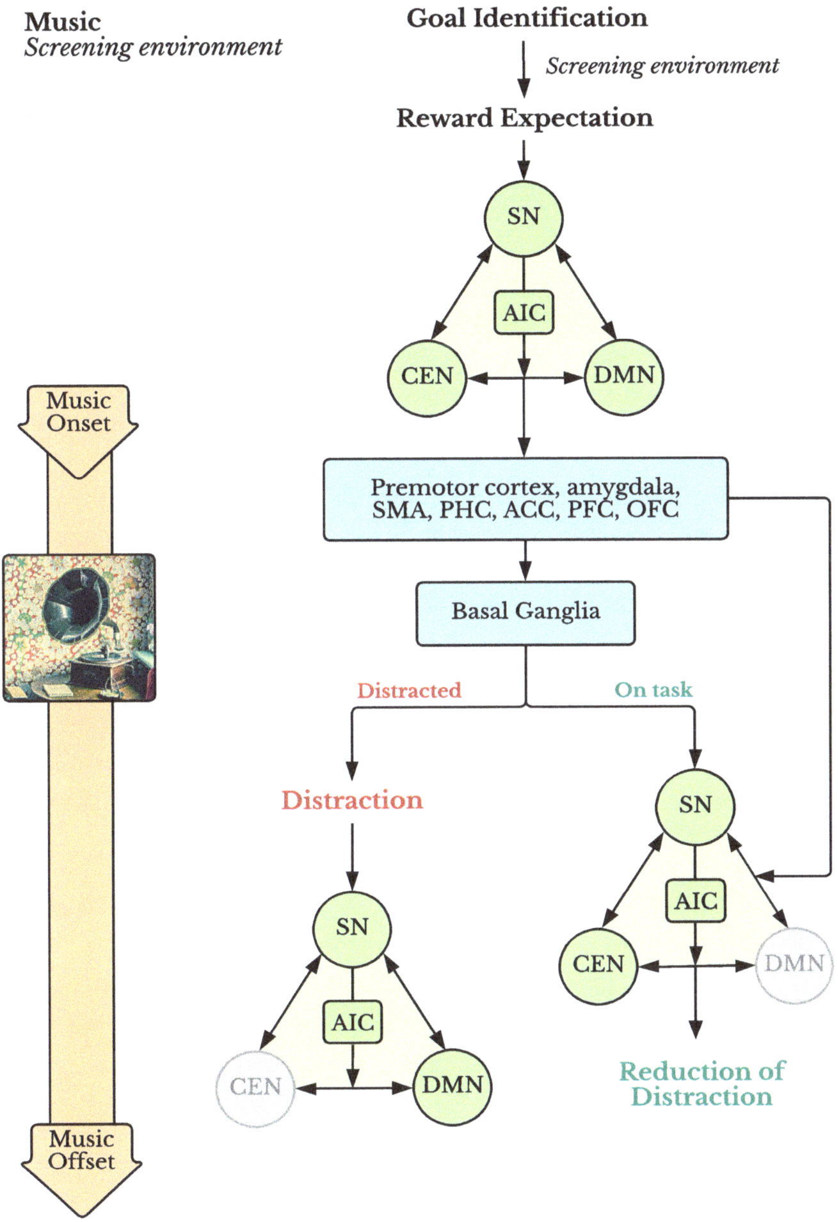

Figure 3.11
Music, screening environment. Musical elements interfere with detection of salient, potentially attention-grabbing, elements of the environment. DMN suppression accompanies reduces distraction, enabling focus on a chosen task. Image credit: Marilyn Perkins.

predictions about states that carry probabilistic weights—it's more or less likely that given a set of circumstances, brain responses will follow a particular pattern. For example, as we have seen, in comparing low and high levels of subjective pleasure for five- and fifteen-second periods of looking, the probability that any individual experiencing high pleasure will be in a state where the DMN and SN dominate is relatively close to 100 percent. Five seconds after exposure, the probability flips, so that DMN and SN co-activation for high pleasure is unlikely, but for low pleasure is greater. This can be illustrated and ultimately tested using a Markov chain.

Markov chains enable one to predict the probability that a system will stay in one state or change into another and can be influenced by a coefficient that multiplies the baseline probabilities.[107] Figure 3.12 shows a basic Markov model.

At homeostatic balance the probability of shifting to CEN or DMN dominance can be experimentally demonstrated, as well as the probabilities of staying in a particular state over time (visualized as the semicircles adjacent to each network). The probability of a shift from one state to another or of staying in a particular state is environmentally influenced. For example, the prevalence of mind-wandering during daily life suggests that task orientation is not necessarily the most frequent everyday state (workday or weekend), every state of health (major depression, or normative mood state, for example), even time of day (evening or morning), or activity (powerful

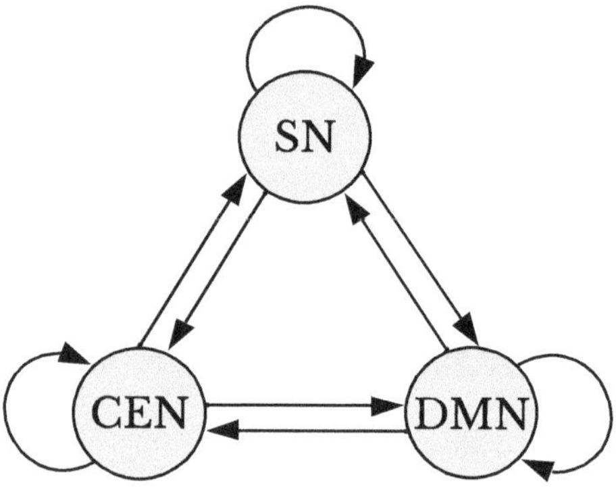

Figure 3.12
Simplified Markov diagram for apex transmodal networks. Straight lines indicate a potential change of state favoring one or more networks. Curved lines represent the potential to remain in a given state. Image credit: Marilyn Perkins.

visual aesthetic experience!). The probability of shifting states can be estimated based on conditions like the ones I have described; for example: is there a distracter? is one immersed in a task? how demanding is the task at hand? what brain regions may be taxed by analysis of an object or experience and how does that influence capacity for networking? and so on.

For aesthetics, it is not a priori easy to determine the probability that any experience will involve a positive response and activation of a reward signal (whether it involves basal ganglia, OFC, substantia nigra), but once a reward associated with a particular goal is reached, there are two primary possibilities: either you enter state B or state C, as shown in figure 3.13.

Goal expectation and rewards should contribute to the probability of how long you remain in a given state, how frequently you shift states, and your path to getting there. For example, at approximately T_{10} in our vision task with fifteen-second exposure (see figure 1.4), the probability of entering state C is going to be determined by whether or not one is rewarded for the image at a high level; for a low reward, it's near 0. For the most highly rated images, the probability of entering state C is nearly 1. This could be understood as the reward signal coming from the basal ganglia acting as a multiplier that increases one's chance of shifting from A or B (a task-oriented state) to state C. For the least preferred images, at T_{20s}, the probability of shifting from state B to state C increases with increasing reward (i.e.,

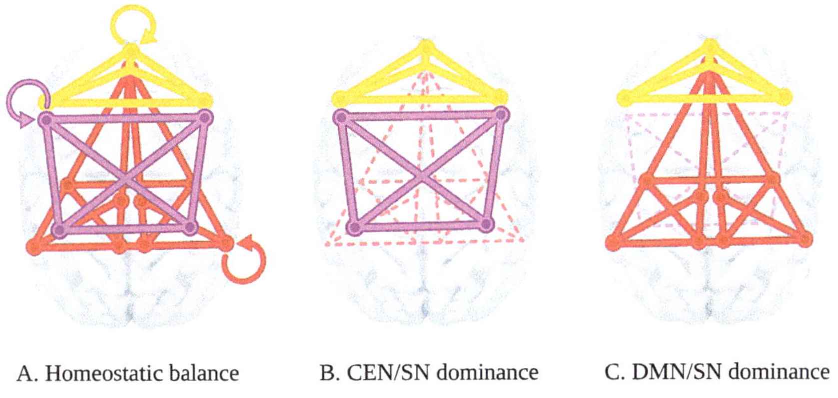

Figure 3.13

Baseline and paired-system dominance. Image credit: Marilyn Perkins. Panel A adapted from Manoliu et al., "Aberrant Dependence of Default Mode/Central Executive Network Interactions on Anterior Insular Salience Network Activity in Schizophrenia."

the disappearance of the image releases the system from negative reward). As reward dips, the probability at T_{20s} of remaining in state C drops for the most preferred images until homeostasis (state A) returns in all cases. Using the idea of a Markov cycle enables a generalizable aesthetic model across modes and across goals, in which the probabilities of an individual's path changes as goals are identified, attained, or lost. In other words, again, we have a probabilistic view of brain states over time.

I've argued throughout this book that the goals we bring to our aesthetic experiences are not neutral and that they often compete with one another. Some goals are socially designated; this means they can also be denigrated. Decorative arts, for example, may be seen as frivolous, wasteful, or gendered in such a way as to devalue them. Attention to one's personal environment and pleasure also may vary in acceptability or possibility at different stages of life, or in different places (whether they are defined by culture—say, stoicism—or by external demand—say, being incarcerated). All of these can be modeled.

Thresholds for pleasure are also thresholds for life, and they are a necessary outcome of how humans are made. Thus, aesthetic pleasures can help people thrive; their absence is painful, weighs against joy, and can hamper human connection. They also may determine how we experience the time course of aesthetic life, and help regulate the temporality of the neural structures and systems that support it.

4 Coda: Future Present

One of the key questions motivating this book has been: what does a model of aesthetics rooted in cognitive neuroscience have to offer? At minimum, it must be able to provide testable predictions about how cognitive architecture functions. It should also be, as far as possible, true to the diversity of experiences as we engage with the range of objects we find aesthetically moving. If we are very lucky, it will teach us something new about experience too. As I have discussed, one of the most significant challenges posed toward cognitive models centers on scope and time.

Neuroscience as a whole has two levels of explanatory reach—one involves the biological parameters of the nervous system, from center to periphery, and the other involves the relationship between observable behavior and neural activity. This means that neuroscience is primed to approach behaviors surrounding the production of art, as well as the range of aesthetic responses to artifacts and natural objects. However, neuroscience has very little to say about works of art themselves. This ramifies, as Alva Noë puts it, in a question of whether or not art can be confronted as a stimulus—that is, for example, an image shown to a set of individuals for a defined amount of time, with behavioral and physiological measurements straddling exposure. The answer is yes and no. Indeed, identifying visual (or other sensory) features of an artwork that influence aesthetic appreciation is not the same thing as describing an artwork in its totality. Artworks have histories, as well as institutional and personal contexts that help define them and that shape encounters with them. This is the work of criticism, and as I close this book I explore some of the ways in which criticism and neuroaesthetics can complement each other.

When it comes to the temporality of aesthetic experience, neuroscience enables researchers to explore phenomena with behavioral and experiential significance, which occur at timescales that are unavailable to conscious perception, and to deconstruct almost instantaneous events. The model of aesthetic time that I lay out depends on rapidly occurring feedback around goals of which we may not even be aware. It also helps understand cyclical processes that take place differently at varying moments in individual development and across individuals. I began with two central premises. The first is that aesthetic experiences are not bounded within discrete, self-enclosed, or self-sufficient windows of time, but that they exceed the boundaries in which one might like to neatly encapsulate them. They begin before we ever encounter an artwork or perceive a flash of light or a tone of music. They also do not have a unitary arc of temporality: aesthetic experiences change the way we experience time, and in their successive, cyclical structures, they require that we look at not just the present but also the future and the past to make sense of what we feel, think, and know.

My models thus focus on a window that begins before an artwork is presented to consciousness and extends until after the artwork has faded from awareness. The shape and sequence of the cycles of aesthetic experience are determined by how the goals that individuals take to aesthetic encounters influence perception, emotion, attention, affect, and action. I have offered an adaptable and expandable framework for deconstructing complex, temporally extended aesthetic experiences, and it can be tested through introspection (e.g., conscious goal identification and compression or dilation of subjective experiences of duration), behavioral psychology (continuous and discrete measures of affect and pleasure, as well as measures of duration of engagement, memory, and changes of these over the maturation or development of individuals), and neuroscience.

What I have called goal time is shaped by the ways we adjust our attention, energy, actions, thoughts, and feelings in interacting with an aesthetic object or its memory over time, based on our own perceptions of pleasure. It is perhaps a truth universally acknowledged that the human brain is a time machine.

> "Clearly," the Time Traveler proceeded, "any real body must have extension in *four* directions: it must have Length, Breadth, Thickness, and—Duration.
>
> . . .
>
> *"There is no difference between Time and any of the three dimensions of Space except that our consciousness moves along it."*—H. G. Wells[1]

Indeed, memory is not traceable to a single brain region or even a small subset of them: the whole brain carries its history within it. Thomas J. Carew and Nikolay Kukushkin make a fascinating argument that sums up this principle. Whatever the unit—neurotransmitter, RNA or protein, or even at the levels of the synapse or pathway—memories are made, accessed, and reconsolidated at discrete timescales. Our brains encode experience in service of the future, enabling us to adapt to whatever life throws our way—until we just can't adapt fast enough, well enough, or at all. And then . . . it's over. It is crucial to acknowledge that most of these timescales are imperceptible to us, even as the larger, dilated, and florid memories that make up our life stories can be startlingly vivid, even gripping. However, Carew and Kukushkin contend that even though the nanosecond isn't perceptible, it is still integral to experience. The bigger picture involves complex summations: "identifying and elucidating specific and unique temporal domains in memory processing falls short of capturing the extremely wide range of *nested* temporal domains that are *simultaneously* operating in the service of encoding and storing long-term memories."[2] In this view, "experience can be seen as a series of temporally limited deviations from homeostasis, the timing of which determines the structure of the resulting memory."[3] These shifts involve probabilities, which can be estimated or determined experimentally, and overall we each move along in a discontinuous stream of data, pixelated moments we can't fully access, until something interrupts that flow: a change in homeostasis, a shift from one state to another.

In that spirit, I return to where this book began. Marcel Proust's extraordinary novel *Remembrance of Things Past* is perhaps the most significant attempt by any artist to capture the persistence of memory, and it is notable thus that the pearls he strings together are memories of the beautiful. My memory of the osprey in flight is accessible to me on demand. Try it yourself right now. Think of your wedding. Your baby. Your art. My late, beloved colleague Arden Reed begins his book *Slow Art* writing about an affair to remember—an engagement, over many years, with Manet's *Young Lady in 1866*. Reed had encountered the painting once and was struck by its "physicality," but:

> seeing it again after a hiatus of several years produced an unexpected reaction. Around the turn of the millennium, I found myself back in the Metropolitan Museum. Heading down a long corridor toward Central Park I glanced to my left,

> curious whether "my" picture was hanging in its usual spot. It was. I decided not to stop. All at once, I felt a certain discomfort, verging on embarrassment. Pausing to breathe, I realized that my strange reaction was provoked by passing the place of my enthrallment, a site-specific reminder of my multiyear preoccupation with one object.[4]

The power of this aesthetic experience pushes Reed so far beyond his normal pattern of being that everything is arrested. There is something, however, in the repetition here that resonates with Kukushkin and Carew's view of memory as a global system. Reed was caught up in a memory even when the memory could be nearly relived in the present. But memory matters to beauty because there are so many moments of beauty that we inevitably lose. Hence Proust searches for them as time passes and memory erodes. Every memory fades; yet I wonder: is beauty part of a special kind of time machine? In the past, I argued that the experience of the beautiful ought to be impossible without memory. It turns out to be more complicated than that.[5]

Aesthetic experience, I contend, is a necessary outcome of the way we learn. Humans sum a variety of error signals when we make decisions, because we need to know how far we are from our goals. Even small decisions or actions require the integration of complex feedback loops. Recall my young archer, sighting along her arrow at a target; she must measure the wind, degrees of light and shade, must know her bow and string as well as her strength of arm, back, and eye. A viewer of Jasper Johns's *Green Target* (1955) is integrating at least as many variables, and most of us probably do so with more room for error, less practice, and an increased potential for surprise. Someone experienced in expert aesthetic evaluations, like Reed, may perhaps more easily adjust their goals or maxima on the fly than the rest of us do. But goals are key because goals and their attainment are one way in which we mark time. It is not just that setting our sights on a target may speed up or slow down our subjective experience; we learn because we remember our biggest failures as well as our greatest successes. Powerful aesthetic experience marks moments when we feel that the world has changed for us or around us, and that the strength of our feeling has marked a kind of unusual success.

In engaging with goal time, we newly confront one of the basic challenges of neuroaesthetics (as with any field that addresses the biological components of human experience): the so far intractable relationship between processes available to consciousness (like the bodily sensations that accompany joy) and the many layers of matter that underlie our experience, layers whose activity is both generally unavailable to perception and functions independently of our ability to perceive it (like the firing of a neuron). This is what David Chalmers has called the "hard problem" of consciousness: how do we match phenomenal experiences of self and world to the biological, chemical, and physical makeup of our being?[6] In this book, I have not sought to close this explanatory gap. Indeed, I seek little in the way of response to the "so what?" school of critique of neuroscience: what does knowing more about neural function add to the understanding of any kind of experience? Simply put, it helps deconstruct the components of experience, breaking down the elements that help build what we see, feel, and think so that we can better understand how they fit together.

What I advance, then, is a model that hovers at the horizon between conscious and unconscious processes, and moves back and forth across it. Each move and change has temporal implications. Goal time, as I have described it, blends conscious and unconscious markers of duration. For example, the rapid filling of the purported information buffer produced by the insula is not subject to introspective view, and its effect is somewhat paradoxical: the faster salient events occur, the slower time appears to unroll. The richness, say, of a tapestry of sound in a concert hall might make time seem to slow down, as we match our attention or movements to changing notes and rhythms. However, the cycles of goal time have other implications. Not all the satisfactions of aesthetic experience come with consciously positing a specific goal, because these cycles can be directed as well as exploratory. At times, for example, we experience aesthetic failures and suffer frustration—often a slow process that, with the defeat of expectations, drags out the conscious sense of time passing: I just don't understand why I'm staring at a target on a wall, or hearing moment after moment of silence. In other cases, as we find our initial expectations foiled, we may switch goals, filling up time with a series of gambits or forays that may or may not meet with success. Sometimes, a truly magical experience occurs, and in hearing bars of music there is a seeming simultaneity of desire and satisfaction, and anticipation is indistinguishable from fruition. Aesthetic pleasure emerges as a rush of joy even before we can understand what has happened, or why.

Shared Pleasure, Criticism, and the Dilation of Pleasure

A goal-oriented view of aesthetics works alongside but not in place of understanding aesthetics through ideas of culture or institution. Each of these may influence the motivations that we take to our aesthetic encounters. For example, my own aesthetic motivations in reading have become in many ways inseparable from criticism as a set of social, conversational, or intellectual practices; indeed, one motivation for criticism can be the dilation of pleasure in time. Literary criticism has long implicitly acknowledged the varied time courses of aesthetic engagement via the practices of close reading, in which moment-to-moment possibilities are dilated and documented by critics. For instance, Maureen McLane's *My Poets* is a tour de force not just of criticism but of the pleasures of rereading, a literary autobiography of a poet who returns to her college notebooks as she rethinks her life as a reader and writer. What is remarkable about *My Poets*, among other things, is McLane's continued reawareness that aesthetic experiences may have troubled beginnings:

> I'm fascinated by that threshold where one hovers not getting it yet wanting to get it, where a tentative desire contends with frustration. Where frustration may be converted into desire, and desire into some provisional illumination. As a poet, as a student, as a critic, as a citizen, I have found this vale of unknowing yet wanting-to-know to be a fruitful vale, a dwelling place with sharing, pondering. This uncomfortable yet not completely unpleasurable affective, cognitive situation presents itself to me as a somatic condition that feels rather like an environment—a kind of tensed haze.[7]

Aesthetic experience here begins with anticipation, not the climactic moment.

This is a lesson offered by one of the oldest forms of poetry—the epic—which begins in the thick of things (in medias res); as Edmund Spenser wrote, "a poet thrusteth into the middest."[8] Take Nobel Laureate Derek Walcott's *Omeros*. There, the beginning is always the middle of something that has gone before: it is a revision of Homer's *Odyssey*. Within a few hundred lines, Wolcott monumentalizes an aesthetic truth—emergent experience hooks onto desire—by staging an encounter with human, not divine, beauty. The goddess Aphrodite was born from the sea, according to legend, and appears rising above the waves. In Emily Wilson's virtuoso translation of the *Odyssey*, she evokes an ancient tool that plays with expectations: parallelism. There are two kinds: semantic parallelism uses repetition to revise or expand upon a scene or idea, and the aural version takes advantage of groups of sounds to create similarities and contrasts. (I break the lines below with a caesura ° and use brackets to identify parallel phrases.) In Homer's version, Aphrodite, jealous of Helen's beauty and that of Helen's daughter Hermione, carries out godlike machinations. Helen says,

° I wanted to go home.
I wished that Aphrodite ° had not made me
go crazy when she ° took me from my country,
and made me leave my daughter ° and the bed
I shared with my fine, ° handsome, clever husband.[9]

In his Caribbean reversal, far from Homer's Greece, Walcott's narrator stares not at the demi-goddess Helen (daughter of Zeus and Helen) but at Antigone. Antigone is fully human, bound in the way of all humans to circumstances over which she has no control, whether because of gods or only because of history. Walcott's postmodern play with parallelism, both aural and semantic, exploits division by forming, violating, and reforming expectations by turn. Some lines refuse the neatness of parallels, while others expand upon them with dizzying replications and contradictions that may be separated by several lines:

I saw how the surf ° printed its lace in patterns
on the shore of her neck, ° the lowering shallows
of silk swirled at her ankles, ° like surf without noise,

and felt that another cold bust, ° not hers, but yours
saw this with stone almonds for eyes, ° its broken nose
turning away, ° as the rustling silk agrees.

But if it could read ° between the lines of her floor
like a white-hot deck ° uncaulked by Antillean heat,
to the shadows in its hold, ° its nostrils might flare

at the stench from manacled ankles, ° the coffled feet
scraping like leaves, ° and perhaps the inculpable marble
would have turned ° its white seeds away, to widen

the bow of its mouth ° at the horror under her table,
from the lyre of her armchair ° draped with its with white chiton,
to do what the past always does: ° suffer and stare.[10]

Shore meets shallows; heat melts the caulking on a white-hot deck; manacled ankles join coffined feet; leaves meet the seeds that gave them birth; and the bow of a statue's mouth sits incongruously near an open-faced lyre. Beauty appears to us because we want it, so we've learned to look for it in even the worst places. Humanity and history clash in one transfixing view of suffering and sensuality; slavery and music; living, feminine beauty; and the cold finality of stone. The seemingly endless interlocking cycles of repetition mark the union of past and present.

Aesthetics, Power, and Learning

Wallace Stevens's oeuvre closes out as a return to the beginning: he finds echoes of his past being in his current self. The model of aesthetic experience I have offered keeps returning to this cyclic notion. I began my discussion of goal time in chapter 3 by pointing out the peculiarity of the role of the DMN in visual aesthetics, where perceptions of the external world and of inner life become intermingled. While it may come as no surprise that the brain data suggests this is about a conformity between sense data and the processes that identify and filter self-relevant data, it is peculiar that these processes work together most easily for visual information and visual art. We now are equipped to understand more about why.

One answer is that the goals we bring to aesthetic encounters combine with the sensory demands of aesthetic objects to shape neural processing so that different systems of self-relevance dominate in differing circumstances—signals of salience (as action preparation, for example) or internal mentation may take center stage. There is a deeper answer, however, that takes us back to human learning. I've argued that aesthetic experience is an emergent property that is a necessary result of the wide range of preferences available to humans as learners. These preferences are the positive outcomes of the numerous decision rules human beings create in our daily exploration of the world around us. We have so many potential goals and ways of satisfying them that the hedonic space we inhabit is accordingly (geometrically or more) complex. If the goal, for example, is social cohesion, one can satisfy it by moving together, feeling together, speaking together, eating together, touching each other, competing with each other, even looking at the same vista together. Equally, humans can act together while having divergent goals. A group of people walking down the same street will be motivated by many more goals than there are individuals. For example, one person may walk for exercise as well as to get home; another is walking in search of dinner; yet another is looking for a pocket to pick; another is simply a flaneur walking to see and be seen.

The complex interrelation of goals and means of satisfaction generates an expansive preference space as everyone pursues a different set of optima. Humans have been designed for a world like this, and aesthetic pleasures emerge at the interstices of this ever-changing space where we can be surprised by a novel combination of pleasures, whether they come with a shift of the breeze or the changing light of evening. The divergence of our aesthetic pleasures is the result of the competing maxima we all must resolve as we choose among competing goods, prioritize competing goals, and find new ways of feeding our need for knowledge. Our search for understanding the patterns in the world has an exquisitely temporal dimension too. The pleasures we take can establish a rhythm whereby we continually seek new patterns that may align with or deviate from what we know. Pleasure sets a metronome for exploration.

The particular neural configurations of aesthetic experience reflect a primal necessity. The three apex transmodal systems compete because we must be able to shift our attention dynamically, based on changing needs and circumstances. Sometimes, external signals take pride of place, and we must focus on a particular task or prepare for and execute a new plan. In these circumstances, bodily awareness often recedes from our focus, and exteroception dominates interoception. For example, as I write, I am far less aware of the feel of my skin on the chair or paper than of the unrolling of text behind my moving pen and fingers. In other circumstances, however, my awareness of my body dominates, and I notice the pain of an inflamed, compressed nerve that requires me to shift in my seat.

Importantly, different sensory systems and different data contribute to our sense of self in varying ways. For example, vision generally takes primacy in sighted individuals, and data travels via the optic nerve to a variety of regions in the occipital cortex. Smell and taste, however, feed directly into interoceptive processing by way of the vagus nerve. Heart rate is integrated into self-monitoring systems by way of nerves in the cardiac wall as well as around the carotid artery in the neck, nerves throughout the peritoneal cavity, and throughout other major arteries. The exteroceptive version of the self, however, is built largely based on what individuals can see—limbs and hands. The interoceptive self-image comes from experiences of one's own facial expressions as well as data about the position of the body and a general sense of how one feels.[11]

In general, and perhaps surprisingly, bodily awareness is the most important kind of information humans have. As important as it is to be aware of one's surroundings, say, when crossing the street, these episodic needs are far dwarfed by the centrality of homeostasis. We constantly must adjust our bodies to maintain the kind of balance necessary for our health, well-being, and even survival. That is why a disease like leprosy is so deadly: if we lose the ability to feel pain, even the clothes we wear can kill, rubbing the skin raw and producing infection; small cuts or wounds balloon into life-threatening conditions; bones break before we even know we were close to tearing ourselves apart. Interoceptive data takes priority, therefore, in our learning; it is a "first prior" that "constrain[s] every aspect of biological function" because "if our internal organs become unreliable, the immediate result is death."[12] Thus, "interoceptive learning [is] much faster to acquire and harder to extinguish than purely external learning."[13] Briefly put, one experience of food poisoning is enough for a lifetime. The powerful nausea and aversion to spoiled chicken, for example, "from the brain's point of view," generates a "highly precise interoceptive prediction [that] represents a potentially fatal event and affords for an equally precise alteration of internal models."[14] The pleasures and displeasures—as the effects of learning—that arise from bodily awareness are excruciatingly important.

Imagine, then, aesthetic experience as one way in which we exercise the integration of internal and external information, information that can be configured in novel, unexpected ways. The continually emerging pleasures and displeasures of aesthetic life reset the competition and hierarchies of interoception and exteroception of different kinds of salient, personally relevant information, and tap into some of the most powerful mechanisms of learning and survival we possess. When it comes to works of art, the senses to which they appeal can help determine how they influence and interact with our sense of self. So, in appealing to the eyes, the visual arts require little in the way of proprioceptive data to move their viewers. Music, however, by prodding listeners to move with the rhythm and by influencing their breath and heartbeat, may strike closer to the core of one's interoceptive sense of self. On the other hand, poetry, in harnessing vision but by demoting visual data in favor of thoughts, imagery, and feelings, can affect readers in yet different ways, by pricking the sense of rhythm and beat.

Whether, then, it is the kind of self-relevance that may harness the DMN, or the gut feelings that may come with music or poetry, aesthetic experiences make us distinctly aware of the trade-offs between inner and outer worlds.[15] No wonder aesthetic life is a universal—present across generations and cultures—yet present differently in almost every instance. Aesthetic experiences are the ultimate in open-form solutions. (This is one reason that while our tastes may be surprising to us as individuals, a large-scale computational method could begin to show trends in and predictors for human taste in general.)[16] In my model, then, as aesthetic objects and our responses to them realigned the balance across transmodal systems, they strike at the core of the sense of self indeed.

Pleasures and Ends

The idea that aesthetic time is cyclical is deeply present in works of art, whether Shakespeare's sonnets ("From fairest creatures we desire increase, / That thereby beauty's rose may never die") or Wallace Stevens's poetry. Pleasures can point toward the cycles that poetry creates in experience (individual) and history (collective). Wallace Stevens's "Banjo Boomer" is one of his final works, and unusual in many ways. It is formally intricate in a quite traditional sense, rhymed through repetition, and with a gentle refrain that is reminiscent of a children's rhyme. (As Tim Armstrong argues, "Mulberry, shade me, shade me awhile" is the older man's version of a playground refrain, "Here we go round the mulberry bush"—even matching its meter, singing its song.[17]) That the poem might be two things at once is clear from the first line, which states, "The mulberry is a double tree"; that those two things might be youth and old age is signaled by the somewhat exhausted repetition at the end of the lines. The poet can't find a rhyme; why try, anyway, when the same word or phrase is just as good: "tree," "awhile," "as well," and even just "word."

However, Stevens suddenly shifts the frame, forgoing the straightforwardness of repetition and the dominating dactyls of the refrain, by introducing near-rhyme and altering the beat: "It is a shape of life described / By another shape without a word."[18] The poem breaks its established shape in order to signal that something has to change for the poem to close. The final two lines return to the fascination that is repetition: "With nothing fixed by a single word. / Mulberry, shade me, shade me awhile." The refrain evokes the search for comfort, the return to gentle rhythmic rocking that is the heart of a lullaby.

Importantly, late in his career, Stevens offers clarification, even simplicity, and not mystery. The poem-as-lullaby recalls a child's experience, that of family, home. Indeed, one needn't know the world of poetry intimately in order to hear the children's song, nor to hear it broken; the song is so familiar any deviation may be clear. Thus, when the comfortable, simple, and shared (cultural) knowledge of the rhythm or the sense of the lullaby begins to falter, that's not an effect of expertise, which is remarkable for a poet who often foregrounds expert knowledge. The bough breaks and the cradle might fall—but here there may be backup. At the end of the poem, a reader might discover that the overall rhythm of the poem—not only the scansion of meter but also the larger repetitions and returns—is not just about the circularity of children moving around a tree. If disruption of expectation can signal pleasure, confirmation of expectation can bring pleasure too. The repetition of the refrain as a phrase means nothing can be fixed by a single word, nor understood by a single beat: "By anóther shápe withóut a wórd." With the return of the refrain at the poem's close, something—poetry, life, joy—has been remade.

What matters ultimately is the circularity of life and of the search for comfort; the comfort of old age returning to childhood and dependence; the cycling of goals and possibilities for achievement; and the pleasure of a poet who mixes the rocking rhythm of a lullaby, seeking shade and rest, with the beat of American music—the hand knocking out an extra rhythm as the banjo player adds an extra beat on the board of the instrument, even as the fingers pursue the complicated rhythm of the song: the banjo boomer of the title. The deep, perhaps surprising irony here is that the banjo is an invention of African American music, and given Stevens's general dismissive stance toward Black people, it is remarkable that an African American beat shapes some of his last work.

Still, while endings are not fully predictable, aesthetic experience always assumes the possibility of closure, of success, finality, or satisfaction. Closure comes in aesthetic experience, even when it is extended by seriality for as long as one keeps wanting it. Some sonnets do this: either published in sequences (as with Vikram Seth's novel *The Golden Gate*) or one by one, they can come in the midst of things. In a powerful revision of a devastating story, US Poet Laureate Rita Dove tells us how the goddess Demeter has wrested her child back from total imprisonment. But there's still no finality, no completion. In "Demeter's Prayer to Hades," the world, love, and the felt experience of pleasure are split in two, where even the line breaks tell us we no longer know what we thought we knew:

> This alone is what I wish for you: knowledge.
> To understand each desire has an edge,
> to know we are responsible for the lives
> we change. No faith comes without cost,
> no one believes without dying.
> Now for the first time
> I see clearly the trail you planted,
> what ground opened to waste,
> though you dreamed a wealth
> of flowers.
>
> There are no curses—only mirrors
> held up to the souls of gods and mortals.
> And so I give up this fate, too.
> Believe in yourself,
> go ahead—see where it gets you.[19]

While we don't know what we thought we knew, it's not always clear what remains. Indeed, while a persistent challenge for neuroaesthetics is temporality, that's not the only one. It is difficult to connect the processes of cells or molecules to our lived experience as humans, and neuroaesthetics poses a particular version of this problem. It's not just a matter of how the mechanisms of cellular interactions connect with or emerge as conscious experience. Indeed, I'm not certain that we will ever have a seamless view of aesthetic life. I don't think we need one though. Human experience is discontinuous, and we sew together the spaces between sleep and wakefulness, past and present. One key feature of aesthetic experience is to highlight why discontinuous moments matter. Seamlessness would belie the lack of power we have over our own conscious lives. Beauty nonetheless persists. Beauty must persist.

For the reasons I have described in this book, among many others, I am disturbed by the evacuation of art, music, and literature from schools across the United States of America. In places that prioritize learning, it is deeply misguided to remove one of the foundational components of human beings' ability to extract meaning from the environment around us. Denying our children the kind of engagement, even if we understand it as play, that comes from experiencing the arts as both creators and audiences cuts them off from part of their humanity.

For different reasons, I also am concerned that when modern America punishes people, we deprive them of aesthetic outlet, even wiping the walls that imprison them clean. If we expect individuals to make good decisions, they must have the freedom to learn how a good decision feels, to tap into their humanity and to learn how to regulate and share pleasures constructively.[20] Several years ago when I and colleagues at New York University cofounded a prison education program, one of the first courses we placed on the books was in drama. The director, writer, and actress Anna Deavere Smith noted in conversation that the first thing people who had been incarcerated needed to do when they left was to pretend they'd never been inside in the first place. Inhabiting another persona enables us to learn more about ourselves; it requires that we subordinate our own thoughts and feelings as we seek to understand people very unlike us.

In this way the arts are good for all of us. We must come in contact with things we must learn to hate and things we must learn to love. They are a prescription for democracy in action, placing responsibility for knowing each other squarely on each of us. Beauty must persist so that we all can survive—and so that we all can thrive. Before we run out of time.

Appendix 1: Table of Key Brain Regions and Networks

Name		Function
AIC	Anterior insular cortex	Physiological interoception; subjective emotional experience; monitoring salient internal and external information; modulating activity of and between the DMN and CEN *Part of the salience network*
amPFC	Anterior medial prefrontal cortex	Self-referential thought; autobiographical memory; sense of self; social mimicry *Part of the default-mode network*
	Basal ganglia	Reward; reinforcement; habit formation; motor control
CEN	Central executive network	Problem-solving; decision-making; working memory; focused attention; completing cognitively demanding tasks
DCNN	Deep convolutional neural network model	A machine learning method used for artificial intelligence analysis of images. DCNN integrates one or more functions into a new function space without assuming linear summation
DMN	Default-mode network	Self-referential thinking; representing others, especially others understood to be like oneself; imagining the future; mind-wandering; imagining the past
OFC	Orbitofrontal cortex	Decision-making; reward value
PFC	Prefrontal cortex	Complex cognition; personality; social behavior; executive function
PCC	Posterior cingulate cortex	Imagining other minds; human awareness; memory retrieval *Part of the default-mode network*
SN	Salience network	Directing attention to important information; modulating activity of and between the DMN and CEN
	Substantia nigra	Reward; dopamine production; motor control

Appendix 2: Experimental Materials and Methods

Vessel, Starr, and Rubin, "The Brain on Art: Intense Aesthetic Experience Activates the Default-mode Network," *Frontiers in Human Neurocience* (2012)

Observers

Sixteen observers were recruited at New York University (NYU) (11 male; 13 right-handed; 27.6 ± 7.7 years) and paid for their participation. All had normal or corrected to normal vision. Informed consent was obtained from all participants, in accordance with the NYU Committee on Activities Involving Human Subjects.

Stimuli

One hundred and nine images were selected from the Catalog of Art Museum Images Online (CAMIO) database (http://www.oclc.org/camio). CAMIO contains more than ninety thousand images of textiles, paintings, architecture, and sculpture from museum collections around the world. The artworks came from a variety of cultural traditions (American, European, Indian, and Japanese) and historical periods (from the fifteenth century to the recent past). Images were representational and abstract and could be roughly classified as either female figure(s) (33), male figure(s) (23), a mixed group (20), still life (11), landscape (14), or abstract painting (8). These classifications did not show significant effects on responses.

Commonly reproduced images were not used, in order to minimize recognition. Most observers recognized no images, and no observer recognized more than a few (3–5) stimulus images as reported by survey responses. Images were scaled such that the largest dimension did not exceed 20° of visual angle, and the area did not exceed 75 percent of a 20° box. Stimulus presentation and response collection were controlled using a Macintosh G4 running MATLAB 6.5 and the Psychophysics Toolbox (Brainard, 1997).

Procedure

Observers were told they would be viewing a set of artworks while lying in the scanner. They were to use a scale of 1–4 by pressing a button on a hand-held response box to answer the question "How strongly does this painting move you?" according to the following instructions:

> Imagine that the images you see are of paintings that may be acquired by a museum of fine art. The curator needs to know which paintings are the most aesthetically pleasing based on how strongly you as an individual respond to them. Your job is to give your gut-level response, based on how much you find the painting beautiful, compelling, or powerful. Note: The paintings may cover the entire range from "beautiful" to "strange" or even "ugly." Respond on the basis of how much this image "moves" you. What is most important is for you to indicate what works you find powerful, pleasing, or profound.

Each observer viewed all 109 artworks; the order was counterbalanced across observers to control for possible serial order effects. Observers were instructed prior to entering the magnet and given practice trials using artworks not in the stimulus set.

Nine-Item Evaluative Questionnaire

After the fMRI session, observers were given a short break and were then taken to a behavioral lab where they sat in front of a computer screen to complete a nine-item questionnaire. They were shown the same set of paintings in the same order as in the scanner. Each painting was shown for six seconds. Observers were asked to rate the intensity with which each artwork evoked the following evaluative and emotional responses: joy, pleasure, sadness, confusion, awe, fear, disgust, beauty, and the sublime. Responses to this nine-item questionnaire were given using mouse clicks on a visual seven-point scale for each item. These items were presented in random order on each trial. Observers could respond to the nine items in any order but could not change ratings.

Observers ranged from those with novice-level experience of art and art history to several having completed some undergraduate study in the history of art (evaluated using a survey at the time of the experiment). Before entering the scanner, observers were also administered the Positive and Negative Affect Schedule (PANAS; Watson et al. 1988). PANAS is a highly stable and internally consistent metric for dispositional affect (mood), used to determine how frequently an observer experiences positive and negative affect in a defined time period. Observers in this study were asked to answer questions with regard to the immediately preceding few days.

fMRI Scanning Procedures

fMRI scans were carried out at the NYU Center for Brain Imaging (CBI), using a 3T Siemens Allegra scanner and a Nova Medical Head coil (NM011 head transmit coil). Artworks were projected onto a screen in the bore of the magnet and viewed through a mirror mounted on the head coil.

The 109 artworks were divided into four sets (different subsets per observer, depending on order) and shown over the course of four functional scans using a slow event-related design. During these functional scans, the BOLD signal was measured from the entire brain using thirty-six 3 mm slices aligned approximately parallel to the AC-PC plane (in plane resolution 3 × 3 mm, TR=2 s, TE=30 ms, FA=80°). Each trial began with a one-second blank period then a blinking fixation point for one second, followed by the artwork for six seconds, and a blank screen for four seconds, during which the observer pressed a key corresponding to recommendation. An additional 0s, 2s, or 4s blank interval was inserted pseudo-randomly between trials to jitter trial timing, with an average trial length of 13.14 seconds.

Observers were also run in a localizer scan containing blocks of objects, scrambled objects, faces, and places. This 320s scan consisted of four 18s blocks of each stimulus type, during which the observer performed a "1-back" task (where observers monitor for exact repeats of an image). Each block contained sixteen stimulus images plus two repeats, each presented for 800 ms with a 200ms inter-stimulus interval. The full-color images were placed on top of phase-scrambled versions of the same stimuli filling a 500 × 500-pixel square to control for differences in size across stimulus categories.

A high-resolution (1 mm^3) anatomical volume (MPRage sequence) was obtained after the functional scans for registration and spatial normalization.

Behavioral Data Analysis

For the observers' recommendations collected during the scanning session, a measure of agreement across individuals was computed by taking the set of 109 recommendations for every pair of observers and computing the Pearson correlation coefficient. Images with any missing recommendation values were excluded from the correlations in a pairwise manner. One observer gave no "4" recommendations and was therefore excluded from subsequent analyses relying on the contrast of 4-vs.-1 responses. Similarly, a measure of across-observer agreement was computed for each item of the nine-item questionnaire collected after the scanning session. For each item, the Pearson correlation coefficient was computed for each pair of observers.

Factor Analysis of Evaluative Questionnaire

The responses on the nine-item questionnaire produced by each observer to each artwork (16 × 109 = 1,744 trials total) were then converted to *z*-scores within observers and concatenated into a single large matrix of scores. Principal components extraction was used to identify factors with eigenvalues greater than one. Two emotional and evaluative factors survived and were rotated using the "direct oblmin" method, which does not require that the factors be orthogonal. Scores on these two factors were computed for each of the 1,744 trials using regression.

fMRI Data Analysis

The scans were preprocessed using the FMRIB Software Library (FSL) to correct for slice-timing and motion, and were high-pass filtered at 0.0125 Hz. Subsequent analyses were performed using BrainVoyager QX. After alignment to observer-specific high-resolution anatomical images, the scans were normalized to Talairach space (Talairach and Tournoux 1988), blurred with an 8 mm Gaussian kernel, and converted to *z*-scores.

4-vs.-1 Whole-Brain Analysis

To identify regions sensitive to observer recommendation, a whole-brain random effects group-level general linear model (GLM) analysis was computed with the responses of each observer on each of the four possible recommendation levels coded as separate regressors (as a 6s "on" period for each image convolved with a standard two-gamma hemodynamic response function, HRF). A contrast of the "4" regressors vs. the "1" regressors was computed and the resulting statistical map was corrected for multiple comparisons at a false discovery rate (FDR) of $q < 0.05$ (Benjamini and Hochberg

1995; Genovese et al. 2002) and a cluster threshold of five 3 mm^3 voxels. This contrast will be referred to as the 4-vs.-1 whole-brain analysis.

ROI Analysis

In order to compare BOLD activation for all four recommendation levels across these regions, the group-level clusters from the 4-vs.-1 analysis were used to draw regions of interest (ROIs) from which we extracted time series for each observer. Using the average (over voxels in the ROI) of nonblurred, z-scored time series for each scan, individual observer parameter estimates for each of the four recommendation levels were obtained using a GLM with a standard two-gamma HRF convolved with a 6s "on" period for each image. Standard errors were computed across observers.

4-vs.-321 Whole-Brain Analysis

To further isolate processes particular to aesthetic response, we computed a second whole-brain contrast relying on the same whole-brain GLM as above, but with a new contrast of only the "4" recommendations versus the average of all the other recommendation levels, balanced to add to zero [e.g., a linear contrast of (–1 –1 –1 3) for the 1, 2, 3, and 4 regressors]. The same statistical threshold was used to correct for multiple comparisons—FDR of $q < 0.05$ and a five 3 mm^3 cluster threshold. This contrast will be referred to as the 4-vs.-321 whole-brain analysis. Note that this contrast may lead to the discovery of new activations not found in the original 4-vs.-1 analysis. Given the widely extended and interconnected nature of the resulting whole-brain map, we do not report the full set of activation coordinates—most of the peak activations were coincident with regions reported for the 4-vs.-1 contrast. Group-level ROIs were isolated for four prominent activations not found in the 4-vs.-1 contrast: the anterior medial pre-frontal cortex (aMPFC), the left hippocampus (HC), left substantia nigra, and the left posterior cingulate cortex (PCC). It was not possible to draw an isolated ROI for the aMPFC from this contrast given the large swath of activation—we therefore drew a more restricted ROI for the aMPFC based on the 4-vs.-1 whole-brain contrast, but with a statistical threshold of $p < 0.001$.

ROI Analysis of Evaluative Factors

The trial-by-trial scores for the two factors extracted from the principal components factor analysis of the nine-item evaluative questionnaire were used to create BOLD predictors by convolving with a standard 2 gamma HRF with a length of 1 TR (2s) and a delay of 1 TR relative to image onset. This middle TR was chosen as a compromise given our uncertainty about when, during a 6s viewing, an observer was able to integrate enough information across successive fixations of an artwork to generate an affective response. The resulting time courses were combined with an "Image On" predictor and orthonormalized using the Gram-Schmidt process before being entered into a GLM predicting BOLD activation in each of the ROIs identified in the whole-brain analysis.

Individual Differences Analysis of Evaluative Questionnaire

We performed an analysis of individual differences in responses to the nine-item evaluative questionnaire and their relationship to BOLD activation. Each observer's recommendations and their subsequent responses on the nine items were converted to *z*-scores and then concatenated into a single large matrix (16 observers × 109 images = 1,744 rows). We performed a stepwise regression analysis in SPSS of observers' recommendations against their responses to the nine items to eliminate redundant terms or terms that had no significant predictive power for recommendations. Individual standardized beta weights were then computed for how well each of the items surviving this procedure predicted recommendations, entered in order from most to least predictive at the group level. The resulting beta weights, which can be conceptualized as reflecting the weight an observer places on a particular emotion or evaluation when making recommendations, were used to predict the size (across observers) of the 4-vs.-1 BOLD effect in the set of ROIs identified in the whole-brain recommendation-based analysis. This yielded an overall R^2 for each ROI and beta weights for each of the items with associated confidence intervals. A significant effect in this analysis would indicate that variability *across* observers in the size of the BOLD effect in an ROI is related to variability in how much individual observers weigh a particular emotion or evaluation when making recommendations.

Belfi et al., "Dynamics of Aesthetic Experience Are Reflected in the Default-Mode Network," *NeuroImage* (2019)

Participants

Thirty participants were recruited at NYU and paid for their participation. Five participants were excluded due to excessive motion, leaving a final group of 25 participants (8 men, 17 women; 24 right-handed; 27.56 ± 6.49 years of age). The Institutional Review Board approved this study and all participants gave informed consent in accordance with the NYU Committee on Activities Involving Human Subjects.

Our sample size was determined by conducting a power analysis based on data from our previous work, which reported effect sizes in DMN ROIs around η^2=0.80 (Vessel et al. 2012). Using G*Power software (Faul et al. 2007), this power analysis indicated a sample of 20 participants would be sufficiently powerful (at a 1-β level of 0.95) to detect an effect this large. Thus, our sample size is more than adequate for the main objective of this study and should allow for sufficient power to detect our predicted effects.

Stimuli

Images selected were chosen from those used in previous work (Vessel et al. 2012). Ninety images were selected from the CAMIO database (http://www.oclc.org/camio). These images are high-quality photographs of paintings from a variety of cultural traditions (American, Asian, European) and time periods (fifteenth century to the present). Commonly reproduced images were not included in order to minimize familiarity; in a previous study using more images (109 artworks; Vessel et al. 2012), very few participants (four of sixteen), some of whom had extensive art history expertise, were able to identify specific artworks that had been seen previously, though a larger number (eleven) expressed vague familiarity with "a few" images. Images were scaled so that the largest dimension did not exceed 20° of visual angle and the area did not exceed 75 percent of a 20° box. Stimulus presentation was controlled using the Psychophysics Toolbox in MATLAB (Brainard 1997; Pelli 1997).

Procedure

Prior to the experiment, participants completed a brief (~10 minute) training session using images not presented in the experiment to familiarize themselves with the task and response modalities. This training session was identical to the experimental procedures, such that participants were not given visual feedback when using the squeeze ball. Before beginning the experiment, participants were debriefed to ensure they were comfortable using the squeeze ball as a response modality.

During the fMRI experiment, participants viewed the 90 stimuli for one of three durations: 1, 5, or 15s. In order to capture participants' initial response to each artwork, and since aesthetic appreciation may change based on prior exposure (Cutting 2003; Park et al. 2010), each stimulus was presented only once over the course of the experiment. Therefore, participants saw thirty stimuli per duration. Image presentation was counterbalanced across participants, across durations, such that each image appeared a roughly equal number of times in each duration.

Each trial began with a 1s blinking fixation cross, followed by an image of an artwork. At the onset of the image, participants began continuously rating the pleasure they felt from the stimulus. Exact instructions to the participants were as follows: "When the image appears on the screen, begin rating the pleasure you experience from the image." These continuous measurements were recorded using an fMRI-compatible squeeze ball and sampled at a rate of 10 Hz. The squeeze ball was used to provide haptic feedback, so participants were aware of their rating without the need for visual feedback (Nielsen 1987). Participants were not aware of the duration of the stimulus prior to stimulus presentation. Following stimulus presentation, the screen remained blank for a 14s "post-stimulus" rating period during which the participants continued to rate the pleasure they were experiencing from having seen the artwork. After this post-stimulus rating period, a visual slider bar appeared on the screen and participants used a trackball in their opposite hand to make a single rating of their "overall" aesthetic appreciation of the image (4s max response window). The instructions given to the participant stated: "Please rate, overall, how much this image 'moved' you. That is, how powerful, pleasing, or profound did you find the image?"

fMRI Scanning Procedures

All fMRI scans took place at the NYU CBI using a 3T Siemens Allegra scanner with a Nova Medical head coil (NM011 head transmit coil). Stimuli were presented using back-projection onto a screen mounted in the scanner and viewed through a mirror on the head coil. The ninety artworks were divided into five runs and presented in an event-related design, with each run containing six trials of each duration. Timing of stimulus onset, ordering of 1s, 5s, and 15s trials, and inter-trial intervals (mean ITI=6.76 s, range=2s–20s) were calculated using the OptSeq2 Toolbox (https://surfer.nmr.mgh.harvard.edu/optseq). Whole-brain BOLD signal was measured from thirty-four 3 mm slices using a custom multi-echo (ME) echo-planar imaging (EPI) sequence (2s TR, 80 × 64 3mm voxels, right-to-left phase encoding, FA=75°). The ME EPI sequence and a tilted slice prescription (15–20° tilt relative to the AC-PC line) were used to minimize dropout near the orbital sinuses. We collected a custom calibration scan to aid in ME reconstruction, unwarping and alignment. Prior to the experimental runs, participants completed a 6-minute eyes-open rest scan. Following the functional scans, participants completed a high-3 resolution (1 mm) anatomical scan (T1 MPRage).

Experimental Design and Statistical Analysis

Behavioral data preprocessing. Continuous rating The continuous rating data underwent a series of preprocessing steps prior to analysis. Due to the mechanics of the squeeze ball used to acquire the continuous data, a high-frequency spike often accompanied the onset of each squeeze. To remove these artifacts and other high-frequency noise, a low-pass filter (cutoff frequency 0.25 Hz) was applied to the continuous rating data. Each run was then normalized by scaling the continuous rating data based on the average of two "maximum" squeezes provided by the participant prior to the start of each run. Participants were instructed to make these maximum squeezes correspond to their maximum rating, not the hardest they could possibly squeeze. They were instructed to pick a level that could be sustained throughout the course of the experiment. All continuous data were scaled in this way for each run for each participant, so that all continuous data for all participants was between 0 and 1.

Overall Rating

Each overall rating was assigned a single value ranging between 0 and 1. Trials were designated as "high," "medium," and "low" aesthetic appreciation based on the value of the overall rating given at the end of each trial. This binning into categories was done separately for each individual participant, not across all trials. Overall, participants tended to use the entire range of the scale when making their responses. Within each duration level (1s, 5s, 15s), trials were divided into thirds, and the top third was designated as being high, the middle third as medium, and the bottom third as low. This post hoc trial categorization resulted in nine total trial types: three durations (1s, 5s, and 15s) and three rating levels (low, medium, and high), with ten trials in each of the nine types. These trial types were used for analysis of both the behavioral and fMRI data.

Behavioral Data Analysis

Continuous pleasure ratings are well fit by a simple model adapted from previous studies (Brielmann and Pelli 2017; Brielmann et al. 2017). To assess how pleasure amplitude, as identified by this model, changes with rating level and stimulus duration, we conducted a 3 × 3 repeated measures analysis of variance (ANOVA).

fMRI Preprocessing

ME EPI images were reconstructed using a custom algorithm designed by the NYU CBI to minimize dropout and distortion, and were tested for data quality (e.g., spikes, changes in signal-to-noise) using custom scripts. The scans were then preprocessed using the FMRIB Software Library (FSL) to correct for motion, align data across scans, and apply a high-pass filter (0.01 Hz cutoff). High-resolution anatomical scans were segmented using FreeSurfer (http://surfer.nmr.mgh.harvard.edu).

ROI Selection and Analysis

Three network ROIs were selected based on our a priori hypotheses regarding visual, reward, and DMN networks. Additionally, the frontoparietal control network (FP), an important network for goal-directed cognition (Spreng et al. 2010), was analyzed for comparison. We selected ROIs in one of two ways. For the DMN, visual and FP network ROIs, we used the rest scan to functionally localize these networks in individual participants. After preprocessing (motion correction, high-pass filtering at 0.005 Hz, spatial smoothing with 6 mm FWHM Gaussian filter), independent component analysis (ICA) was performed on individual participants' scans using FSL's Multivariate Exploratory Linear Optimized Decomposition into Independent Components (MELODIC). MELODIC determines the appropriate size of the lower-dimensional space using the Laplace approximation to the Bayesian evidence of the model order (Beckmann et al. 2001; Minka 2000). This process resulted in an average of 24 spatial components (SD=9.5) for each participant. These ICA components were then moved into MNI standard space and compared to a set of predefined network maps (Smith et al. 2009) using Pearson correlation.

The component with the highest correlation to the Smith et al. (2009) DMN map was then visually inspected to ensure that its spatial distribution appeared similar to the canonical DMN. For six participants, the DMN was split between two ICA components, which were combined to form a single component. The final DMN ROI for each participant was then defined as the voxels from this component that also belonged to gray matter (as defined by the FreeSurfer gray matter segmentation).

After transformation of these volumetric DMN maps to cortical surface space, a set of five subregions (anterior medial prefrontal cortex, aMPFC; dorsal medial prefrontal cortex, dMPFC; ventral medial prefrontal cortex, vMPFC; posterior cingulate cortex, PCC; inferior parietal lobule, IPL) were identified in each hemisphere by masking the DMN map with a set of "master" ROIs delineated on the FreeSurfer fsaverage brain.

These master ROIs, which each covered a contiguous region of cortex larger than the corresponding DMN subregion in any one participant, were drawn from the distribution of locations of these subregions observed in an independent sample of 16 participants. This method was used in order to identify previously characterized, spatially specific nodes of the DMN from each individual's own functional connectivity in a manner that required minimal manual intervention. For the higher-level visual network, the component with the highest correlation to the Smith et al. (2009) "lateral visual" network was used, and the ROI was created in the same manner as the DMN. More specifically, we selected the lateral visual network since the inferior temporal sulcus (ITS; MNI coordinates –49 –61 –2) activation reported in Vessel et al. (2012) falls within this network mask. For the FP network, the components with highest correlation to Smith et al. (2009) "left frontoparietal" and "right frontoparietal" networks were identified.

Eleven participants had a single bilateral component, twelve had two lateralized components that were combined, and two had no acceptable match, leaving twenty-three participants for FP. Basal ganglia ROIs were defined anatomically based on the FreeSurfer "aparc" automatic segmentation. The caudate, putamen, pallidum, and nucleus accumbens were individually identified (bilaterally) and then combined to form the whole basal ganglia ROI. General linear modeling was implemented using custom software written in MATLAB. Following extraction of an average time series from each ROI, residual signal variation due to head motion was removed by projecting out the framewise displacement vector and its absolute value. Since the post hoc trial sorting (by overall rating) resulted in an unequal number of trials in each condition per scan, the time courses from all five scans were *z*-scored and concatenated. This ROI time course was then modeled using a set of finite impulse response (FIR) functions time-locked to stimulus onset, one for each of the nine conditions (3 presentation durations × 3 rating groups). Each FIR included image presentation, the post-stimulus rating period, the overall-response period and eight trailing timepoints. The resulting parameter estimates were then averaged across participants for each time bin, resulting in estimates of fMRI signal change across the entire trial for each trial type, as well as an estimate of error at each timepoint (standard error of the mean; SEM).

The high-, medium-, and low-rated trial conditions were compared using repeated measures ANOVA for each ROI at each presentation duration (i.e., 1s, 5s, 15s). These ANOVAs were conducted with time (from image onset until end of post-stimulus period) and condition (high, medium, and low) as within-subjects factors (e.g., Shulman et al. 1999). As our goal is to identify at which time points high trials differ from low trials, we sought to identify any time by condition interactions. In this way, we chose to treat the low-rated trials as a "control" condition, as opposed to using a more standard control of, say, scrambled visual images. Importantly, including modified images (such as scrambled images) would interfere with the content of the stimuli (Fairhall and Ishai 2008), which would likely have large effects on the aesthetic appeal of the images. This would then introduce a confound into the experiment, as it is likely that scrambled images would be more likely to fall within the low-rated group. Instead, considering the low-rated trials themselves as a neutral control preserves the same content across the three categories, as all low-, medium-, and high-rated images are still intact artworks. All interactions are reported and include measures of effect size ($\eta2$). Any significant interactions were followed up by tests of simple main effects for pairwise comparisons; all were corrected for multiple comparisons using Bonferroni correction (all p-values reported are corrected p-values) and included measures of effect size (using Cohen's d as measure).

Starr and Belfi, "Pleasure," *Further Reading* (2020)

Participants

Research was performed at NYU under the approval of the NYU Committee on Activities Involving Human Subjects. Participants were recruited online using Amazon's Mechanical Turk (MTurk). We restricted participation to individuals with approval ratings of at least 95 percent on at least 1,000 previous MTurk tasks. We limited the geographic location of participants to the United States. Participants consisted of 141 adults who were native English speakers (data from eight additional participants were excluded due to incomplete responses). These participants were divided into three groups: those who read short (n=48), medium (n=47), and complete (n=46) versions of the sestina.

Procedure

Each participant read one version (short, medium, or complete) of each of the twelve sestinas and answered several questions after each (titles/first lines are available upon request). No one read multiple versions of the same poem, and each read one version of every poem. After each item, participants rated what they read on four dimensions in the following order: (1) vividness of imagery; (2) valence of emotions experienced while reading; (3) strength of their emotional arousal; and (4) aesthetic pleasure derived from reading the work. Each rating was made on a continuous scale using a slider bar with values ranging between 0 and 100. Each excerpt or poem and the four questions were presented on one screen. After responding to the questions, participants advanced to the next poem or excerpt.

Analysis

To identify differences between groups (short, medium, and complete), we conducted a MANOVA, with length as the between-subjects variable, and our five characteristics of interest as dependent variables. The overall MANOVA did not show a significant effect of length, [$F(8, 270)=1.62$, $p=0.11$, $\eta 2=0.04$]. When examining the post hoc one-way ANOVAs, we found no significant effects of length on vividness [$F(2,138)=2.39$, $p=0.09$, $\eta 2=0.03$], valence [$F(2,138)=1.53$, $p=0.22$, $\eta 2=0.02$], emotional strength [$F(2,138)=0.12$, $p=0.88$, $\eta 2=0.01$], or aesthetic pleasure [$F(2,138)=0.52$, $p=0.53$, $\eta 2=0.01$].

Individual subject regressions were computed to measure how well the factors of vividness, valence, and emotional strength predicted ratings of aesthetic appeal, and whether the predictive ability of these variables differed as a function of length. On average, strength of emotional arousal was the best predictor of aesthetic pleasure (average standardized β: 0.39 for short, 0.43 for medium, 0.45 for long), followed by the valence of felt emotions (average standardized β: 0.30 for short, 0.24 for medium, 0.23 for long) and vividness of imagery (average standardized β: 0.15 for short, 0.20 for medium, 0.21 for long). When comparing the regression results between the three lengths, a one-way MANOVA revealed no significant differences in the predictive ability of the three ratings between the three poem lengths [$F(6,274)=0.43$, $p=0.85$, $\eta 2=0.01$].

We also investigated agreement among the raters for short, medium, and complete conditions. We calculated ICCs from single measures for each characteristic using the ICC (2,1) consistency measure. As assessed by ICC (2,1), participants showed similar patterns of agreement for short, medium, and complete conditions. For all lengths, participants showed the highest agreement for valence, followed by vividness, then arousal and aesthetic pleasure. Overall, agreement was quite low for each rating scale. To compare ICC values between the three lengths, we calculated 95 percent confidence intervals to assess the degree of overlap between the three lengths. This indicated that there were no significant differences between ICC values for any of the ratings.

Belfi et al., "Individual Ratings of Vividness Predict Aesthetic Appeal in Poetry," *Psychology of Aesthetics, Creativity and the Arts* (2019)

Participants

Participants were recruited using Amazon's Mechanical Turk (MTurk). While online samples, like any other method, have limitations, substantial previous work has indicated the reliability of MTurk data (Rand 2012). In addition to allowing data collection from a large sample of participants, MTurk has the benefit of giving access to a more diverse population than the typical undergraduate sample used in psychological studies (Buhrmester et al. 2018). MTurk results are also consistent with those obtained in a traditional laboratory setting (Paolacci et al. 2010).

We restricted participation to workers in the United States who have completed at least 1,000 previous MTurk tasks and obtained approval ratings of at least 95 percent. In total, 402 participants completed the experiment. Participants were divided into two groups: haiku (n=302) and sonnet (n=100). Four participants from the haiku group were excluded for giving the same response for each item. Despite consistencies between online and in-lab samples, others have identified that around 10 percent of survey respondents are "careless" (Meade and Craig 2012). One way of discarding such careless raters is to identify those who give inconsistent responses. In the present study, participants rated five (haiku) or two (sonnet) repeated poems to assess test–retest reliability. We identified participants whose test–retest reliability scores were below 0.5 for all ratings (interpreted as "poor" reliability; Koo and Li 2016). Twenty-five participants who read haiku and ten who read sonnets fell below this threshold. These participants were removed, leaving a total of 90 participants in the sonnet group and 273 participants in the haiku group.

Because the stimulus set was much larger for haiku than sonnets (see Materials) each participant in the haiku group read one-third of the total number of haiku. To ensure that all poems were read approximately the same number of times, a larger number of subjects were assigned to the haiku group.

In the haiku group, participants (163 M, 110 F) were an average of 34.24 years old (*SD*=10.18) with an age range between 18 and 69 years. Participants had taken, on average, 2.59 (*SD*=1.56) poetry or writing classes at the high school level or above, 3.00 (*SD*=1.71) literature classes, and 1.60 (*SD*=1.35) aesthetics classes. They spent, on average, 1.79 hr (*SD*=1.38) each week writing creatively. In the sonnet group, participants (43 M, 47 F) were an average of 34.93 years old (*SD*=9.31) with an age range between 21 and 68 years old. Participants had taken, on average, 2.48 (*SD*=1.59) poetry or writing classes at the high school level or above, 2.92 (*SD*=1.61) literature classes, and 1.61 (*SD*=1.29) aesthetics classes. They spent, on average, 1.58 hr (*SD*=1.04) each week writing creatively. There were no significant differences between haiku and sonnet groups on any demographic variables. In addition, there were no differences in positive (PA) or negative (NA) affect at the time of the experiment between the haiku (mean PA=18.03; mean NA=7.54) and sonnet (mean PA=17.03, mean NA=7.19) groups, as measured by the PANAS (Meade and Craig 2012). All participants self-identified as native English speakers.

Materials

The haiku poetry set consisted of 111 haiku chosen to exhibit a variety of subject matter. Of these, 68 were translated into English from the original Japanese, 32 were "standard" haiku in original English, and 11 were "alternate" haiku in original English. Standard haiku consisted of haiku in a prescribed 5-7-5 syllable form, while alternate did not follow this prescription (the 5-7-5 syllable form is not universally adopted in haiku, whether they are Japanese or not). Translated haiku were originally written by Basho (*n*=5), Bushon (*n*=29), and Issa (*n*=34). English translations from Japanese were written by American poet Robert Hass, and did not adhere to the 5-7-5 form. All original English haiku were written by Richard Wright.

Sixteen sonnets were selected from published collections. All were in their original language and form, and were chosen to include equal numbers of the two main forms of English-language sonnets, Elizabethan (with a rhyme scheme of abab cdcd efef gg) and Petrarchan (abbaabbaabba cde cde), as well as a broad range of subjects. The poems range in date from the early seventeenth century to 2011. The sonnets also exhibited stylistic range, so that, for example, three Petrarchan and three Elizabethan sonnets did not have the traditional "volta" or "turn," and varied in degree of enjambment. Both stimulus sets may be made available to any researcher by request.

Procedure

All procedures were conducted in compliance with the APA Ethical Principles and were approved by the Committee on Activities Involving Human Subjects. First, participants received a general description of the study. Next, participants completed the PANAS scale to measure their current affect. Participants then received detailed instructions about rating the poems. After reading the instructions, participants read and rated the poems on a set of dimensions. To reduce participant fatigue and to ensure total reading time was equivalent between haiku and sonnet readers, each subject saw approximately one-third of the 111 haiku presented in a random order. To assess test–retest reliability within participants, each participant saw the first five haiku again at the end of the testing session. In the sonnet group, participants read all sixteen sonnets and read the first two sonnets again at the end of the testing session.

Participants rated each poem on four dimensions in the following order: (a) vividness ("How vivid is the imagery evoked from this poem?"), (b) arousal ("How relaxing or stimulating is this poem?"), (c) valence ("How positive or negative is the content of this poem?"), and (d) aesthetic appeal ("How enjoyable or aesthetically appealing did you find this poem?"). Each rating was made on a continuous scale using a slider bar with values ranging between 0 and 100. Each poem and the four questions were presented on one screen. After responding to the questions, participants advanced to the next poem.

After rating the poems, participants completed the Vividness of Visual Imagery Questionnaire (VVIQ; Marks 1973), which assesses individual differences in visual imagery abilities. Finally, participants completed a short demographic questionnaire that included questions about prior experience with poetry and creative writing. The experiment took approximately thirty minutes to complete and subjects were paid $3 for completing the task.

Analysis

A primary goal was to investigate which characteristics (vividness, arousal, or valence) best predict aesthetic appeal in poems, and whether there is an influence of genre. This was assessed by computing a linear mixed effects model using the *lme4* package (Bates et al. 2014) in R (version 3.4.0). Predictors were centered within each subject (i.e., "group mean centering") before being submitted to the model (Enders and Tofighi 2007). A restricted maximum likelihood linear mixed-model analysis was run on aesthetic ratings using vividness, arousal, and valence ratings, VVIQ scores, and PANAS scores (both positive and negative composite scores), as well as the interaction of each of these variables with poem genre, as fixed effects. As random effects, we included intercepts for subjects and stimuli, as well as by-subject and by-stimulus random slopes for the effects of valence, arousal, and vividness. Genre was coded as follows: haiku = 0.5, sonnet = –0.5. The *car* package in R was used to obtain *p*-values for regression coefficients (Fox and Weisberg 2011).

Next, to further explore individual differences in ratings, we sought to assess the agreement among raters for haiku and sonnets. To summarize agreement using a single statistic, we calculated ICCs from single measures for each characteristic for haiku and sonnets using the ICC (2,1) consistency measure. We assessed test–retest reliability for repeated poems using Pearson's correlations.

Finally, a secondary goal of the present article was to characterize our set of haiku for use in further research, similar to what has been done for visual images or words (Bradley and Lang 1999; Lang and Bradley 2007; Kurdi et al. 2017). We calculated descriptive statistics for each haiku based on four characteristics: vividness, arousal, valence, and aesthetic appeal.

Belfi et al., "Rapid Timing of Musical Aesthetic Judgments," ***Journal of Experimental Psychology: General*** **(2018)**

Experiment 1

Participants Twenty students from NYU participated in this study (sex: 2 M, 18 F; age: M=19.25, SD=1.25). This target number of participants was determined by an a priori power analysis based on effect sizes reported in the literature from previous studies using a gating paradigm in music (Huijgen et al. 2015). Using these reported effect sizes (η^2 ranging from 0.20 to 0.61), our power analysis indicated that a sample of twelve participants would be sufficiently powerful (at a level of 0.95) to detect an effect of this size. Along these lines, previous studies using the gating paradigm in music have typically used sample sizes of around ten to twenty participants (Filipic et al. 2010; Huijgen et al. 2015; Tillmann et al. 2014). In the present study, participants had 5.8 years of formal musical training on average (SD=4.62). All participants were undergraduate students enrolled in psychology courses at NYU and received credit for participating in the current study. All procedures were approved by the NYU Institutional Review Board and participants provided written informed consent before participating.

Materials Sixty musical excerpts were chosen from three genres, referred to here as "classical," "jazz," and "electronica." For classical music, all excerpts were chosen from nineteenth-century small ensemble music of the Romantic era. Nineteenth-century classical was selected because it tends to have a wider range of dynamic and emotional intensity than earlier classical-era music. No composer was included more than once in the stimulus set, and no particularly well-known composers were selected (in an effort to ensure that all pieces are unfamiliar). All pieces were from the European tradition and ranged in tempo from 69 to 160 beats per minute (M=117.15, SD=28.00). Jazz music consisted of 1960s music with bop or postbop elements, avoiding avant-garde styles of the later 1960s. Ensembles and instrumentation were all traditional jazz, consisting of piano, guitar, saxophone, brass, and so forth. Jazz pieces ranged in tempo from 104 to 192 beats per minute (M=137.7, SD=28.71). Electronic music consisted of electronic dance music with a distinctive beat structure (i.e., no ambient music) that contained no lyrics or human vocalizations. All electronic pieces were contemporary and ranged in tempo from 60 to 150 beats per minute (M=111.05, SD=23.41).

From each piece, one 10s excerpt was selected for the present experiment. These excerpts were selected by the experimenters to represent portions of the piece that contained "dynamic" information; that is, the excerpts were selected to contain changes in instrumentation, loudness, and other musical qualities. The goal here was to select pieces that were likely to be unfamiliar to the participants in the present study, but to represent enough of a variety to see varied responses.

Procedure Participants heard musical excerpts blocked by genre. Excerpts were blocked by genre to prevent listeners from making ratings based solely on between-genre comparisons (e.g., a listener who strongly prefers classical over jazz may be influenced by hearing a classical excerpt immediately preceding a jazz excerpt). Instead, listeners were instructed to make judgments about the individual excerpts themselves. Within each genre block, each of the twenty excerpts was presented in six subblocks of increasing duration (250 ms, 500 ms, 750 ms, 1,000 ms, 2000 ms, 10,000 ms). That is, listeners heard each excerpt at each duration. Excerpts were blocked by increasing duration to ensure that listeners would rate just the portion they heard, as opposed to rating the memory of a longer excerpt. For example, if durations were intermixed, a listener might hear the 10s excerpt first, and all subsequent shorter versions of this excerpt may be judged based on the memory of the entire excerpt. The excerpts for each clip started at the same starting point in the piece. After each excerpt, participants were asked to answer the question "How much did you like the clip you just heard?" using a 1–9 point Likert scale, where 1 represented "not at all" and 9 represented "very much." Genre order was counterbalanced across participants.

Analysis The central question of the experiment is to identify at which duration listeners make accurate aesthetic judgments of music. To assess this, we first calculated an accuracy score for each trial compared to the listener's final rating of the longest duration. If a listener's rating on a given trial matched that of their rating of the same piece on the final trial (within ± 1 points on the scale), that trial was scored a 1 for "correct." For example: a listener hears classical piece #1 for 250 ms and gives it a rating of 2. If their rating of this piece at the 10,000 ms duration was a 6, the 250 ms trial would be scored a 0 for "incorrect." If their rating of this piece at the 10,000 ms duration was a 3, their rating on the 250 ms duration would be scored a 1 for "correct."

To assess at which time point listeners made accurate judgments, we conducted two complementary analyses. First, we performed a generalized linear mixed-effect model analysis using the glmer function from the *lme4* package (Bates et al. 2015) implemented in R (Version 3.4.0). The anova function from the R package car was used to conduct significance tests (Fox and Weisberg 2011). This model included fixed effects for genre, duration, their interaction, and years of musical experience, as well as random intercepts for participants and items. While this model will test for differences in accuracy between durations and genres, it does not indicate whether listeners' performance differs from what would be expected by chance. In our second analysis, we conducted one-sample *t* tests to compare actual performance to chance performance. All *t* tests were corrected using Bonferroni corrections for multiple comparisons. These analyses together assess 1) when listeners' accuracy differed between durations and 2) when accuracy differed from chance. Finally, we also analyzed our data with a more standard method used in prior gating tasks (Filipic et al. 2010; Huijgen et al. 2015; Tillmann et al. 2014). These analyses evaluate the raw "liking" ratings and compare between clips identified as "liked" or "disliked." The results of these analyses converge.

Experiment 2

In Experiment 1, listeners heard excerpts of the same duration (e.g., 500 ms, 750 ms), but these excerpts were taken from musical pieces of various tempos. It is likely that a piece with a faster tempo contains more notes in 500 ms than a piece with a slower tempo. In Experiment 2, we controlled for the potential effect of tempo by gating the stimuli by "note values." One way this is frequently done is by playing a one-line melody note-by-note and identifying the number of notes required for a successful judgment (Bailes 2010; Dalla Bella et al. 2003). Here, we designed a similar task with the more naturalistic stimuli used in Experiment 1. Identifying note onsets in music is a challenging problem currently being undertaken in the field of music information retrieval (Miron et al. 2015; Shao et al. 2016). Therefore, instead of gating by note onset, as done in prior work with one-line melodies, here we gated by the estimated duration a note would take given the tempo of a piece. Using the tempo of each piece, we calculated the approximate duration of one eighth note, quarter note, and so forth, and gated our stimuli by these values. In this way, Experiment 2 explicitly controlled for tempo by gating each piece based on its tempo. Participants heard musical clips gated by note value (e.g., eighth note, quarter note) as opposed to absolute time (e.g., 250 ms, 500 ms).

Participants Twenty students from NYU participated in this study (sex: 6 M, 14 F; age: M=19.10, SD=0.96). In the present study, participants had 7.5 years of formal musical training on average (SD=4.82). Participants were undergraduate students enrolled in Psychology courses at NYU and received credit for participating in the current study. All procedures were approved by the NYU Institutional Review Board, and participants provided written informed consent before participating.

Materials Materials are as in Experiment 1. However, instead of designating duration blocks of absolute time, as in Experiment 1, excerpts in Experiment 2 were blocked by the note duration. That is, we first determined the duration of each note value (e.g., eighth note, quarter note) for each piece of music given its tempo. For example, an eighth note would last approximately 270 ms in a piece with a tempo of 110 beats per minute. The tempo of each piece was identified using the MIRToolbox (Lartillot and Toiviainen 2007) and was confirmed manually by an experienced musician using a metronome. Blocks were as follows: eighth note, quarter note, half note, dotted half note, whole note, and full excerpt. On average, the absolute durations for these were as follows: 260 ms, 520 ms, 1,000 ms, 1,500 ms, 2,000 ms. These durations roughly correspond to those used in Experiment 1, but importantly were calculated based on the tempo of each individual musical piece. A one-way MANOVA comparing each of the note values across all three genres revealed significant differences between genres for all note values [$F(2, 57)=4.61$, p=.01, $\eta^2=0.13$]. Pairwise comparisons indicated that all note values of electronic music were significantly longer than all note values of jazz music (ps < 0.01).

Procedure and Data Analysis Participants heard the sixty musical excerpts blocked by genre. Within each genre block, each of the twenty excerpts was presented in six subblocks of increasing note length (eighth note, quarter note, half note, dotted half note, whole note, and full excerpt). The excerpts for each clip began at the same starting point in the piece. After each excerpt, participants were asked to answer the question "How much did you like the clip you just heard?" using a nine-point Likert scale, where 1 represented "not at all" and 9 represented "very much." Excerpts were presented in a different random order for each participant and genre block order was counterbalanced across participants. Data were analyzed in the same manner described in Experiment 1.

Vessel et al., "The Default-Mode Network Represents Aesthetic Appeal That Generalizes across Visual Domains," *Proceedings of the National Academy of Sciences* (2019)

Participants

Eighteen participants were recruited at NYU and paid for their participation. Two participants were excluded due to excessive head motion that led to visible signal distortions and difficulties with registration, leaving a final group of 16 participants (10 female, 16 right-handed; 25.7 ± 6.3 y). All had normal or corrected to normal vision and no history of neurological disorders. Informed consent was obtained from all participants. All experimental procedures, including informed consent, were approved by the NYU Committee on Activities Involving Human Subjects. Images were presented using back-projection (Eiki LC-XG250 projector) onto a screen mounted in the scanner and viewed through a mirror on the head coil. Stimulus presentation was controlled by a Macintosh Pro running OS 10.6 and MATLAB R2011b (MathWorks) with Psychophysics Toolbox-3 extensions (http://psychtoolbox.org).

Visual Art

The set consisted of 148 photographs of visual artworks (paintings, collages, woven silks, excluding sculpture) sourced from the CAMIO database. A subset of these (109) were used in a previous study (Vessel et al. 2012). The set covered a variety of periods (fifteenth century to the twentieth), styles, and genres (landscape, portrait, abstract, still life), and diversely represented cultures of Europe, the Americas, and Asia. While all the images were taken from museum collections, special care was used to ensure that only lesser-known artworks were included. When necessary, stimuli were cropped to remove the artist's signature. Due to the large differences in size and color content across different artworks, contrast equalization was not possible.

Architecture

For architecture, 148 photographs (74 exterior, 74 interior) were selected, with the majority collected from Artstor, a database of high-quality images representing multiple cultures and periods. Images containing people were excluded. Interior images were chosen to highlight architectural detail, not interior décor. An effort was also made to utilize exterior images that gave an impression of building detail as well as its place in a given setting, while excluding images that gave primary emphasis to features of the landscape. Images represented a variety of structures (e.g., skyscraper vs. single residence), styles (e.g., Gothic vs. classical), materials, and time periods. Images were cropped to a 4:3 (landscape) or 3:4 (portrait) aspect ratio and presented at a size of 13 degrees of visual angle for the longer dimension. The images were contrast-equalized and displayed using a linearized color lookup table. Natural landscapes. For natural landscapes, 148 photographs were obtained from a variety of sources, including the SUN Database (Xiao et al. 2013), IMSI MasterClips, and MasterPhotos Premium Image Collection, and also from images publicly available on the internet. Images were cropped to a 4:3 aspect ratio and presented at 13 degrees of visual angle for the horizontal dimension. The images were contrast-equalized and displayed using a linearized color lookup table.

Procedure

The experiment took place over two sessions. Participants were instructed in the task and given a short practice (ten trials) to familiarize them with the types of images they would be seeing, the task timing, and the response method. Participants were told that they would be viewing and evaluating images from three different aesthetic domains: natural landscapes, architecture, and visual art. They were asked to rate how aesthetically moving they found each depicted scene, structure, or artwork. In each session, participants completed six experimental scans composed of thirty-seven trials each. Each scan contained images of only a single domain (artwork, natural landscape, interior or exterior architecture) in order to allow participants to fully engage with this domain over a several-minute period. One session therefore contained two artwork scans, two landscape scans, one interior architecture scan, and one exterior architecture scan. Scan order was counterbalanced across participants, and image order within each scan was pseudorandomized and also counterbalanced by assigning alternating participants the reverse order of another participant. Each participant saw each image only once. Across the two sessions, this resulted in a total of 148 trials for each of the three domains. Each trial began with a blinking 1s fixation cross followed by image presentation for four seconds.

After the image disappeared, a visual "slider" bar appeared on the screen, and participants had up to four seconds to indicate their response on a continuous interval (marked with *L* and *H* at the ends) using a trackball. The mapping between observer movement (up/down) and movement of the slider (left/right) was counterbalanced across participants to remove any confounds associated with direction of hand movement. This was followed by a variable intertrial interval drawn from a discrete approximation of an exponential function with a mean of 2.6 seconds. Each scan also included 20 seconds of blank screen at the 10 seconds at the end to allow for better baseline signal estimation and removal of T1 saturation effects.

fMRI Acquisition and Reconstruction

All fMRI scans took place at the NYU CBI using a 3T Siemens Allegra scanner with a Nova Medical head coil (NM011 head transmit coil). The whole-brain BOLD signal was measured from thirty-four 3 mm slices using a custom ME echo-planar imaging (EPI) sequence (2s repetition time [TR], 80 × 64 3 mm voxels, right-to-left phase encoding, flip angle=75°). The ME EPI sequence and a tilted slice proscription (15° to 20° tilt relative to the anterior commissure–posterior commissure [AC-PC] line) were used to minimize dropout near the orbital sinuses. Cardiac and respiration signals were collected using BIOPAC hardware and AcqKnowledge software.

We collected a custom calibration scan to aid in ME reconstruction, unwarping, and alignment. ME EPI images were reconstructed using a custom algorithm designed by the NYU CBI to minimize dropout and distortion, and were tested for data quality (e.g., spikes, changes in signal-to-noise) using custom scripts. Following the session 1 experimental runs, we collected a high-resolution (1 mm^3) anatomical volume (T1 magnetization-prepared rapid gradient echo [MPRage]) for registration and segmentation using FreeSurfer (http://surfer.nmr.mgh.harvard.edu). Following the session 2 experimental runs, participants completed a 360s eyes-open "rest" scan plus a 320s visual localizer scan that contained blocks of objects, places, faces, and scrambled objects. The visual localizer scan is fully described in Vessel et al. (2012).

Analysis

Identification of individual DMN maps and DMN sub-ROIs Participant-specific maps of the DMN were obtained using the rest scan. Motion correction, high-pass filtering at 0.005 Hz, and spatial smoothing with 6-mm FWHM Gaussian filter were applied using the FMRIB Software Library (FSL). Independent component analysis (ICA) was then performed on individual subjects' scans using FSL's MELODIC tool. MELODIC determines the appropriate size of the lower-dimensional space using the Laplace approximation to the Bayesian evidence of the model order (Beckmann et al. 2001; Minka 2000). This process resulted in an average of 21.88 spatial components (*SD*=3.70) for each subject. These ICA components were spatially thresholded at a *z*-score cutoff of 2.3, moved into MNI standard space, and compared to a set of predefined network maps (Smith et al. 2009) using Pearson correlation.

The component with the highest correlation to the Smith et al. (Smith et al. 2009) DMN map was then visually inspected to ensure that its spatial distribution appeared similar to the canonical DMN. For three participants, the DMN was split between two ICA components similar to those seen Andrews-Hanna 2010b, which were combined to form a single map. The final DMN ROI for each subject was then defined as the voxels from this component that also belonged to gray matter (as defined by the FreeSurfer gray matter segmentation).

Volumetric DMN maps were transformed to participant-specific surface space. The following six subregions of the DMN were then identified in both hemispheres from the DMN ICA maps of individual subjects by combining anatomically defined boundaries with the participant-specific DMN maps: aMPFC, dMPFC, vMPFC, PCC, IPL, and LTC.

Identification of VOT ROIs

For comparison to the DMN, three category-selective regions of the ventral occipitotemporal cortex (VOT) were identified using standard methods. Finally, an overall VOT ROI was created by identifying a larger region of the VOT that included all three of these category-selective ROIs plus the voxels between them (Hasson et al. 2004). This ROI was first drawn on the FreeSurfer fsaverage cortical surface bilaterally using category-selective ROIs from three representative participants as a guide and then projected onto individual hemispheres. The borders of the resulting ROI extended from the depth of the occipitotemporal sulcus laterally to the center of the lingual/parahippocampal gyrus medially, and from the posterior collateral transverse sulcus to the anterior collateral transverse sulcus (approximate

MNI coordinates y = –72 to y = –31). All ROIs were combined across left and right hemispheres to form bilateral ROIs.

ROI Classification Analysis of Aesthetic Appreciation

A beta-series GLM (83) implemented using custom MATLAB code was used to extract an estimate of response amplitude for each trial, at each voxel in gray matter. Experimental scans were first preprocessed using FSL to correct for motion, align data across scans, and apply a high-pass filter (0.01-Hz cutoff). Nuisance signals were then removed from the BOLD time courses of all twelve scans by projecting out motion estimates and nuisance time series derived from a second-order Taylor series expansion of cardiac and respiration measurements (RetroIcor method) (Glover et al. 2000). The cleaned time courses were then converted to percent signal change. Individual trials were modeled using a 4s "on" period convolved with a canonical hemodynamic response function from the SPM12 Toolbox (Wellcome Centre for Human Neuroimaging), and the resulting trial-wise amplitude estimates were *z*-scored separately for each scan.

A series of participant-specific classifiers were then trained to distinguish high versus low aesthetic appreciation trials using the beta-series amplitude estimates from all voxels in an individual ROI. This analysis used the ten trials with the highest rating (out of thirty-seven; top 27 percent) and the ten trials with the lowest rating from each scan (bottom 27 percent). "Within-domain" classification performance was evaluated by training logistic regression classifiers (logreg.m from Princeton MVPA Toolbox, https://github.com/princetonuniversity/princeton-mvpa-toolbox) with high and low trials from three scans of one domain and then measuring classification accuracy on the high and low trials of one heldout scan of the same domain (fourfold cross-validation). The classifier penalty parameter was set to equal 5 percent of the total number of voxels in an ROI. Across-domain classification performance was evaluated by training on high and low trials from three scans of one domain and then measuring classification accuracy on high and low trials in one scan from a different domain (again with fourfold cross-validation). This resulted in a three-by-three matrix of classification scores with within-domain scores along the diagonal and across-domain scores off the diagonal.

The three within-domain scores along the diagonal were averaged for each participant to produce an overall within-domain score, and the six off-diagonal across-domain scores were also averaged to produce an overall across-domain score. Maximum likelihood estimation was then used to compute the average and 95 percent confidence interval for both of these scores, across all eleven ROIs.

An area under the curve (AUC) measure was also computed for each ROI and participant by averaging probabilistic classifier predictions. Significance of classification performance across all participants was assessed through permutation testing. For each subject, five thousand permutations of the high and low trial-wise labels were computed and used to generate a null distribution of the two summary statistics in each ROI. We tested the hypothesis that classification performance was better than chance (one-tailed) at two critical alpha values, 0.05 and 0.005, Bonferroni corrected for twenty-two total tests (eleven ROIs by two statistics).

Searchlight Analysis

Maps of classification performance were computed across the cortical surface using a "searchlight" approach. For each participant, linear support-vector machine classifiers were trained and tested in a series of 5mm-radius spheres (thirty-three 3 mm voxels) centered on each voxel where data were collected. Three within-domain maps and six across-domain maps were created from the average of a fourfold cross-validation procedure for each participant. Maps of above-chance performance (> 0.5) for the average of the across-domain classifiers (e.g., train on art, test on landscape) and all three within-domain classifiers (art, architecture, landscape) were created for each participant, and then averaged across participants on the FreeSurfer "fsaverage" surface. The resulting four maps were corrected for comparisons using cluster-wise thresholding derived from Monte Carlo simulations (mri_glmfit-sim; (Hagler Jr. et al. 2006) with a voxel-wise threshold of $p <$ 0.001 and a cluster threshold of 0.05 across the entire cortical surface (two hemispheres).

Correlation with behavioral discrimination The distribution of rating responses differed from observer to observer; some generated largely bimodal distributions, some uniform, and some strongly unimodal near the neutral point. Therefore, the ratings of the distributions of images subsequently labeled "high" (top 40 of 148 in each domain) and those labeled "low" (bottom 40 of 148 in each domain) also differed across observers, with some showing a greater separation than others. In order to quantify this individual variability, a distance measure (d′; e.g., distance between the mean of the two distributions, rescaled in units of SD) was computed between the distributions of raw ratings for "high" and "low" labeled trials for each participant, in each aesthetic domain. The average d′ scores across the three domains were then used in a linear regression analysis as predictors for DMN domain-general classification performance. Data are available at https://dx.doi.org/10.17617/3.2r.

Notes

Preface

1. Proust, *Remembrance of Things Past,* 1:706–707; cf. Pléiade edition, *A la recherche du temps perdu,* 2:18.

2. Nehamas and Woodruff, trans., *Plato,* 53. See also the elucidation in Scarry, *On Beauty and Being Just.*

Introduction

1. Thank you to Marcia Fowle for educating me about ospreys and dwelling with me in that moment of beauty.

2. Hopkins, *Poems and Prose,* 51.

3. Hopkins, *Poems and Prose,* 51.

4. Hopkins, *Poems and Prose,* 30–31.

5. Dewey, *Art as Experience,* 49.

6. Dewey, *Art as Experience,* 5. In chapter 1, I will discuss some of the challenges of an account of aesthetics that privileges positive affect.

7. Johns, *Target with Plaster Casts,* 1955, encaustic and collage on canvas with objects, 51 × 44", 1955, private collection.

8. Troxler, "Uber Das Vcrschwindern Gegehener Gegenstande Innerhalh Unsers Gesichtskreises," 1–53; Bonneh et al., "Motion-Induced Blindness and Troxler Fading," e92894.

9. Mennemeier et al., "Contributions of the Parietal and Frontal Lobes to Sustained Attention and Habituation," 703–716.

10. Johns, *Green Target*, 1955, encaustic on newspaper and cloth over canvas, 60 × 60", 1955, Museum of Modern Art, New York.

11. Hogarth, *Analysis of Beauty*, 33; emphasis in the original. See also Burke, *A Philosophical Enquiry into the Sublime and Beautiful*, Part 4, sections 13, 21, 22. In those sections, beauty is exemplary when it involves what is round or green.

12. Dissanayake, *Homo Aestheticus*, 190, 205. On affordances, see Gibson, *Ecological Approach to Visual Perception.*

13. My argument here about the legibility of the target and number series as alternating between abstraction and denotation owes much to teacher and mentor Philip Fisher. See Fisher, *Making and Effacing Art.*

14. Stoltzfus, "Appendix," 99–108.

15. Johns, *Seven*, 1955, encaustic and collage on canvas, 1955, LACMA.

16. Belfi et al., "Dynamics of Aesthetic Experience Are Reflected in the Default-Mode Network," 584–597.

17. See Menninghaus et al., "Towards a Psychological Construct of Being Moved," e0128451; Ngai, *Ugly Feelings.*

18. Fingerhut and Prinz, "Aesthetic Emotions Reconsidered," 229.

19. Dissanayake, *Art and Intimacy*, 190, 205.

20. Clayton, Sager, and Will, "In Time with the Music," 1–82; Tierney and Kraus, "Neural Entrainment to the Rhythmic Structure of Music," 400–408; Doelling et al., "An Oscillator Model Better Predicts Cortical Entrainment to Music," 10113–10121; Doelling and Poeppel, "Cortical Entrainment to Music and Its Modulation by Expertise," E6233–E6242.

21. See, for example, DeNora, *Music in Everyday Life*; Gouk, "Music as a Means of Social Control," 307–314.

22. Tomlinson, *A Million Years of Music*, 38. The term "musicking" is coined by and detailed in Small, *Musicking.*

23. The cross-cultural universality and sociality of music may seem to support the idea that aesthetic responses (to music and other arts) are universally shared. Immanuel Kant argues that a claim that something is beautiful is generally a claim not just that something is beautiful to an individual, but that it is "universally so": see *Critique of Judgment*, Part I, sections 7–9. He takes this as a feature of the structure of cognition, and even the universals of human perception; but this idea of universality is also a social claim, a claim to a shared basis of reality. Earlier in the European philosophical tradition, this is a claim for a "common sense"—that is, the basic for aesthetic taste (as well as for conversation and manners). See also Shaftesbury,

Characteristics of Men, Manners, Opinions, Times; and Hutcheson, *An Inquiry into the Original of Our Ideas of Beauty and Virtue*. It is notable that this "common sense" was in fact reserved for white Europeans: see, for example, Kant, *Observations on the Feeling of the Beautiful and Sublime*; Lovejoy, *The Great Chain of Being*; and Gates Jr., *The Signifying Monkey*.

24. On the relation between perception and art, see, for example, Livingstone and Hubel, *Vision and Art*; and Zeki, *Inner Vision*. On disparate taste, see Vessel et al., "Stronger Shared Taste for Natural Aesthetic Domains than for Artifacts of Human Culture," 121–131.

25. Luhmann, *Art as a Social System*, 22; emphasis in the original. See also Dissanayake, *Homo Aestheticus*.

26. Arstila and Lloyd, *Subjective Time*, 323.

27. Haggard, Clark, and Kalogeras, "Voluntary Action and Conscious Awareness," 382–385. For a good review, see Moore and Obhi, "Intentional Binding and the Sense of Agency," 546–561.

28. Priming occurs when an object is presented to the senses below the threshold of conscious perception, but the perceptual apparatus nonetheless feeds information forward into, and influences outcomes for, later stages of processing. This includes subliminal influences that introduce bias. For a good summary, see Wittenbrink and Schwarz, *Implicit Measures of Attitudes*. Paul Armstrong makes the case that the multidimensionality of time in our perception of cause and effect creates the conditions under which we experience narrative in life and art. Armstrong, *Stories and the Brain*.

29. Hasson et al., "Intersubject Synchronization of Cortical Activity during Natural Vision," 1634–1640.

30. Stephens, Silbert, and Hasson, "Speaker-Listener Neural Coupling Underlies Successful Communication," 14425–14430.

31. Sachs et al., "Dynamic Intersubject Neural Synchronization Reflects Affective Responses to Sad Music," 116512.

32. Tartt, *The Goldfinch*, 758.

33. Noë, *Strange Tools*, 4–5. It is somewhat disturbing to me that many of the examples Noë offers of mutually constituted behaviors involve women's bodies. For example, he writes, "When it comes to breast-feeding, the striking thing about human beings is that . . . We do it very badly. . . . Our frailty as feeders is . . . far-reaching. . . . Our babies are liable to wander during the task. They get distracted by noises. Or they blissfully fall asleep. Or they indulge in the pleasures of biting and chewing to the neglect of the main business at hand" (3–4). It is a biological fact that breastfeeding is successful for our species, even as it is challenging at times for any parent, and nearly impossible for some individuals. The experiences that Noë

chooses to elevate, like breastfeeding, raise the question for me of whether what he describes is truly mutual in his view, or only an ideal toward which he gestures, which is built from a vantage point of external observation and power. Given the centrality of mutuality and maternal–child relations in Ellen Dissanayake's account of art, it is surprising to me that he does not pursue this question. See Dissanayake, *Art and Intimacy*.

34. Descartes, "Meditations on First Philosophy."

35. Hume, *An Enquiry Concerning Human Understanding*, 164–171.

36. Aristotle, *Nicomachean Ethics*.

37. Zysset et al., "The Anterior Frontomedian Cortex and Evaluative Judgment," 983–991; Moran, Kelley, and Heatherton, "What Can the Organization of the Brain's Default Mode Network Tell Us about Self-Knowledge?"; Jessica R. Andrews-Hanna et al., "Functional-Anatomic Fractionation of the Brain's Default Network," 550–562.

38. Buckner and DiNicola, "The Brain's Default Network," 593–608.

39. Supekar et al., "Development of Functional and Structural Connectivity within the Default Mode Network in Young Children," 290–301; Fair et al., "The Maturing Architecture of the Brain's Default Network," 4028–4032.

40. Vessel, Starr, and Rubin, "The Brain on Art," 66; Cela-Conde et al., "Dynamics of Brain Networks in the Aesthetic Appreciation," 10454–10461. The connection with the DMN(s) is further underscored by research that shows that individuals remember artworks they have found aesthetically appealing better than they do neutral ones, in what is often called the self-reference effect. See Lee et al., "Beauty Is in the Eye of the Beholder"; Leshikar, Dulas, and Duarte, "Self-Referencing Enhances Recollection in Both Young and Older Adults," 388–412; Moran, Kelley, and Heatherton, "What Can the Organization of the Brain's Default Mode Network Tell Us about Self-Knowledge?," 391.

41. Gusnard and Raichle, "Searching for a Baseline"; Smith et al., "Correspondence of the Brain's Functional Architecture during Activation and Rest," Laufs et al., "Electroencephalographic Signatures of Attentional and Cognitive Default Modes in Spontaneous Brain Activity Fluctuations at Rest."

42. Krueger, "Empathy, Enaction, and Shared Musical Experience," 188, 187.

43. This study found that older adults rely on emotional response as a driver in their judgments of the beauty of metaphor. See McQuire, McCollum, and Chatterjee, "Aptness and Beauty in Metaphor," 316–331.

44. James, "What Is an Emotion?," 188–205; Aristotle, *On Rhetoric*.

45. Salimpoor et al., "Anatomically Distinct Dopamine Release during Anticipation and Experience of Peak Emotion to Music," 257; Salimpoor et al., "Interactions

between the Nucleus Accumbens and Auditory Cortices Predict Music Reward Value," 216–219; Salimpoor et al., "The Rewarding Aspects of Music Listening Are Related to Degree of Emotional Arousal," e7487; Salimpoor et al., "Predictions and the Brain," 86–91; Panksepp, "The Emotional Sources of 'Chills' Induced by Music," 171–207; Doelling et al., "An Oscillator Model."

46. Bambini et al., "Time Course and Neurophysiological Underpinnings of Metaphor in Literary Context," 77–97; Citron et al., "Conventional Metaphors in Longer Passages Evoke Affective Brain Response," 218–230; Citron, Lee, and Michaelis, "Affective and Psycholinguistic Norms for German Conceptual Metaphors (COMETA)," 1056–1072; Lüdtke, Meyer-Sickendieck, and Jacobs, "Immersing in the Stillness of an Early Morning," 363; Menninghaus et al., "The Emotional and Aesthetic Powers of Parallelistic Diction," 47–59; Ullrich et al., "On the Relation between the General Affective Meaning and the Basic Sublexical, Lexical, and Inter-Lexical Features of Poetic Texts," 2073; Wassiliwizky et al., "The Emotional Power of Poetry," 1229–1240.

47. Vessel, Starr, and Rubin, "The Brain on Art"; Leder and Nadal, "Ten Years of a Model of Aesthetic Appreciation and Aesthetic Judgments," 443–464.

48. See, for example, Kirsch, Urgesi, and Cross, "Shaping and Reshaping the Aesthetic Brain," 56–68.

49. Evidence from a variety of disciplines suggests that both fiction and film support the development of empathy. However, empathy is not an unmitigated social good, as one can empathize with negative emotions and acts, from anger or cruelty to contempt. See, for example, Grodal and Kramer, "Film, Neuroaesthetics, and Empathy," 271–291; Keen, *Empathy and the Novel*; Kidd and Castano, "Reading Literary Fiction Improves Theory of Mind," 377–380.

50. Gates Jr., Smith, and Benston, eds., *The Norton Anthology of African American Literature*, 3rd ed.

51. Bortolussi and Dixon, "Transport," 525–540.

52. Hogan, *Affective Narratology*, 42. On literature's almost preternatural potential to heighten perception, and appear more vivid in imagination than in daily life, see Clune, *Writing against Time*.

53. Brielmann, Vale, and Pelli, "Beauty at a Glance," 9; Belfi et al., "Dynamics of Aesthetic Experience Are Reflected in the Default-Mode Network."

54. Starr, *Feeling Beauty*.

55. Fredrickson, "The Role of Positive Emotions in Positive Psychology," 218; Starr and Belfi, "Pleasure," 282–293.

56. See Carver, "Pleasure as a Sign You Can Attend to Something Else," 246; Chiew and Braver, "Dissociable Influences of Reward Motivation and Positive Emotion on Cognitive Control," 509–529.

57. Biederman and Vessel, "Perceptual Pleasure and the Brain," 247–253; Schoeller and Perlovsky, "Aesthetic Chills."

58. Neurological distinctions are important as well. First, there are at least two different neural systems involved in visual aesthetic pleasures. One involves systems for reward (defined as positive or negative reinforcement for reaching or failing to reach a goal), and its activity is relatively linear in relation to increased aesthetic pleasure. The other, as mentioned, is nonlinear, involves regions in the canonical DMN, and selectively kicks in at very high levels of aesthetic response.

59. Vessel et al., "Stronger Shared Taste for Natural Aesthetic Domains than for Artifacts of Human Culture."

60. Belfi, Vessel, and Starr, "Individual Ratings of Vividness Predict Aesthetic Appeal in Poetry," 341–350.

61. On motor brain regions and aesthetics, see Battaglia, Lisanby, and Freedberg, "Corticomotor Excitability during Observation and Imagination of a Work of Art," 79; Massaro et al., "When Art Moves the Eyes," e37285; Thakral, Moo, and Slotnick, "A Neural Mechanism for Aesthetic Experience," 310–313; Di Dio et al., "Human, Nature, Dynamism," 705; Humphries et al., "Movement in Aesthetic Experiences," 1329–1342.

62. Zhao et al., "The Neural Mechanism of Aesthetic Judgments of Dynamic Landscapes," 1–11.

63. Failing and Theeuwes, "Reward Alters the Perception of Time," 19–26.

64. Craig, "Emotional Moments across Time," 1933–1942.

65. On the involvement of other brain regions in timing and action prediction or execution, see especially Grondin, "Timing and Time Perception," 561–582. It is important to note that negative stimuli that elicit sympathetic arousal, especially involuntary threat responses, slow down time, while parasympathetic arousal (e.g., tears, sexual drive) may speed it up. See also Ogden et al., "Time Distortion under Threat," e0216704.

66. See, for example, Brielmann and Pelli, "Beauty Requires Thought," 1506–1513; Salimpoor et al., "The Rewarding Aspects of Music Listening Are Related to Degree of Emotional Arousal."

67. Roeske et al., "Listening to Birdsong Reveals Basic Features of Rate Perception and Aesthetic Judgements," 20193010; emphasis in the original.

68. For information about the tradition of the sister arts, see especially Hagstrum, *Sister Arts*; and Starr, *Feeling Beauty*.

69. Music, the "static" visual arts (including painting, sculpture, mosaics), and poetry have been grouped as the sister arts in a tradition dating to Western classical antiquity; see Hagstrum, *Sister Arts*. Recent work in neuroaesthetics has expanded to include film, dance, and drama. However, the twentieth-century consumption of drama and dance has meant that these forms are almost exclusively encountered in performance; film and television have emerged with new venues and media, and while music and painting are still frequently encountered in public spaces, music, painting, and poetry are now available in individual, on-demand encounters of varying kinds. In order to be able to treat the question of time with adequate focus, I chose to restrict this discussion to the genres I address.

Chapter 1

1. Members of the New York University Global Institute for Advanced Studies on Aesthetic Experience and the Brain included Amy Belfi, Felicity Callard, Anjan Chatterjee, Andrea Halpern, Rob Hopkins, Helmut Leder, Denis Pelli, Natalie M. Phillips, David Poeppel (co-principal investigator), Lauren Vale, and Edward A. Vessel. Funding for GIAS Neuroaesthetics was provided generously by NYU's office of the provost. I am deeply grateful to this team for their brilliance, kindness, and camaraderie. Unless otherwise noted, my interpretations are not those of the group, and mistakes are, of course, my own.

2. For descriptions of pleasure, the agreeable, and the universality of the judgment of beauty, see Kant, *Critique of Judgment*, Part 1, sections 7–9. Other accounts that make a distinction between the aesthetic and other pleasures include Hogarth, *Analysis of Beauty*; Burke, *A Philosophical Enquiry into the Sublime and Beautiful*; Brown et al., "Naturalizing Aesthetics," 250–258; and Brown, "Toward a Unification of the Arts," 1938. For a unifying description of the aesthetic and the everyday, see also Hogarth, *Analysis of Beauty*; Burke, *A Philosophical Enquiry into the Sublime and Beautiful*; and Dewey, *Art as Experience*. For a recent argument that assimilates aesthetic emotions with others, contra Menninghaus et al., "What Are Aesthetic Emotions?," see Skov and Nadal, "There Are No Aesthetic Emotions."

3. Kawabata and Zeki, "Neural Correlates of Beauty"; Pearce et al., "Neuroaesthetics." For excellent reviews, see Chatterjee, "Neuroaesthetics: A Coming of Age Story"; Leder, "Next Steps in Neuroaesthetics"; and Chatterjee and Vartanian, "Neuroaesthetics."

4. See, respectively, Belfi et al., "Dynamics of Aesthetic Experience Are Reflected in the Default-Mode Network"; Belfi, Vessel, and Starr, "Individual Ratings of Vividness Predict Aesthetic Appeal in Poetry"; Vessel et al., "The Default-Mode Network

Represents Aesthetic Appeal That Generalizes across Visual Domains"; Belfi et al., "Rapid Timing of Musical Aesthetic Judgments"; and Vessel, Starr, and Rubin, "The Brain on Art." It is notable that a later study finds similar brain activations to Vessel, Starr, and Rubin by asking whether or not an artwork was beautiful rather than how "moving" it might be. See Cela-Conde et al., "Dynamics of Brain Networks in the Aesthetic Appreciation."

5. On the complexity of the relation between aesthetic experiences understood to be positive and emotions that are generally understood to be negative, see especially Brattico, "The Neuroaesthetics of Music"; Hanich et al., "Why We Like to Watch Sad Films." As I will discuss, I'm not certain that "being moved" is something other than a special kind of reward, and I believe that "pleasure" is the best term we have.

6. Brielmann and Pelli, "Intense Beauty Requires Intense Pleasure."

7. See, for example, Winkielman and Cacioppo, "Mind at Ease Puts a Smile on the Face." On spontaneous aesthetic judgments during reading, see Bohrn et al., "When We Like What We Know." There is also evidence that we are continually judging facial attractiveness, even when we do not think we are explicitly doing so. See Chatterjee et al., "The Neural Response to Facial Attractiveness." Lebreton and colleagues argue for a domain-general evaluation system that is always on; see Lebreton et al., "An Automatic Valuation System in the Human Brain: Evidence from Functional Neuroimaging." On pleasure and aesthetics, see, among others, Chatterjee, *Aesthetic Brain*; and Hanich et al., "Why We Like to Watch Sad Films."

8. Jacobellis v. Ohio, 378 US. Justice Stewart of course meant this in reference to obscenity.

9. Harter, "Excitability Cycles and Cortical Scanning."

10. Adaptation of neurons in human visual perception has been explored perhaps most prominently in research on the wagon wheel illusion, in which spinning meals at times appear to rotate backward. Attention can modulate this effect. See Macdonald, Cavanagh, and VanRullen, "Attentional Sampling of Multiple Wagon Wheels."

11. For a detailed discussion of perceptual adaptation in vision, see Kanwisher and Wojciulik, "Visual Attention."

12. Hume, *A Treatise of Human Nature*; Hume, *An Enquiry Concerning Human Understanding*; Bergson, *Henri Bergson*.

13. Droit-Volet, "What Emotions Tell Us about Time," 482.

14. Dutke, "Remembered Duration."

15. For a good overview of current thinking, see Barrett, Lewis, and Haviland-Jones, *Handbook of Emotions*.

16. See Robinson, *Deeper than Reason*; and Walton, *Mimesis as Make-Believe*.

17. See especially Fingerhut and Prinz, "Aesthetic Emotions Reconsidered"; Frijda and Sundararajan, "Emotion Refinement," 2007; Menninghaus et al., "What Are Aesthetic Emotions?" Several thinkers have made a connection between aesthetic emotions and moral emotions, dating at least back to the work of Plato in the *Symposium* and the *Phaedrus*, and persisting in work by researchers across a variety of disciplines, including philosophy, psychology, criticism and neuroscience.

18. Hosoya et al., "Mapping the Conceptual Domain of Aesthetic Emotion Terms"; Schindler et al., "Measuring Aesthetic Emotions"; Zentner, Grandjean, and Scherer, "Emotions Evoked by the Sound of Music"; Miu, Pițur, and Szentágotai-Tătar, "Aesthetic Emotions across Arts."

19. Hanich et al., "Why We Like to Watch Sad Films"; Brattico et al., "It's Sad but I Like It"; Jacobs et al., "10 Years of BAWLing into Affective and Aesthetic Processes in Reading: What Are the Echoes?"; Menninghaus et al., "Towards a Psychological Construct of Being Moved"; Menninghaus et al., "The Distancing-Embracing Model of the Enjoyment of Negative Emotions in Art Reception"; Hosoya et al., "Mapping the Conceptual Domain of Aesthetic Emotion Terms"; Wassiliwizky et al., "The Emotional Power of Poetry"; Eerola et al., "An Integrative Review of the Enjoyment of Sadness Associated with Music"; Brattico, "The Neuroaesthetics of Music."

20. Droit-Volet and Meck, "How Emotions Colour Our Perception of Time."

21. See in particular the striatum and the substantia nigra: Crocker, "The Regulation of Motor Control"; Joshua, Adler, and Bergman, "The Dynamics of Dopamine in Control of Motor Behavior."

22. Frijda and Sundararajan, "Emotion Refinement," 2007.

23. Joshua, Adler, and Bergman, "The Dynamics of Dopamine in Control of Motor Behavior."

24. Menninghaus et al., "Towards a Psychological Construct of Being Moved"; Hanich et al., "Why We Like to Watch Sad Films." On dwelling in "subjective feeling" in the absence of an action tendency, see the section on motivational tendencies in Menninghaus et al., "What Are Aesthetic Emotions?" See also Frijda and Sundararajan, "Emotion Refinement," 2007.

25. For example, Cicero, *De oratore*.

26. Menninghaus and colleagues note that sadly moving instances are more prevalent in artistic than in daily life. See "Towards a Psychological Construct of Being Moved."

27. On low-arousal, high-intensity emotional responses and aesthetics, see Menninghaus et al., "The Distancing-Embracing Model of the Enjoyment of Negative Emotions in Art Reception."

28. Vessel, Starr, and Rubin, "The Brain on Art."

29. On mixed valence and varying arousal emotions, see Brattico, "The Neuroaesthetics of Music"; Menninghaus et al., "Towards a Psychological Construct of Being Moved"; Schindler et al., "Measuring Aesthetic Emotions"; Wassiliwizky et al., "The Emotional Power of Poetry"; Hanich et al., "Why We Like to Watch Sad Films"; Starr, *Feeling Beauty*, 120–127.

30. Fredrickson, "The Role of Positive Emotions in Positive Psychology."

31. Carver, "Pleasure as a Sign You Can Attend to Something Else," 209. On the other hand, it is also relatively clear how negative emotions and pain narrow our field of vision and attention; see, for example, Scarry, *The Body in Pain*; and Marcuse, *Eros and Civilization*. Kimberly Chiew and Todd Braver have proposed a mechanism by which this may occur, indicating that positive affect may increase, in a small but measurable way, the ability to control attention proactively and focus on tasks of our choice. Chiew and Braver, "Dissociable Influences of Reward Motivation and Positive Emotion on Cognitive Control."

32. Craig, "How Do You Feel—Now?," 67.

33. Carver and Scheier, "A Self-Regulatory Viewpoint on Human Behavior."

34. For a good overview, see Carver and Scheier, "A Self-Regulatory Viewpoint on Human Behavior."

35. Carver and Scheier, "A Self-Regulatory Viewpoint on Human Behavior," 31–32.

36. Note that a negative difference is a shift in a positive direction.

37. Roeske et al., "Listening to Birdsong Reveals Basic Features of Rate Perception and Aesthetic Judgements."

38. On social entrainment, see McGrath, Kelly, and Machatka, "The Social Psychology of Time."

39. Jones, "Music as a Stimulus for Psychological Motion."

40. Craig argues that there is an important nexus here as well: "The engagement of the AIC by emotional feelings, by the feeling of movement and by the sense of time encourages the view that this model can explain the observed activation of the AIC by rhythm and by musical enjoyment, as well as the primal emotional effects of communal music-making, because music would inherently involve the core of awareness." Craig, "How Do You Feel—Now?," 68.

41. Failing and Theeuwes, "Reward Alters the Perception of Time."

42. On arousal and perceived time, see Droit-Volet, "What Emotions Tell Us about Time."

43. Wearden et al., "Subjective Duration in the Laboratory and the World Outside," 293.

44. Eerola et al., "An Integrative Review of the Enjoyment of Sadness Associated with Music," 108–109.

45. Eerola et al., "An Integrative Review of the Enjoyment of Sadness Associated with Music," 109.

46. Morrison, *Beloved*, 158.

47. Morrison, *Beloved*, 257.

48. Burke, *A Philosophical Enquiry into the Sublime and Beautiful*, 28–32.

49. Morrison, *Beloved*, 148.

50. Morrison, *Beloved*, 256–257.

51. Menninghaus et al., "Towards a Psychological Construct of Being Moved."

52. It is not just distant tragedy that may raise the clash of aesthetics and ethics, but tragicomedy as well, as I have argued around the poetry of Ovid; see Starr, "Burney, Ovid, and the Value of the Beautiful"; and Ovid Defoe, "Narrative and Poiesis."

53. Pascal, *Pensées*, n. 347: "Man is only a reed, the most weak thing in nature, but he is a thinking reed. The entire universe need not arm itself to crush him. A vapor, a drop, of water suffices to kill him. But if the universe were to crush him, man would still be more noble than that which killed him, because he knows that he dies and . . . all our dignity consists in thought. It is there that we must elevate ourselves, and not by space and time which we know we cannot fill. Let us, strive, then, to think well; this is the principle of morality" (my translation): "L'homme n'est qu'un rouseau, le plus faible de la nature; mais c'est un roseau pensant. Il ne faut pas que l'univers entire, s'arme pour l'écraser: une vapeur, une goutte d'eau, suffit pour le tuer. Mais, quand l'univers l'ecraserait, l'homme serait encore plus noble que ce qui le tue, parce qu'il sait qu'il meurt. . . . Toute notre dignité consiste donc en la pensée. C'est de là qu'il nous faut elever et non de l'espace et de la durée, que nous ne saurons remplir. Travaillons donc à bien penser: voilà le principe de la morale."

54. Brumm et al., "Oldest Cave Art Found in Sulawesi"; Turk, Turk, and Otte, "The Neanderthal Musical Instrument from Divje Babe I Cave (Slovenia)"; Fritz et al., "First Record of the Sound Produced by the Oldest Upper Paleolithic Seashell Horn."

55. On the congruence between emotions in aesthetic and other daily life (art in this way does not require specially evolved emotion systems), see Skov and Nadal, "There Are No Aesthetic Emotions."

56. Cf. Pinker, *The Blank Slate*, where he argues that art is like cheesecake: a delicious creation that takes advantage of the evolutionarily-driven human delight in fat and sugar.

57. Johnson-Laird and Oatley, "Emotions in Music, Literature, and Film," 83.

58. Tamar Gendler describes and offers solution to the philosophical conundrum around belief and emotional responses to art in "Alief in Action (and Reaction)"; "Alief and Belief."

59. This line of argument has been called social intuitionist. For a good defense, see Haidt, "The Emotional Dog and Its Rational Tail." The examples adduced here are at times tendentious, and indulge in a spectacle of disgust (and at times also times flawed by ignoring cultural concepts like ritual impurity), but the general argument holds.

60. For a foundational account of the common currency theory, see Levy and Glimcher, "The Root of All Value."

61. Fingerhut and Prinz, "Aesthetic Emotions Reconsidered," 230.

62. Belfi et al., "Dynamics of Aesthetic Experience Are Reflected in the Default-Mode Network." This research was carried out at New York University with approval of the IRB. Images were taken from actual museum collections, via the CAMIO database. Continuous ratings were taken using a squeeze ball. Three practice trials were conducted before the experiment began so that participants were trained on the task to ensure they understood what was being asked of them. Participants were not experts in art or art history.

63. See, for example, Locher, "The Aesthetic Experience with Visual Art 'at First Glance,'" 75–88. On music, see Belfi et al., "Rapid Timing of Musical Aesthetic Judgments"; Bigand, Filipic, and Lalitte, "The Time Course of Emotional Responses to Music"; Gjerdingen and Perrott, "Scanning the Dial."

64. Cf. Brielmann and Pelli, "Beauty Requires Thought"; and Brielmann, Vale, and Pelli, "Beauty at a Glance."

Chapter 2

1. DeNora, *Music in Everyday Life*, 102–103.

2. Vessel et al., "Stronger Shared Taste for Natural Aesthetic Domains than for Artifacts of Human Culture"; Germine et al., "Individual Aesthetic Preferences for Faces Are Shaped Mostly by Environments, Not Genes"; Leder et al., "Private and Shared Taste in Art and Face Appreciation"; Vessel and Rubin, "Beauty and the Beholder"; Belfi, Vessel, and Starr, "Individual Ratings of Vividness Predict Aesthetic Appeal in Poetry."

3. Smith and Baker, "Conditioning in the Horseshoe Crab."

4. On the conservation of the central nervous system for horseshoe crabs, see Chamberlain and Wyse, "An Atlas of the Brain of the Horseshoe Crab Limulus Polyphemus"; Walls, Berkson, and Smith, "The Horseshoe Crab, Limulus Polyphemus"; Bicknell et al., "Central Nervous System of a 310-Million-Year-Old Horseshoe Crab."

5. Nadal and Chatterjee, "Neuroaesthetics and Art's Diversity and Universality."

6. On the rapid development of cortical folding and the DMN, see Buckner and Krienen, "The Evolution of Distributed Association Networks in the Human Brain." On this rapid folding and aesthetics, see Cela-Conde and Ayala, "Art and Brain Coevolution."

7. See Hutcheson, *An Inquiry into the Original of Our Ideas of Beauty and Virtue*, treatise I, sections 5, 6, and 8, and treatise II, section 1. For Hutcheson, God provides human beings with pleasures in beauty so that we will be able to make quick and reliable judgments about effort and reward, as well as learn to recognize moral beauty and to seek it out in God himself: "the author of Nature has determin'd us to receive, by our external Senses, pleasant or disagreeable Ideas of Objects, according as they are useful or hurtful to our Bodys; and to receive from uniform Objects the Pleasures of Beauty and Harmony, to excite us to the Pursuit of Knowledge, and to reward us for it; or to be an Argument to us of his Goodness" (99).

8. Clayton, Sager, and Will, "In Time with the Music," 28.

9. Clayton, Sager, and Will, "In Time with the Music," 28.

10. Jones and Boltz, "Dynamic Attending and Responses to Time."

11. Clayton, Sager, and Will, "In Time with the Music," 29.

12. Clayton, Sager, and Will note that such shifts of attention are less likely to happen in events of low temporal coherence. "In Time with the Music," 27.

13. Wassiliwizky et al., "Art-Elicited Chills Indicate States of Being Moved"; Salimpoor et al., "Anatomically Distinct Dopamine Release during Anticipation and Experience of Peak Emotion to Music."

14. Natural objects will carry natural affordances—easy interfaces humans can grasp (on the idea of affordances, see Gibson, *The Ecological Approach to Visual Perception*). Natural objects are not the only things with affordances—cups with handles afford grasping, for example—as well as socially shared or designed means of engagement. These could be the undetermined possibilities of a diving spot, naturally made over millennia, or the rout outcrops that seem made to climb, and which over time have become known to humans and worn clear by human maintenance.

15. While vicarious learning has long been part of the theory of literary value (dating back to at least Plato's concern that poets would mislead their listeners in

the *Republic*), cognitive psychologists have been exploring this idea more recently regarding media and advertising. See, for example, Schunk and Usher, "Social Cognitive Theory and Motivation."

16. Robbe-Grillet and Johns, *The Target*.

17. Biederman and Vessel have posited the need for information as a basic aesthetic goal. Biederman and Vessel, "Perceptual Pleasure and the Brain."

18. Indeed, Lüdtke et al. found that style was the strongest predictor of "aesthetic liking." Lüdtke, Meyer-Sickendieck, and Jacobs, "Immersing in the Stillness of an Early Morning."

19. Shklovsky, "Art as Technique," 12.

20. For the modern statement of poetry being the real language of mankind, see the preface to *Lyrical Ballads*: Wordsworth and Coleridge, *Lyrical Ballads, 1798*. On the difficulties of differentiation, see, for example, Miall and Kuiken, "Foregrounding, Defamiliarization, and Affect." For a good summary of experimental work, see Lüdtke, Meyer-Sickendieck, and Jacobs, "Immersing in the Stillness of an Early Morning."

21. Alter, *Art of Biblical Poetry*.

22. See, for example, Jacobs and Willems, "The Fictive Brain," 149–151.

23. Welke, Purton, and Vessel, "Inspired by Art."

24. Starr and Belfi, "Pleasure," 282–293.

25. Berridge and Kringelbach, "From Pleasure to Happiness," 136.

26. Coleridge, *Biographia Literaria*, chap. 14; Bell, *Art*.

27. Stevens, *Letters of Wallace Stevens*, 340.

28. Myklebust, "'Bergamo on a Postcard,'" 146.

29. Myklebust, "'Bergamo on a Postcard,'" 146.

30. Myklebust, "'Bergamo on a Postcard,'" 146. See Tsur, *Poetic Rhythm*.

31. Stevens, *Collected Poetry and Prose*, 370; scansion added.

32. Stevens, *Collected Poetry and Prose*, 371.

33. Stevens, *Collected Poetry and Prose*, 909.

34. Stevens, *Collected Poetry and Prose*, 370.

35. Stevens, *Collected Poetry and Prose*, 370.

36. Stevens, *Collected Poetry and Prose*, 371.

37. Twombly, *Untitled*, 1970.

38. Stevens, *Collected Poetry and Prose*, 397.

39. Stevens, *Collected Poetry and Prose*, 57.

40. Levine, *Forms*, 13.

41. Dewey, *Art as Experience*, 57.

42. See, for example, Noë, *Strange Tools*.

43. Respectively, see Smith and Smith, "Spending Time on Art"; and Tröndle et al., "A Museum for the Twenty-First Century." Another study shows a median of thirty-eight seconds: Brieber, Forster, and Leder, "On the Mutual Relation between Art Experience and Viewing Time"; Brieber et al., "Art in Time and Space." See appendix 2 for further details.

44. Much of the recent discussion of temporality in the recent past has been shaped by responses to Husserl, as well as attempts to reconcile what part of current experience needs to sum backward and what must, in active prediction of the future, sum forward. See Husserl, *The Phenomenology of Internal Time-Consciousness*.

45. Dainton, "The Phenomenal Continuum," 101–138.

46. The question of how we integrate interrupted or altered consciousness is quite old. One example includes the question of how we maintain our identities over time. For example, as David Hume pointed out, we have interruptions in consciousness at least every night when we fall asleep, but we still generally infer or experience a continual sense of self. See Hume, *An Enquiry Concerning Human Understanding*.

47. Brieber et al., "Art in Time and Space."

48. Verhavert, Wagemans, and Augustin, "Beauty in the Blink of an Eye."

49. Belfi et al., "Rapid Timing of Musical Aesthetic Judgments."

50. For an influential account of the influence of anthologies, see Price, *The Anthology and the Rise of the Novel*.

51. We selected twelve poems with stanzas that could stand alone grammatically (occasionally adding final punctuation to an individual stanza). The "short" versions were the sestinas' first two stanzas (60–134 words); the "medium" versions were the first four stanzas (131–287 words), and finally "long" were the complete sestinas (207–461 words). All the poems were first published in the twentieth or twenty-first century, composed in English, and taken from published anthologies, though we avoided poems frequently taught in literature courses or likely to be recognized (e.g., Elizabeth Bishop's "One Art"). Poems came from Nester, ed., *Incredible Sestina Anthology*; Whitlow and Krysl, *Obsession*.

52. When comparing the regression results between the three lengths, a one-way MANOVA revealed no significant differences in the predictive ability of the three ratings between the three poem lengths [$F(6,274)=0.43$, $p=0.85$, $\eta^2=0.01$].

53. Smith, *Poetic Closure.*

54. Wassiliwizky et al., "The Emotional Power of Poetry."

55. Kraxenberger and Menninghaus, "Emotional Effects of Poetic Phonology, Word Positioning and Dominant Stress Peaks in Poetry Reading."

56. Burke, *The Philosophy of Literary Form.*

57. In a fascinating study, Clynes and Walker show that over thirteen years, different versions (with different performers) of Brahms's *Haydn Variations* varied only by seconds in duration. See "Neurobiologic Function of Rhythm, Time, and Pulse in Music," 171–216. I am grateful to an anonymous press reviewer for drawing my attention to this case.

58. Brielmann and Pelli, "Beauty Requires Thought"; Lang and Bradley, "The International Affective Picture System (IAPS) in the Study of Emotion and Attention." Note that the candy was Jolly Ranchers—hard candy with a simple flavor. More complex foods by flavor or texture might have a different effect. We tend to want to savor what is truly a delicacy.

59. DeNora, *Music in Everyday Life,* 11–14.

60. James, *The Golden Bowl,* 106.

61. James, *The Golden Bowl,* 109.

62. James, *The Golden Bowl,* 111.

63. James, *The Golden Bowl,* 102.

64. James, *The Golden Bowl,* 500.

65. James, *The Golden Bowl,* 508.

66. James, *The Golden Bowl,* 581.

67. James, *The Golden Bowl,* 582.

68. James, *The Golden Bowl,* 595.

69. James, *The Golden Bowl,* 595.

Chapter 3

1. For a good meta-analysis, see Tiihonen et al., "Constituents of Music and Visual-Art Related Pleasure." See also, among others, Chatterjee, "Neuroaesthetics: A

Coming of Age Story"; Mastandrea, Fagioli, and Biasi, "Art and Psychological Well-Being"; Vartanian and Skov, "Neural Correlates of Viewing Paintings"; Boccia et al., "Where Does Brain Neural Activation in Aesthetic Responses to Visual Art Occur?"; Brown et al., "Naturalizing Aesthetics."

2. For a foundational discussion of the parameters that engender and ground artworks, see especially Davis, *A General Theory of Visual Culture*.

3. Buckner and DiNicola, "The Brain's Default Network."

4. Di Dio et al., "Human, Nature, Dynamism"; Starr, *Feeling Beauty*; Thakral, Moo, and Slotnick, "A Neural Mechanism for Aesthetic Experience"; Gallese and Freedberg, "Mirror and Canonical Neurons Are Crucial Elements in Esthetic Response"; Ticini et al., "Enhancing Aesthetic Appreciation by Priming Canvases with Actions That Match the Artist's Painting Style."

5. Brielmann and Pelli, "Intense Beauty Requires Intense Pleasure."

6. Brielmann and Pelli, "Beauty Requires Thought," 1059.

7. On reevaluation and poetry, see O'Sullivan et al., "'Shall I Compare Thee.'" On reading networks in general, see Smallwood et al., "The Default Modes of Reading."

8. Vendler, *Art of Shakespeare's Sonnets*, 333.

9. Vendler, *Art of Shakespeare's Sonnets*, 333–334.

10. Swift, *Complete Poems*.

11. On aesthetic pleasure and imagery, see Belfi, "Emotional Valence and Vividness of Imagery Predict Aesthetic Appeal in Music"; Belfi, Vessel, and Starr, "Individual Ratings of Vividness Predict Aesthetic Appeal in Poetry." On overlapping of DMN regions with imagery networks, see Moulton and Kosslyn, "Imagining Predictions"; Mellet et al., "Functional Anatomy of High-Resolution Visual Mental Imagery." On costliness of imagery as reading strategy, see Citron, Lee, and Michaelis, "Affective and Psycholinguistic Norms for German Conceptual Metaphors (COMETA)."

12. On the PCC and musical features, see Alluri et al., "Large-Scale Brain Networks Emerge from Dynamic Processing of Musical Timbre, Key and Rhythm." On the PCC and other minds, see Spreng, Mar, and Kim, "The Common Neural Basis of Autobiographical Memory, Prospection, Navigation, Theory of Mind, and the Default Mode."

13. Raichle, "The Brain's Default Mode Network."

14. Buckner and DiNicola, "The Brain's Default Network."

15. Van den Heuvel and Sporns, "Rich-Club Organization of the Human Connectome."

16. They also point out that their "initial high-resolution analysis revealed the rich club to be a distributed set of nodes participating in the default mode network (e.g., posterior cingulate cortex/precuneus, medial orbitofrontal cortex), the salience network (e.g., insula, caudal anterior cingulate cortex), the visual (cuneus, lingual gyrus) and auditory (superior temporal cortex) networks, and to some extent the executive control network (e.g., superior frontal and left superior parietal)." Van den Heuvel and Sporns, "Rich-Club Organization of the Human Connectome," 15785. See also Van den Heuvel et al., "High-Cost, High-Capacity Backbone for Global Brain Communication," 11376: "rich-club connections constitute a feature of human brain connectivity that results from a trade-off between conserving material resources and boosting dynamic performance."

17. Goulden et al., "The Salience Network Is Responsible for Switching between the Default Mode Network and the Central Executive Network: Replication from DCM." Their results build upon Sridharan, Levitin, and Menon, "A Critical Role for the Right Fronto-Insular Cortex in Switching between Central-Executive and Default-Mode Networks."

18. Sridharan, Levitin, and Menon, "A Critical Role for the Right Fronto-Insular Cortex in Switching between Central-Executive and Default-Mode Networks"; Goulden et al., "The Salience Network Is Responsible for Switching between the Default Mode Network and the Central Executive Network." The mechanisms supporting switching are not fully understood. See Buckner and DiNicola, "The Brain's Default Network." On insula and aesthetics (primarily attributing activation to appraisal), see, among others, Brown et al., "Naturalizing Aesthetics"; and Cupchik et al., "Viewing Artworks."

19. Nadal and Chatterjee, "Neuroaesthetics and Art's Diversity and Universality."

20. Vessel et al., "Stronger Shared Taste for Natural Aesthetic Domains than for Artifacts of Human Culture." For a broad account of aesthetic responses across visual art and natural objects, see Chatterjee, *The Aesthetic Brain*.

21. Aharon et al., "Beautiful Faces Have Variable Reward Value." Work was measured by a button-press task, whereby participants could keep an image on-screen for longer the more they exerted effort.

22. On liking and wanting and aesthetics in general, see Chatterjee and Vartanian, "Neuroaesthetics." On music, chills, and reward expectation, see Salimpoor et al., "Anatomically Distinct Dopamine Release during Anticipation and Experience of Peak Emotion to Music." On lack of caudate-striatal distinction in visual aesthetics, see Vessel, Starr, and Rubin, "The Brain on Art."

23. Levy and Glimcher, "The Root of All Value." There are of course anatomical distinctions for differing kinds of aesthetically salient objects as well. See, for example,

Pegors et al., "Common and Unique Representations in PFC for Face and Place Attractiveness."

24. See Mastandrea, Fagioli, and Biasi, "Art and Psychological Well-Being": "experiencing art is a self-rewarding activity, irrespective of the emotional content of the artwork." On information foraging and aesthetics, see Biederman and Vessel, "Perceptual Pleasure and the Brain."

25. Kirsch, Urgesi, and Cross, "Shaping and Reshaping the Aesthetic Brain." By temporal dynamics, here, they refer to the distinction between wanting and liking or anticipatory and consummatory pleasure. One side of these distinctions involves temporally extended buildup, the other a relatively faster resolution of desire.

26. On the multiplicity of goals, implicit and explicit, see Menninghaus et al., "What Are Aesthetic Emotions?"

27. Burke, *A Philosophical Enquiry into the Sublime and Beautiful*; Hutcheson, *An Inquiry into the Original of Our Ideas of Beauty and Virtue*; Kant, *Critique of Judgment*; Hume, "Of the Standard of Taste," 230–247. For a neurocognitive approach, see Tsukiura and Cabeza, "Shared Brain Activity for Aesthetic and Moral Judgments."

28. Noë, *Strange Tools*, 59, 55.

29. For a good broad analysis, see Jones, *Gender and the Formation of Taste in Eighteenth-Century Britain.*

30. Paulson, *The Beautiful, Novel, and Strange*; Starr, "Cavendish, Aesthetics, and the Anti-Platonic Line."

31. See Dickie, "The Myth of the Aesthetic Attitude"; and Stolnitz, "On the Origins of 'Aesthetic Disinterestedness.'" Noë also argues for a special aesthetic attitude that applies only to art, not the natural world: see Noë, *Strange Tools*, chapter 5. Arthur Coleman Danto, perhaps the most significant thinker on art in the twentieth century, writes: "To see something as art at all . . . demands . . . an art theory, which is so powerful a thing as to detach objects from the real world and make them part of an artworld, a world of interpreted things." Danto, *Transfiguration of the Commonplace*, 135.

32. Danto, *Transfiguration of the Commonplace*, 135.

33. Regarding multiple goals, see Carver and Scheier, "A Self-Regulatory Viewpoint on Human Behavior." On excitatory and inhibitory processes and circuits in reward, see Reeve and Lee, "Motivational Neuroscience."

34. Schultz, Dayan, and Montague, "A Neural Substrate of Prediction and Reward."

35. Miu, Piţur, and Szentágotai-Tătar, "Aesthetic Emotions across Arts."

36. See, for example, Kirk et al., "Modulation of Aesthetic Value by Semantic Context"; Leder, Carbon, and Ripsas, "Entitling Art"; Gerger, Leder, and Kremer, "Context Effects on Emotional and Aesthetic Evaluations of Artworks and IAPS Pictures."

37. Leder and Nadal, "Ten Years of a Model of Aesthetic Appreciation and Aesthetic Judgments"; Pelowski et al., "Move Me, Astonish Me . . . Delight My Eyes and Brain."

38. Augustin et al., "Style Follows Content."

39. Brieber et al., "Art in Time and Space." See also Smith and Smith, "Spending Time on Art"; Tschacher et al., "Physiological Correlates of Aesthetic Perception of Artworks in a Museum." Indeed, even in very brief engagements, there are at least two distinct phases of processing. See Cela-Conde et al., "Dynamics of Brain Networks in the Aesthetic Appreciation."

40. Burke, *Philosophy of Literary Form*. See "Trial Translation," 344–349.

41. Brattico, "Neuroaesthetics of Music." For a comprehensive model of music and emotion, see Juslin and Sakka, "Neural Correlates of Music and Emotion," 285.

42. On expertise, see, for example, Kirk et al., "Modulation of Aesthetic Value by Semantic Context"; Locher, Krupinski, and Schaefer, "Art and Authenticity"; Kirsch, Urgesi, and Cross, "Shaping and Reshaping the Aesthetic Brain." On long-term effects, including calm, see Wang et al., "An Investigation of the Neural Substrates of Mind Wandering Induced by Viewing Traditional Chinese Landscape Paintings." On age-related differences, see Ferreri et al., "Music and the Aging Brain"; McQuire, McCollum, and Chatterjee, "Aptness and Beauty in Metaphor"; Halpern and O'Connor, "Stability of Art Preference in Frontotemporal Dementia"; Halpern et al., "'I Know What I Like.'"

43. There are some exceptions to this, however. As Anjan Chatterjee reminded me, Persian and Arabic script, as well as calligraphy in many languages (including English), can be a key component for aesthetic response. See also Zhang et al., "Neural Substrates of Embodied Natural Beauty and Social Endowed Beauty."

44. Jacobs, "Towards a Neurocognitive Poetics Model of Literary Reading," 135–159. For a good cognitive historicist analysis of reading, see Armstrong, *Stories and the Brain*; and Elfenbein, *The Gist of Reading*.

45. Lutterbie, "Feeling Beauty, Time, and the Body in Neuroaesthetics." See also the very clear critique offered in Nadal and Skov, "Top–down and Bottom–up."

46. Noguchi and Murota, "Temporal Dynamics of Neural Activity in an Integration of Visual and Contextual Information in an Esthetic Preference Task."

47. Roeske et al., "Listening to Birdsong Reveals Basic Features of Rate Perception and Aesthetic Judgements."

48. A deep convolutional neural network model (DCNN) does not presume linear summation of different functions but rather that one or more functions can be integrated in a new function space. In neural terms, this would mean that an initial function (say, an analysis of color) would then feed forward to a new analysis pattern (e.g., for motion), to a further one (location), and so on. A DCNN also does not automatically assume the relationship between the function spaces (e.g., additive, multiplicative, high- and low-pass filtration). Iigaya et al., "Aesthetic Preference for Art Can Be Predicted from a Mixture of Low-and High-Level Visual Features."

49. Belfi et al., "Dynamics of Aesthetic Experience Are Reflected in the Default-Mode Network."

50. Belfi et al., "Rapid Timing of Musical Aesthetic Judgments." See appendix 2 for details.

51. Iigaya, O'Doherty, and Starr, "Progress and Promise in Neuroaesthetics."

52. On trait influence and aesthetic experience, see, for example, Fayn et al., "Aesthetic Emotions and Aesthetic People"; Fayn et al., "Nuanced Aesthetic Emotions"; Eerola, Vuoskoski, and Kautiainen, "Being Moved by Unfamiliar Sad Music Is Associated with High Empathy"; and Silvia and Nusbaum, "On Personality and Piloerection."

53. For useful instruments, see Watson and Clark, "The PANAS-X"; Watson, Clark, and Tellegen, "Development and Validation of Brief Measures of Positive and Negative Affect"; Gard et al., "Anticipatory and Consummatory Components of the Experience of Pleasure"; Ho et al., "Factor Structure and Construct Validity of the Temporal Experience of Pleasure Scales"; and Chatterjee et al., "The Assessment of Art Attributes." For an influential expertise scale, see Smith and Smith, "The Nature and Growth of Aesthetic Fluency," 47–58.

54. The VIMAP suggests a variety of elements of prior experience that might shape potential aesthetic encounters. These include expertise, autobiographical memory, context, mood or emotion, whether one is solo or in a group, personality, and an initial attitude (e.g., detachment, openness, critique). The model proposes several different brain networks that should engage, defining networks as connected brain regions engaged in the evaluation of particular classes of information. The first involves emotion and modes of focus on aesthetic processing: a "detached" aesthetic mode switching with a "self-related pragmatic" one (Pelowski et al., "Move Me, Astonish Me," 114). This network involves "frontal cortical and subcortical regions, including the OFC, tied to basic assessment of affective valence [with input from the thalamus and hypothalamus as well as the amygdala] . . . via the OFC to the dorsal lateral and ventral lateral PFC" (114–115). From there, "the lateral PFC, [via] . . . the rostral ACC, may then connect with, and modulate activity within, the amygdala . . . to the insula, related to interoception of affective/bodily response, and to the MPFC." In the VIMAP, this is not understood as a pleasure network, but

"only allows for more or less subjectively felt emotion itself." The second key network they suggest is focused on "self relevance/congruency and engages the DMN" (115). However, this proposal needs testing precisely from a systematic perspective. The importance of regions in the SN (e.g., the insula) and the CEN (e.g., dlPFC) in the first network raises questions of other ways regions implicated in the evaluation of art could be interconnected and function, both in visual art and across sensory modalities.

55. On the importance of the insula in aesthetics, see Juslin and Sakka, "Neural Correlates of Music and Emotion"; Brown et al., "Naturalizing Aesthetics"; Janzen and Thaut, "Cerebral Organization of Music Processing," 1–41; and Brown, "Toward a Unification of the Arts."

56. They suggest aesthetic processing is a special case of "all cognitive processes that involve viscerality." Brown et al., "Naturalizing Aesthetics," 256.

57. Vessel, Starr, and Rubin, "The Brain on Art." We should note, however, as described in chapter 1, prioritizing powerful experiences (e.g., "moving") can be problematic for a complete understanding of aesthetic life.

58. On pleasure as an implicit goal, see Eerola et al., "An Integrative Review of the Enjoyment of Sadness Associated with Music."

59. See, for example, Kühn and Gallinat, "The Neural Correlates of Subjective Pleasantness."

60. Brielmann and Pelli, "Intense Beauty Requires Intense Pleasure." On the persistence of mind-wandering in daily life, see Killingsworth and Gilbert, "A Wandering Mind Is an Unhappy Mind." On the balance between goal-oriented and exploratory thought, see Sripada, "An Exploration/Exploitation Trade-off between Mind Wandering and Goal-Directed Thinking," 23–34.

61. There is some TMS evidence for the necessity of particular regions in different kinds of aesthetic evaluation. TMS uses a magnetic field to interrupt the conduction of electricity in cortical tissue within around five centimeters of the skull (a small induction coil is placed above the scalp in the desired location). This essentially takes the target region offline for neural activity, and in a behavioral experiment allows for causal inferences between brain activity and a behavioral condition. See Cattaneo et al., "The Role of the Lateral Occipital Cortex in Aesthetic Appreciation of Representational and Abstract Paintings," 2015; Cattaneo et al., "A TMS Study on the Contribution of Visual Area V5 to the Perception of Implied Motion in Art and Its Appreciation"; Ferrari, Schiavi, and Cattaneo, "TMS over the Superior Temporal Sulcus Affects Expressivity Evaluation of Portraits"; Ferrari et al., "The Dorsomedial Prefrontal Cortex Mediates the Interaction between Moral and Aesthetic Valuation"; Fiori et al., "Modulation of Corticospinal Excitability during Paintings Viewing"; Stupacher et al., "Musical Groove Modulates Motor Cortex Excitability"; Cattaneo,

"Noninvasive Brain Stimulation"; and Cattaneo, "Neural Correlates of Visual Aesthetic Appreciation."

62. For a network analysis, see Belfi et al., "Dynamics of Aesthetic Experience Are Reflected in the Default-Mode Network." For individual brain structures in the ventral visual pathway and their role in aesthetic perception, see, in particular, Cattaneo et al., "The Role of the Lateral Occipital Cortex in Aesthetic Appreciation of Representational and Abstract Paintings"; Kim et al., "Temporal Isolation of Neural Processes Underlying Face Preference Decisions"; Yue, Vessel, and Biederman, "The Neural Basis of Scene Preferences"; Jacobsen et al., "Brain Correlates of Aesthetic Judgment of Beauty"; Vartanian and Goel, "Neuroanatomical Correlates of Aesthetic Preference for Paintings."

63. Fingerhut and Prinz, "Grounding Evaluative Concepts."

64. Cela-Conde et al., "Dynamics of Brain Networks in the Aesthetic Appreciation," 10458. The authors argue that the perception of the beautiful is similar to the "a-ha!" moment in problem-solving, "the sudden result of a complex process," and the evolutionary "by-product of the capacity for mind-wandering" (10460).

65. There is evidence that goal switching "is costly in cognitive-affective terms, because any change, even the successful achievement of a goal, has consequences for many other goals." See Choe et al., "To Search or to Like." See also Conway, Meares, and Standart, "Images and Goals"; and Conway, "Memory and the Self."

66. On DMN rebound as later stage response, see Cela-Conde et al., "Dynamics of Brain Networks in the Aesthetic Appreciation."

67. Esposito et al., "Independent Component Model of the Default-Mode Brain Function"; Friston et al., "Functional Connectivity"; Greicius et al., "Functional Connectivity in the Resting Brain."

68. Cela-Conde et al., "Dynamics of Brain Networks in the Aesthetic Appreciation," 10456.

69. Cela-Conde et al., "Dynamics of Brain Networks in the Aesthetic Appreciation," 10457.

70. Cela-Conde et al., "Dynamics of Brain Networks in the Aesthetic Appreciation," 10458.

71. Cela-Conde et al., "Dynamics of Brain Networks in the Aesthetic Appreciation," 10459.

72. Fingerhut and Prinz suggest that with processing ease, "having accomplished its goal, the visual system may instruct the body to relax" ("Aesthetic Emotions Reconsidered," 230). I don't see this as instruction from the visual system, but certainly input from vision would matter to goal resolution.

73. Vartanian makes this claim in "Internal Orientation in Aesthetic Experience," 23–34.

74. On the self-relevance effect in general, see Conway, "Memory and the Self"; Cunningham et al., "Yours or Mine?"; Cunningham, Brady-Van den Bos, and Turk, "Exploring the Effects of Ownership and Choice on Self-Memory Biases"; Leshikar, Dulas, and Duarte, "Self-Referencing Enhances Recollection in Both Young and Older Adults."

75. Nadal, Marty, and Munar, "The Search for Objective Measures of Aesthetic Judgment"; Choe et al., "To Search or to Like."

76. Lee et al., "Beauty Is in the Eye of the Beholder."

77. The VIMAP emphasizes self-relevance checks as part of positive aesthetic responses, both on an emotional level and at the level of a broader conceptualizations of the self: for example, where do I fit? How does this artwork challenge me and who I am? It also places the DMN in this analysis.

78. Kasdan and Belfi, "Investigating a Self-Reference Effect in Musical Aesthetics."

79. Belfi, Karlan, and Tranel, "Music Evokes Vivid Autobiographical Memories." Emotional and arousal are key for better recollection of music; see Jäncke, "Music and Memory." Their model suggests that emotion directs attention, which is key for encoding music. Taxing auditory tasks depressed the DMN, though familiar music may be different. See Wilkins et al., "Network Science and the Effects of Music Preference on Functional Brain Connectivity."

80. Taxing working memory or cognitive load with a two-back task also seems to interrupt one's ability to detect or experience visual beauty: Brielmann and Pelli, "Beauty Requires Thought." An *n*-back task involves giving participants a list of items and asking them whether they have encountered a target within the last *n* presentations of items. Because it is generally accepted that working memory can hold a limited number of items, the *n*-back task is generally seen as a good test of strain on working memory. It is not entirely clear, however, exactly what components of cognition underpin the task. See Miller, "The Magical Number Seven, Plus or Minus Two: Some Limits on Our Capacity for Processing Information"; and Jaeggi et al., "The Concurrent Validity of the N-Back Task as a Working Memory Measure."

81. One well-known example involves phantom limb syndrome. As Vilayanur S. Ramachandran has shown, when an injury leads to amputation, areas of the brain that map our bodies rewire, so that an adjacent area (say, the forearm) begins to map onto brain regions previously mapped by the missing limb (e.g., the hand). See Ramachandran and Rogers-Ramachandran, "Phantom Limbs and Neural Plasticity." The foundational example here is perhaps the study of hippocampal changes in London cab drivers; see Maguire, Woollett, and Spiers, "London Taxi Drivers and

Bus Drivers." Music also encourages brain plasticity; see, for example, Ferreri et al., "Music and the Aging Brain."

82. Wilkins et al., "Network Science and the Effects of Music Preference on Functional Brain Connectivity."

83. DeNora, *Music in Everyday Life*; Hanich et al., "Why We Like to Watch Sad Films."

84. See the account of processing stages in Brattico, "The Neuroaesthetics of Music"; Juslin and Sakka, "Neural Correlates of Music and Emotion."

85. See Huron, *Sweet Anticipation*, 132–141.

86. I am grateful to Anjan Chatterjee for suggesting this possibility.

87. On tears and goosebumps, see Wassiliwizky et al., "Tears Falling on Goosebumps."

88. On the DMN and goal-switching, see Pallesen et al., "Cognitive and Emotional Modulation of Brain Default Operation."

89. Seeley, "Art, Meaning, and Aesthetics," 30.

90. Chatterjee and Vartanian, "Neuroaesthetics"; Chatterjee and Vartanian, "Neuroscience of Aesthetics."

91. Vessel, Starr, and Rubin, "The Brain on Art."

92. See Carver and Scheier, "A Self-Regulatory Viewpoint on Human Behavior."

93. Vessel, Starr, and Rubin, "Art Reaches within."

94. On the subjective general unpredictability of strong aesthetic responses, see Vessel et al., "Stronger Shared Taste for Natural Aesthetic Domains than for Artifacts of Human Culture." On reward, Schultz, Dayan, and Montague, "A Neural Substrate of Prediction and Reward." For literature on peak experience, see also Gabrielsson, Whaley, and Sloboda, "Peak Experiences in Music," 745–758; Pelowski et al., "Move Me, Astonish Me."

95. Huron, *Sweet Anticipation*, 33–39.

96. Salimpoor et al., "Anatomically Distinct Dopamine Release during Anticipation and Experience of Peak Emotion to Music."

97. Zamorano et al., "Insula-Based Networks in Professional Musicians"; Luo et al., "Long-Term Effects of Musical Training and Functional Plasticity in Salience System."

98. Bey, *Light on the Swamp*, black-and-white gel photography, 2019. I am grateful to Victoria Sancho Lobis for showing me these photographs.

99. The particular time course Wassiliwizky describes may be unique for poetic chills, but this may reflect the frequency with which individuals respond with chills to music or poetry as compared to visual art. On localization for caudate and thalamus for visual art, see Vessel, Starr, and Rubin, "The Brain on Art." Striatal regions also show differential localization with other the time course of other anticipatory pleasurable responses. On taste, see O'Doherty et al., "Neural Responses during Anticipation of a Primary Taste Reward." On money, see Knutson et al., "Anticipation of Increasing Monetary Reward Selectively Recruits Nucleus Accumbens."

100. Frost, *Frost*, 229.

101. See, for example, Zunshine, *Why We Read Fiction*; Flesch, *Comeuppance*; Tomlinson, *A Million Years of Music*; Dissanayake, *What Is Art For?*

102. Smallwood et al., "The Default Modes of Reading"; Zhang et al., "Distinct Individual Differences in Default Mode Network Connectivity Relate to Off-Task Thought and Text Memory during Reading."

103. Armstrong, *How Literature Plays with the Brain*. For a nuanced narratological account of reading, see Armstrong, *Stories and the Brain*; Armstrong argues that the discontinuity of narrative, especially the ways in which causation requires that we move back and forward in a narrative as we assimilate details to make sense of motivation, inner life, and feelings, depends on the general discontinuity of time as the brain encodes it.

104. Csikszentmihalyi, Abuhamdeh, and Nakamura, "The Nature of Flow," 230–231. See also Nakamura, Tse, and Shankland, "Flow: The Experience of Intrinsic Motivation."

105. Milton, *Paradise Lost*, Book IV, l. 639.

106. On the importance of motor planning, see, among others, Vuilleumier and Trost, "Music and Emotions"; and Janzen and Thaut, "Cerebral Organization of Music Processing."

107. On the applicability of Markov models to brain states beginning with single-cell recordings, see Beck and Pouget, "Exact Inferences in a Neural Implementation of a Hidden Markov Model"; and Escola et al., "Hidden Markov Models for the Stimulus-Response Relationships of Multistate Neural Systems."

Chapter 4

1. Wells, *The Time Machine and the Invisible Man*.

2. Kukushkin and Carew, "Memory Takes Time," 260.

3. Kukushkin and Carew, "Memory Takes Time," 260.

4. Reed, *Slow Art*, 2.

5. As opposed to Choe et al., "To Search or to Like."

6. Chalmers, "Facing up to the Problem of Consciousness."

7. McLane, *My Poets*, 16.

8. Spenser, *The Faerie Queene*.

9. Wilson, *The Odyssey*, Book 4, ll. 261–264.

10. Walcott, *Omeros*, 14–15.

11. Babo-Rebelo and Tallon-Baudry, "Interoceptive Signals, Brain Dynamics, and Subjectivity," 54.

12. Allen and Tsakiris, "The Body as First Prior," 30, 31.

13. Allen and Tsakiris, "The Body as First Prior," 32.

14. Allen and Tsakiris, "The Body as First Prior," 33.

15. On interoceptive signals (heartrate and the DMN), see Babo-Rebelo and Tallon-Baudry, "Interoceptive Signals, Brain Dynamics, and Subjectivity," 54.

16. O'Doherty and colleagues, as described in chapter 2, have been able to use a neural network model to identify a limited number of high-level features of visual art that can be assembled from lower-level visual features, and which can be used to predict the strength of aesthetic responses for a given artwork across individuals. See Iigaya et al., "Aesthetic Preference for Art Can Be Predicted from a Mixture of Low-and High-Level Visual Features." Their model depends on understanding how computations are made within the brain, and refining and fully understanding their implications requires detailed understanding of neural systems and hierarchies.

17. Armstrong, "Stevens' 'Last Poem' Again," 36.

18. Stevens, *Collected Poetry and Prose*, 475.

19. Dove, "Demeter's Prayer to Hades."

20. For a revealing account of the impact of aesthetic deprivation on high-stakes decision-making and well-being, see Vessel and Russo, "Effects of Reduced Sensory Stimulation and Assessment of Countermeasures for Sensory Stimulation Augmentation." I do not mean to imply that what prisons punish as crime is always the result of bad choices by individuals.

Bibliography

Aharon, Itzhak, Nancy Etcoff, Dan Ariely, Christopher F. Chabris, Ethan O'Connor, and Hans C. Breiter. "Beautiful Faces Have Variable Reward Value: fMRI and Behavioral Evidence." *Neuron* 32, no. 3 (2001): 537–551.

Allen, Micah, and Manos Tsakiris. "The Body as First Prior: Interoceptive Predictive Processing and the Primacy of Self-Models." In *The Interoceptive Mind: From Homeostasis to Awareness*, edited by Manos Tsakiris and Helena De Preester, 27–45. New York: Oxford University Press, 2019.

Alluri, Vinoo, Petri Toiviainen, Iiro P. Jääskeläinen, Enrico Glerean, Mikko Sams, and Elvira Brattico. "Large-Scale Brain Networks Emerge from Dynamic Processing of Musical Timbre, Key and Rhythm." *NeuroImage* 59, no. 4 (2012): 3677–3689.

Alter, Robert. *The Art of Biblical Poetry*. New York: Basic Books, 1985.

Andrews-Hanna, Jessica R., Jay S. Reidler, Jorge Sepulcre, Renee Poulin, and Randy L. Buckner. "Functional-Anatomic Fractionation of the Brain's Default Network." *Neuron* 65, no. 4 (2010): 550–562.

Aristotle. *Nicomachean Ethics*. Translated by Terence Irwin. 2nd ed. Indianapolis: Hackett, 1999.

Aristotle. *On Rhetoric*. Translated by George A. Kennedy. New York: Oxford University Press, 1991.

Armstrong, Paul B. *How Literature Plays with the Brain: The Neuroscience of Reading and Art*. Baltimore: Johns Hopkins University Press, 2013.

Armstrong, Paul B. *Stories and the Brain: The Neuroscience of Narrative*. Baltimore: Johns Hopkins University Press, 2020.

Armstrong, Tim. "Stevens' 'Last Poem' Again." *The Wallace Stevens Journal* 12, no. 1 (1988): 35–43.

Arstila, Valtteri, and Dan Lloyd. *Subjective Time: The Philosophy, Psychology, and Neuroscience of Temporality*. Cambridge, MA: MIT Press, 2014.

Augustin, M. Dorothee, Helmut Leder, Florian Hutzler, and Claus-Christian Carbon. "Style Follows Content: On the Microgenesis of Art Perception." *Acta Psychologica* 128, no. 1 (2008): 127–138. https://doi.org/10.1016/j.actpsy.2007.11.006.

Babo-Rebelo, Marianna, and Catherine Tallon-Baudry. "Interoceptive Signals, Brain Dynamics, and Subjectivity." In *The Interoceptive Mind: From Homeostasis to Awareness*, edited by Manos Tsakiris and Helena De Preester, 46–62. New York: Oxford University Press, 2019.

Bailes, Freya. "Dynamic Melody Recognition: Distinctiveness and The Role of Musical Expertise." *Memory & Cognition* 38, no. 5 (2010): 641–650.

Bambini, Valentina, Paolo Canal, Donatella Resta, and Mirko Grimaldi. "Time Course and Neurophysiological Underpinnings of Metaphor in Literary Context." *Discourse Processes* 56, no. 1 (2019): 77–97. https://doi.org/10.1080/0163853X.2017.1401876.

Barrett, Lisa Feldman, Michael Lewis, and Jeannette M. Haviland-Jones, eds. *Handbook of Emotions*. 4th ed. New York: Guilford Publications, 2016.

Battaglia, Fortunato, Sarah H. Lisanby, and David Freedberg. "Corticomotor Excitability during Observation and Imagination of a Work of Art." *Frontiers in Human Neuroscience* 5 (2011): 79.

Bates, Douglas, Martin Mächler, Ben Bolker, and Steve Walker. "Fitting Linear Mixed-Effects Models Using Lme4." Journal of Statistical Software 67, no. 1 (2015): 1-48.

Beck, Jeffrey M., and Alexandre Pouget. "Exact Inferences in a Neural Implementation of a Hidden Markov Model." *Neural Computation* 19, no. 5 (2007): 1344–1361.

Beckmann, C. F., J. A. Noble, and S. M. Smith. "Investigating the Intrinsic Dimensionality of fMRI Data for ICA." In *Seventh International Conference on Functional Mapping of the Human Brain. Neuroimage* 13, no. 6 (2001).

Belfi, Amy M. "Emotional Valence and Vividness of Imagery Predict Aesthetic Appeal in Music." *Psychomusicology: Music, Mind, and Brain* 29, nos. 2–3 (2019): 128.

Belfi, Amy M., Brett Karlan, and Daniel Tranel. "Music Evokes Vivid Autobiographical Memories." *Memory* 24, no. 7 (2016): 979–989.

Belfi, Amy M., Anna Kasdan, Jess Rowland, Edward A. Vessel, G. Gabrielle Starr, and David Poeppel. "Rapid Timing of Musical Aesthetic Judgments." *Journal of Experimental Psychology: General* 147, no. 10 (2018): 1531.

Belfi, Amy M., Edward A. Vessel, Aenne Brielmann, Ayse Ilkay Isik, Anjan Chatterjee, Helmut Leder, Denis G. Pelli, and G. Gabrielle Starr. "Dynamics of Aesthetic Experience Are Reflected in the Default-Mode Network." *NeuroImage* 188 (March 2019): 584–597. https://doi.org/10.1016/j.neuroimage.2018.12.017.

Belfi, Amy M., Edward A. Vessel, and G. Gabrielle Starr. "Individual Ratings of Vividness Predict Aesthetic Appeal in Poetry." *Psychology of Aesthetics, Creativity, and the Arts* 12, no. 3 (2018): 341–350. https://doi.org/10.1037/aca0000153.

Bell, Clive. *Art*. London: Pickering and Chatto, 1914.

Benjamini, Yoav, and Yosef Hochberg. "Controlling the False Discovery Rate: A Practical and Powerful Approach to Multiple Testing." *Journal of the Royal Statistical Society: Series B (Methodological)* 57, no. 1 (1995): 289-300.

Bergson, Henri. *Henri Bergson: Key Writings*, edited by Keith Ansell Pearson and John Mullarkey. New York: Continuum, 2002.

Berridge, Kent C., and Morten L. Kringelbach. "From Pleasure to Happiness: 'Liking' and 'Wanting' in Mind and Brain." In *Handbook of Emotions*, 4th ed., edited by Lisa Feldman Barrett, Michael Lewis, and Jeannette M. Haviland-Jones, 133–145. New York: Guilford Publications, 2016.

Bey, Dawoud. *Light on the Swamp*. Black-and-white gel photography. 2019.

Bicknell, Russell, Javier Ortega-Hernández, Gregory Edgecombe, Robert Gaines, and John Paterson. "Central Nervous System of a 310-Million-Year-Old Horseshoe Crab: Expanding the Taphonic Window for Nervous System Preservation." *Geology* (July 2021): https://doi.org/10.1130/G49193.1.

Biederman, Irving, and Edward A. Vessel. "Perceptual Pleasure and the Brain: A Novel Theory Explains Why the Brain Craves Information and Seeks It through the Senses." *American Scientist* 94, no. 3 (2006): 247–253.

Bigand, Emmanuel, Suzanne Filipic, and Philippe Lalitte. "The Time Course of Emotional Responses to Music." *Annals of the New York Academy of Sciences* 1060, no. 1 (2005): 429–437.

Boccia, Maddalena, Sonia Barbetti, Laura Piccardi, Cecilia Guariglia, Fabio Ferlazzo, Anna Maria Giannini, and D. W. Zaidel. "Where Does Brain Neural Activation in Aesthetic Responses to Visual Art Occur? Meta-Analytic Evidence from Neuroimaging Studies." *Neuroscience & Biobehavioral Reviews* 60 (2016): 65–71.

Bohrn, Isabel C., Ulrike Altmann, Oliver Lubrich, Winfried Menninghaus, and Arthur M. Jacobs. "When We Like What We Know—A Parametric fMRI Analysis of Beauty and Familiarity." *Brain and Language* 124, no. 1 (2013): 1–8. https://doi.org/10.1016/j.bandl.2012.10.003.

Bonneh, Yoram S., Tobias H. Donner, Alexander Cooperman, David J. Heeger, and Dov Sagi. "Motion-Induced Blindness and Troxler Fading: Common and Different Mechanisms." *PLOS ONE* 9, no. 3 (2014): e92894.

Bortolussi, Marisa, and Peter Dixon. "Transport: Challenges to the Metaphor." In *The Oxford Handbook of Cognitive Literary Studies*, edited by Lisa Zunshine, 525–540. New York: Oxford University Press, 2015.

Bradley, Margaret M., and Peter J. Lang. *Affective Norms for English Words (ANEW): Instruction Manual and Affective Ratings*. Gainesville, FL: The Center for Research in Psychophysiology, 1999.

Brattico, Elvira, Brigitte Bogert, Vinoo Alluri, Mari Tervaniemi, Tuomas Eerola, and Thomas Jacobsen. "It's Sad but I Like It: The Neural Dissociation between Musical Emotions and Liking in Experts and Laypersons." *Frontiers in Human Neuroscience* 9 (2016): 676.

Brattico, Elvira. "The Neuroaesthetics of Music: A Research Agenda Coming of Age." In *Oxford Handbook of Music and the Brain*, edited by Michael H. Thaut and Donald A. Hodges, 364–390. New York: Oxford University Press, 2019.

Brieber, David, Marcos Nadal, Helmut Leder, and Raphael Rosenberg. "Art in Time and Space: Context Modulates the Relation between Art Experience and Viewing Time." *PLOS ONE* 9, no. 6 (2014): e99019.

Brieber, David, Michael Forster, and Helmut Leder. "On the Mutual Relation between Art Experience and Viewing Time." *Psychology of Aesthetics, Creativity, and the Arts* 14, no. 2 (2020): 197–208. https://doi.org/10.1037/aca0000210.

Brainard, D. H. "The Psychophysics Toolbox," *Spatial Vision* 10, no. 4 (1997): 433–436. https://doi.org/10.1163/156856897X00357.

Brielmann, Aenne A., and Denis G. Pelli. "Beauty Requires Thought." *Current Biology* 27, no. 10 (2017): 1506–1513. e3.

Brielmann, Aenne A., and Denis G. Pelli. "Intense Beauty Requires Intense Pleasure." *Frontiers in Psychology* 10 (2019): 2420.

Brielmann, Aenne A., Lauren Vale, and Denis G. Pelli. "Beauty at a Glance: The Feeling of Beauty and the Amplitude of Pleasure Are Independent of Stimulus Duration." *Journal of Vision* 17, no. 14 (2017): 9. https://doi.org/10.1167/17.14.9.

Brown, Steven. "Toward a Unification of the Arts." *Frontiers in Psychology* 9 (2018): 1938.

Brown, Steven, Xiaoqing Gao, Loren Tisdelle, Simon B. Eickhoff, and Mario Liotti. "Naturalizing Aesthetics: Brain Areas for Aesthetic Appraisal across Sensory Modalities." *NeuroImage* 58, no. 1 (2011): 250–258.

Brumm, Adam, Adhi Agus Oktaviana, Basran Burhan, Budianto Hakim, Rustan Lebe, Jian-xin Zhao, Priyatno Hadi Sulistyarto, Marlon Ririmasse, Shinatria Adhityatama, and Iwan Sumantri. "Oldest Cave Art Found in Sulawesi." *Science Advances* 7, no. 3 (2021): eabd4648.

Buckner, Randy L., and Lauren M. DiNicola. "The Brain's Default Network: Updated Anatomy, Physiology and Evolving Insights." *Nature Reviews Neuroscience* 20, no. 10 (2019): 593–608.

Buckner, Randy L., and Fenna M. Krienen. "The Evolution of Distributed Association Networks in the Human Brain." *Trends in Cognitive Sciences* 17, no. 12 (2013): 648–665.

Burke, Edmund. *A Philosophical Enquiry into the Sublime and Beautiful*, edited by Paul Guyer. New York: Oxford University Press, 2015.

Burke, Kenneth. *The Philosophy of Literary Form.* Vol. 266. Berkeley: University of California Press, 1974.

Buhrmester, Michael, Tracy Kwang, and Samuel D. Gosling. "Amazon's Mechanical Turk: A New Source of Inexpensive, Yet High-Quality, Data?" *Perspectives on Psychological Science* 6, no. 1 (2011): 3–5.

Carver, Charles. "Pleasure as a Sign You Can Attend to Something Else: Placing Positive Feelings within a General Model of Affect." *Cognition and Emotion* 17, no. 2 (2003): 241–261.

Carver, Charles, and Michael F. Scheier. "A Self-Regulatory Viewpoint on Human Behavior." In *Oxford Handbook of Human Motivation*, edited by Richard M. Ryan, 27–46. New York: Oxford University Press, 2019. https://doi.org/10.1093/oxfordhb/9780190666453.013.3.

Cattaneo, Zaira. "Noninvasive Brain Stimulation: An Overview of Available Approaches for Research in Neuroaesthetics." *Empirical Studies of the Arts* 37, no. 2 (2019): 153–171. https://doi.org/10.1177/0276237418818637.

Cattaneo, Zaira. "Neural Correlates of Visual Aesthetic Appreciation: Insights from Non-Invasive Brain Stimulation." *Experimental Brain Research* 238, no. 1 (2020): 1–16.

Cattaneo, Zaira, Carlotta Lega, Chiara Ferrari, Tomaso Vecchi, Camilo José Cela-Conde, Juha Silvanto, and Marcos Nadal. "The Role of the Lateral Occipital Cortex in Aesthetic Appreciation of Representational and Abstract Paintings: A TMS Study." *Brain and Cognition* 95 (2015): 44–53.

Cattaneo, Zaira, Susanna Schiavi, Juha Silvanto, and Marcos Nadal. "A TMS Study on the Contribution of Visual Area V5 to the Perception of Implied Motion in Art and Its Appreciation." *Cognitive Neuroscience* 8, no. 1 (2017): 59–68.

Cela-Conde, Camilo J., Juan García-Prieto, José J. Ramasco, Claudio R. Mirasso, Ricardo Bajo, Enric Munar, Albert Flexas, Francisco del-Pozo, and Fernando Maestú. "Dynamics of Brain Networks in the Aesthetic Appreciation." *Proceedings of the National Academy of Sciences* 110, Supplement 2 (2013): 10454–10461.

Cela-Conde, Camilo José, and Francisco J. Ayala. "Art and Brain Coevolution." *Progress in Brain Research* 237 (2018): 41–60.

Chalmers, David. "Facing up to the Problem of Consciousness." *Journal of Consciousness Studies* 2 (1995): 200–210.

Chamberlain, Steven C., and Gordon A. Wyse. "An Atlas of the Brain of the Horseshoe Crab Limulus Polyphemus." *Journal of Morphology* 187, no. 3 (1986): 363–386.

Chatterjee, Anjan. "Neuroaesthetics: A Coming of Age Story." *Journal of Cognitive Neuroscience* 23, no. 1 (2011): 53–62.

Chatterjee, Anjan. *The Aesthetic Brain: How We Evolved to Desire Beauty and Enjoy Art*. New York: Oxford University Press, 2014.

Chatterjee, Anjan, Amy Thomas, Sabrina E. Smith, and Geoffrey K. Aguirre. "The Neural Response to Facial Attractiveness." *Neuropsychology* 23, no. 2 (2009): 135.

Chatterjee, Anjan, and Oshin Vartanian. "Neuroaesthetics." *Trends in Cognitive Sciences* 18, no. 7 (2014): 370–375.

Chatterjee, Anjan, and Oshin Vartanian. "Neuroscience of Aesthetics." *Annals of the New York Academy of Sciences* 1369, no. 1 (2016): 172–194.

Chatterjee, Anjan, Page Widick, Rebecca Sternschein, William B. Smith, and Bianca Bromberger. "The Assessment of Art Attributes." *Empirical Studies of the Arts* 28, no. 2 (2010): 207–222. https://doi.org/10.2190/EM.28.2.f.

Chiew, Kimberly S., and Todd S. Braver. "Dissociable Influences of Reward Motivation and Positive Emotion on Cognitive Control." *Cognitive, Affective, & Behavioral Neuroscience* 14, no. 2 (2014): 509–529.

Choe, Kyoung Whan, Omid Kardan, Hiroki P. Kotabe, John M. Henderson, and Marc G. Berman. "To Search or to Like: Mapping Fixations to Differentiate Two Forms of Incidental Scene Memory." *Journal of Vision* 17, no. 12 (2017): 8.

Cicero, Marcus Tullius. *De oratore*. Translated by Kazimierz Kumaniecki. Editio stereotypa editionis primae (MCMLXIX). Scripta quae manserunt omnia; Fasc. 3. Stutgardiae: In Aedibus B.G. Teubneri, 1995.

Citron, Francesca M. M., Jeremie Güsten, Nora Michaelis, and Adele E. Goldberg. "Conventional Metaphors in Longer Passages Evoke Affective Brain Response." *NeuroImage* 139 (October 2016): 218–230. https://doi.org/10.1016/j.neuroimage.2016.06.020.

Citron, Francesca M. M., Mollie Lee, and Nora Michaelis. "Affective and Psycholinguistic Norms for German Conceptual Metaphors (COMETA)." *Behavior Research Methods* 52, no. 3 (2020): 1056–1072. https://doi.org/10.3758/s13428-019-01300-7.

Clayton, Martin, Rebecca Sager, and Udo Will. "In Time with the Music: The Concept of Entrainment and Its Significance for Ethnomusicology." *European Meetings in Ethnomusicology* 11 (2005): 1–82.

Clune, Michael W. *Writing against Time*. Stanford, CA: Stanford University Press, 2013.

Clynes, Manfred, and Janice Walker. "Neurobiologic Function of Rhythm, Time, and Pulse in Music." In *Music, Mind and Brain*, edited by Manfred Clynes, 171–216. New York: Plenum, 1982.

Coleridge, Samuel Taylor. *Biographia Literaria, or, Biographical Sketches of My Literary Life and Opinions*. Vol. 7. Princeton, NJ: Princeton University Press, 1984.

Conway, Martin A. "Memory and the Self." *Journal of Memory and Language* 53, no. 4 (2005): 594–628. https://doi.org/10.1016/j.jml.2005.08.005.

Conway, Martin, Kevin Meares, and Sally Standart. "Images and Goals." *Memory* 12, no. 4 (2004): 525–531.

Craig, A. D. "Emotional Moments across Time: A Possible Neural Basis for Time Perception in the Anterior Insula." *Philosophical Transactions of the Royal Society B: Biological Sciences* 364, no. 1525 (2009): 1933–1942.

Craig, A. D. "How Do You Feel—Now? The Anterior Insula and Human Awareness." *Nature Reviews Neuroscience* 10, no. 1 (2009): 59–70. https://doi.org/10.1038/nrn2555.

Crocker, Ann D. "The Regulation of Motor Control: An Evaluation of the Role of Dopamine Receptors in the Substantia Nigra." *Reviews in the Neurosciences* 8, no. 1 (1997): 55–76.

Csikszentmihalyi, Mihaly, Sami Abuhamdeh, and Jeanne Nakamura. "The Nature of Flow." In *Flow and the Foundations of Positive Psychology*, edited by Mihaly Csikszentmihalyi, 227–238. Dordrecht: Springer, 2014.

Cunningham, Sheila, Mirjam Brady-Van den Bos, and David Turk. "Exploring the Effects of Ownership and Choice on Self-Memory Biases." *Memory* 19, no. 5 (2011): 449–461.

Cunningham, Sheila J., David J. Turk, Lynda M. Macdonald, and C. Neil Macrae. "Yours or Mine? Ownership and Memory." *Consciousness and Cognition* 17, no. 1 (2008): 312–318. https://doi.org/10.1016/j.concog.2007.04.003.

Cupchik, Gerald C., Oshin Vartanian, Adrian Crawley, and David J. Mikulis. "Viewing Artworks: Contributions of Cognitive Control and Perceptual Facilitation to Aesthetic Experience." *Brain and Cognition* 70, no. 1 (2009): 84–91. https://doi.org/10.1016/j.bandc.2009.01.003.

Cutting, J. E. "Gustave Caillebotte, French Impressionism, and Mere Exposure." *Psychonomic Bulletin & Review* 10, no. 2 (2003): 319–343.

Dalla Bella, Simone, Isabelle Peretz, and Neil Aronoff. "Time Course of Melody Recognition: A Gating Paradigm Study." *Perception & Psychophysics* 65, no. 7 (2003): 1019–1028.

Dainton, Barry. "The Phenomenal Continuum." In *Subjective Time: The Philosophy, Psychology, and Neuroscience of Temporality*, edited by Valtteri Arstila, 101–138. Cambridge, MA: MIT Press, 2014.

Danto, Arthur Coleman. *The Transfiguration of the Commonplace: A Philosophy of Art*. Cambridge, MA: Harvard University Press, 1981.

Davis, Whitney. *A General Theory of Visual Culture*. Princeton, NJ: Princeton University Press, 2017.

Defoe, Ovid. "Narrative and Poiesis." In *Narrative Developments from Chaucer to Defoe*, edited by Gerd Bayer and Ebbe Kiltgard, 161–177. New York: Routledge, 2011.

DeNora, Tia. *Music in Everyday Life*. New York: Cambridge University Press, 2000.

Descartes, René. "Meditations on First Philosophy." In *Discourse on Method and Meditations on First Philosophy*, translated by Donald A. Cress, 46–103. Indianapolis: Hackett, 1998.

Dewey, John. *Art as Experience*. New York: Penguin, 2005.

Di Dio, Cinzia, Martina Ardizzi, Davide Massaro, Giuseppe Di Cesare, Gabriella Gilli, Antonella Marchetti, and Vittorio Gallese. "Human, Nature, Dynamism: The Effects of Content and Movement Perception on Brain Activations during the Aesthetic Judgment of Representational Paintings." *Frontiers in Human Neuroscience* 9 (2016): 705.

Dickie, George. "The Myth of the Aesthetic Attitude." *American Philosophical Quarterly* 1, no. 1 (1964): 56–65.

Dissanayake, Ellen. *Art and Intimacy: How the Arts Began*. Seattle: University of Washington Press, 2000.

Dissanayake, Ellen. *Homo Aestheticus: Where Art Comes from and Why*. Seattle: University of Washington Press, 2001.

Dissanayake, Ellen. *What Is Art For?* Seattle: University of Washington Press, 2015.

Doelling, Keith B., M. Florencia Assaneo, Dana Bevilacqua, Bijan Pesaran, and David Poeppel. "An Oscillator Model Better Predicts Cortical Entrainment to Music." *Proceedings of the National Academy of Sciences* 116, no. 20 (2019): 10113–10121.

Doelling, Keith B., and David Poeppel. "Cortical Entrainment to Music and Its Modulation by Expertise." *Proceedings of the National Academy of Sciences* 112, no. 45 (2015): E6233–E6242.

Dove, Rita. "Demeter's Prayer to Hades." *Poetry* 161, no. 1 (October 1992): 23.

Droit-Volet, Sylvie. "What Emotions Tell Us about Time." In *Subjective Time: The Philosophy, Psychology, and Neuroscience of Temporality*, edited by Valtteri Arstilla and Dan Lloyd, 477–506. Cambridge, MA: MIT Press, 2014.

Droit-Volet, Sylvie, and Warren H. Meck. "How Emotions Colour Our Perception of Time." *Trends in Cognitive Sciences* 11, no. 12 (2007): 504–513.

Dutke, Stephan. "Remembered Duration: Working Memory and the Reproduction of Intervals." *Perception & Psychophysics* 67, no. 8 (2005): 1404–1413.

Eerola, Tuomas, Jonna K. Vuoskoski, and Hannu Kautiainen. "Being Moved by Unfamiliar Sad Music Is Associated with High Empathy." *Frontiers in Psychology* 7 (2016). https://doi.org/10.3389/fpsyg.2016.01176.

Eerola, Tuomas, Jonna K. Vuoskoski, Henna-Riikka Peltola, Vesa Putkinen, and Katharina Schäfer. "An Integrative Review of the Enjoyment of Sadness Associated with Music." *Physics of Life Reviews* 25 (August 2018): 100–121. https://doi.org/10.1016/j.plrev.2017.11.016.

Elfenbein, Andrew. *The Gist of Reading*. Stanford: Stanford University Press, 2020.

Enders, Craig K., and Davood Tofighi. "Centering Predictor Variables in Cross-Sectional Multilevel Models: A New Look at an Old Issue." *Psychological Methods* 12, no. 2 (2007): 121.

Escola, Sean, Alfredo Fontanini, Don Katz, and Liam Paninski. "Hidden Markov Models for the Stimulus-Response Relationships of Multistate Neural Systems." *Neural Computation* 23, no. 5 (2011): 1071–1132.

Esposito, Fabrizio, Adriana Aragri, Ilaria Pesaresi, Sossio Cirillo, Gioacchino Tedeschi, Elio Marciano, Rainer Goebel, and Francesco Di Salle. "Independent Component Model of the Default-Mode Brain Function: Combining Individual-Level and Population-Level Analyses in Resting-State FMRI." *Magnetic Resonance Imaging* 26, no. 7 (2008): 905–913.

Failing, Michel, and Jan Theeuwes. "Reward Alters the Perception of Time." *Cognition* 148 (2016): 19–26.

Fair, Damien A., Alexander L. Cohen, Nico U. F. Dosenbach, Jessica A. Church, Francis M. Miezin, Deanna M. Barch, Marcus E. Raichle, Steven E. Petersen, and Bradley L. Schlaggar. "The Maturing Architecture of the Brain's Default Network." *Proceedings of the National Academy of Sciences* 105, no. 10 (2008): 4028–4032.

Fairhall, Scott L., and Alumit Ishai. "Neural Correlates of Object Indeterminacy in Art Compositions." *Consciousness and Cognition* 17, no. 3 (2008): 923–932.

Fayn, Kirill, Carolyn MacCann, Niko Tiliopoulos, and Paul J. Silvia. "Aesthetic Emotions and Aesthetic People: Openness Predicts Sensitivity to Novelty in the Experiences of Interest and Pleasure." *Frontiers in Psychology* 6 (2015). https://doi.org/10.3389/fpsyg.2015.01877.

Fayn, Kirill, Paul J. Silvia, Yasemin Erbas, Niko Tiliopoulos, and Peter Kuppens. "Nuanced Aesthetic Emotions: Emotion Differentiation Is Related to Knowledge of the Arts and Curiosity." *Cognition and Emotion* 32, no. 3 (2018): 593–599. https://doi.org/10.1080/02699931.2017.1322554.

Ferrari, Chiara, Marcos Nadal, Susanna Schiavi, Tomaso Vecchi, Camilo J. Cela-Conde, and Zaira Cattaneo. "The Dorsomedial Prefrontal Cortex Mediates the Interaction between Moral and Aesthetic Valuation: A TMS Study on the Beauty-Is-Good Stereotype." *Social Cognitive and Affective Neuroscience* 12, no. 5 (2017): 707–717.

Ferrari, Chiara, Susanna Schiavi, and Zaira Cattaneo. "TMS over the Superior Temporal Sulcus Affects Expressivity Evaluation of Portraits." *Cognitive, Affective, & Behavioral Neuroscience* 18, no. 6 (2018): 1188–1197.

Ferreri, Laura, Aline Moussard, Emmanuel Bigand, and E. Glenn Schellenberg. "Music and the Aging Brain." In *The Oxford Handbook of Music and the Brain*, edited by Michael H. Thaut and Donald A. Hodges, 623–644. New York: Oxford University Press, 2019.

Filipic, Suzanne, Barbara Tillmann, and Emmanuel Bigand. "Judging Familiarity and Emotion from Very Brief Musical Excerpts." *Psychonomic Bulletin & Review* 17, no. 3 (2010): 335–341.

Fingerhut, Joerg, and Jesse J. Prinz. "Grounding Evaluative Concepts." *Philosophical Transactions of the Royal Society B: Biological Sciences* 373, no. 1752 (2018): 20170142.

Fingerhut, Joerg, and Jesse J. Prinz. "Aesthetic Emotions Reconsidered." *The Monist* 103, no. 2 (2020): 223–239. https://doi.org/10.1093/monist/onz037.

Fiori, Francesca, Ela Plow, Maria Luisa Rusconi, and Zaira Cattaneo. "Modulation of Corticospinal Excitability during Paintings Viewing: A TMS Study." *Neuropsychologia* 149 (2020): 107664.

Fisher, Philip. *Making and Effacing Art*. New York: Oxford University Press, 1991.

Flesch, William. *Comeuppance: Costly Signaling, Altruistic Punishment, and Other Biological Components of Fiction*. Cambridge, MA: Harvard University Press, 2007.

Fredrickson, Barbara L. "The Role of Positive Emotions in Positive Psychology: The Broaden-and-Build Theory of Positive Emotions." *American Psychologist* 56, no. 3 (2001): 218.

Frijda, Nico H., and Louise Sundararajan. "Emotion Refinement: A Theory Inspired by Chinese Poetics." *Perspectives on Psychological Science* 2, no. 3 (2007): 227–241.

Friston, K. J., C. D. Frith, P. F. Liddle, and R.S.J. Frackowiak. "Functional Connectivity: The Principal-Component Analysis of Large (PET) Data Sets." *Journal of Cerebral Blood Flow & Metabolism* 13, no. 1 (1993): 5–14.

Fritz, Carole, Gilles Tosello, Guillaume Fleury, Emmanuel Kasarherou, Philippe Walter, Francis Duranthon, Pascal Gaillard, and Julien Tardieu. "First Record of the Sound Produced by the Oldest Upper Paleolithic Seashell Horn." *Science Advances* 7, no. 7 (2021): eabe9510.

Frost, Robert. *Frost: Collected Poems, Prose, & Plays*. Edited by Richard Poirier and Mark Richardson. New York: Library of America, 1995.

Fox, J., and S. Weisberg. *An R Companion to Applied Regression*. 2nd ed. Thousand Oaks, CA: Sage, 2011.

Gabrielsson, Alf, John Whaley, and John Sloboda. "Peak Experiences in Music." In *The Oxford Handbook of Music Psychology*, edited by Michael H. Thaut and Donald A. Hodges, 745–758. New York: Oxford University Press, 2016.

Gallese, Vittorio, and David Freedberg. "Mirror and Canonical Neurons Are Crucial Elements in Esthetic Response." *Trends in Cognitive Sciences* 11, no. 10 (2007): 411.

Gard, David E., Marja Germans Gard, Ann M. Kring, and Oliver P. John. "Anticipatory and Consummatory Components of the Experience of Pleasure: A Scale Development Study." *Journal of Research in Personality* 40, no. 6 (2006): 1086–1102.

Gates Jr., Henry Louis. *The Signifying Monkey: A Theory of African American Literary Criticism*. New York: Oxford University Press, 2014.

Gates Jr., Henry Louis, Valerie A. Smith, and Kimberly W. Benston, eds. *The Norton Anthology of African American Literature*. 3rd ed. New York: Norton, 2014.

Gendler, Tamar Szabó. "Alief and Belief." *The Journal of Philosophy* 105, no. 10 (2008a): 634–663.

Gendler, Tamar Szabó. "Alief in Action (and Reaction)." *Mind & Language* 23, no. 5 (2008b): 552–585.

Genovese, Christopher R., Nicole A. Lazar, and Thomas Nichols. "Thresholding of Statistical Maps in Functional Neuroimaging Using the False Discovery Rate." *NeuroImage* 15, no. 4 (2002): 870–878.

Gerger, Gernot, Helmut Leder, and Alexandra Kremer. "Context Effects on Emotional and Aesthetic Evaluations of Artworks and IAPS Pictures." *Acta Psychologica* 151 (2014): 174–183.

Germine, Laura, Richard Russell, P. Matthew Bronstad, Gabriëlla A. M. Blokland, Jordan W. Smoller, Holum Kwok, Samuel E. Anthony, Ken Nakayama, Gillian Rhodes, and Jeremy B. Wilmer. "Individual Aesthetic Preferences for Faces Are Shaped Mostly by Environments, Not Genes." *Current Biology* 25, no. 20 (2015): 2684–2689. https://doi.org/10.1016/j.cub.2015.08.048.

Gibson, James Jerome. *The Ecological Approach to Visual Perception.* New York: Psychology Press, 1986.

Gjerdingen, Robert O., and David Perrott. "Scanning the Dial: The Rapid Recognition of Music Genres." *Journal of New Music Research* 37, no. 2 (2008): 93–100.

Gouk, Penelope. "Music as a Means of Social Control: Some Examples of Practice and Theory in Early Modern Europe." In *The Emotional Power of Music: Multidisciplinary Perspectives on Musical Arousal, Expression, and Social Control*, edited by Tom Cochrane, Bernardino Fantini, and Klaus R. Scherer, 307–314. New York: Oxford University Press, 2013.

Goulden, Nia, Aygul Khusnulina, Nicholas J. Davis, Robert M. Bracewell, Arun L. Bokde, Jonathan P. McNulty, and Paul G. Mullins. "The Salience Network Is Responsible for Switching between the Default Mode Network and the Central Executive Network: Replication from DCM." *NeuroImage* 99 (2014): 180–190.

Greicius, Michael D., Ben Krasnow, Allan L. Reiss, and Vinod Menon. "Functional Connectivity in the Resting Brain: A Network Analysis of the Default Mode Hypothesis." *Proceedings of the National Academy of Sciences* 100, no. 1 (2003): 253–258.

Grodal, Torben, and Mette Kramer. "Film, Neuroaesthetics, and Empathy." In *An Introduction to Neuroaesthetics*, edited by John O. Lauring, 271–291. Copenhagen: Museum Tusculanum Press, 2014.

Grondin, Simon. "Timing and Time Perception: A Review of Recent Behavioral and Neuroscience Findings and Theoretical Directions." *Attention, Perception, & Psychophysics* 72, no. 3 (2010): 561–582.

Gusnard, Debra A., and Marcus E. Raichle. "Searching for a Baseline: Functional Imaging and the Resting Human Brain." *Nature Reviews Neuroscience* 2, no. 10 (2001): 685–694.

Haggard, Patrick, Sam Clark, and Jeri Kalogeras. "Voluntary Action and Conscious Awareness." *Nature Neuroscience* 5, no. 4 (2002): 382–385.

Hagstrum, Jean H. *The Sister Arts: The Tradition of Literary Pictorialism and English Poetry from Dryden to Gray*. Chicago: University of Chicago Press, 1958.

Haidt, Jonathan. "The Emotional Dog and Its Rational Tail: A Social Intuitionist Approach to Moral Judgment." *Psychological Review* 108, no. 4 (1995): 814–834.

Halpern, Andrea R., Jenny Ly, Seth Elkin-Frankston, and Margaret G. O'Connor. "'I Know What I Like': Stability of Aesthetic Preference in Alzheimer's Patients." *Brain and Cognition* 66, no. 1 (2008): 65–72.

Halpern, Andrea R., and Margaret G. O'Connor. "Stability of Art Preference in Frontotemporal Dementia." *Psychology of Aesthetics, Creativity, and the Arts* 7, no. 1 (2013): 95.

Hanich, Julian, Valentin Wagner, Mira Shah, Thomas Jacobsen, and Winfried Menninghaus. "Why We Like to Watch Sad Films: The Pleasure of Being Moved in Aesthetic Experiences." *Psychology of Aesthetics, Creativity, and the Arts* 8, no. 2 (2014): 130–143. https://doi.org/10.1037/a0035690.

Harter, M. Russell. "Excitability Cycles and Cortical Scanning: A Review of Two Hypotheses of Central Intermittency in Perception." *Psychological Bulletin* 68, no. 1 (1967): 47.

Hasson, Uri, Michal Harel, Ifat Levy, and Rafael Malach. "Large-Scale Mirror-Symmetry Organization of Human Occipito-Temporal Object Areas." *Neuron* 37, no. 6 (2003): 1027–1041.

Hasson, Uri, Yuval Nir, Ifat Levy, Galit Fuhrmann, and Rafael Malach. "Intersubject Synchronization of Cortical Activity during Natural Vision." *Science* 303, no. 5664 (2004): 1634–1640.

Ho, Paul M., Andrew J. Cooper, Phillip J. Hall, and Luke D. Smillie. "Factor Structure and Construct Validity of the Temporal Experience of Pleasure Scales." *Journal of Personality Assessment* 97, no. 2 (2015): 200–208.

Hogan, Patrick Colm. 2011. *Affective Narratology: The Emotional Structure of Stories.* Lincoln: University of Nebraska Press.

Hogarth, William. *The Analysis of Beauty*, edited by Ronald Paulson. New Haven, CT: Yale University Press, 1997.

Homer. *The Odyssey*. Translated by Emily Wilson. New York: W. W. Norton, 2017.

Hopkins, Gerard Manley. *Poems and Prose*, edited by W. H. Gardner. New York: Penguin, 1985.

Hosoya, Georg, Ines Schindler, Ursula Beermann, Valentin Wagner, Winfried Menninghaus, Michael Eid, and Klaus R. Scherer. "Mapping the Conceptual Domain of Aesthetic Emotion Terms: A Pile-Sort Study." *Psychology of Aesthetics, Creativity, and the Arts* 11, no. 4 (2017): 457–473. https://doi.org/10.1037/aca0000123.

Huijgen, J., D. Dellacherie, B. Tillmann, S. Clément, E. Bigand, S. Dupont, and S Samson. "The Feeling of Familiarity for Music in Patients with a Unilateral Temporal Lobe Lesion: A Gating Study." *Neuropsychologia* 77, no. 9 (2015): 313–320.

Hume, David. *A Treatise of Human Nature*, edited by David Fate Norton and Mary J. Norton. New York: Penguin, 1986.

Hume, David. *An Enquiry Concerning Human Understanding: A Letter from a Gentleman to His Friend in Edinburgh*. Indianapolis: Hackett, 1993.

Hume, David. "Of the Standard of Taste." In *Eighteenth-Century British Aesthetics*, edited by Dabney Townsend, 230–247. Foundations and Frontiers in Aesthetics. Amityville, NY: Baywood, 1999.

Humphries, Stacey, Jacqueline Rick, Daniel Weintraub, and Anjan Chatterjee. "Movement in Aesthetic Experiences: What We Can Learn from Parkinson Disease." *Journal of Cognitive Neuroscience* 33, no. 7 (2021): 1329–1342.

Huron, David. *Sweet Anticipation: Music and the Psychology of Expectation*. Cambridge, MA: MIT Press, 2008.

Husserl, Edmund. *The Phenomenology of Internal Time-Consciousness*. Bloomington: Indiana University Press, 2019.

Hutcheson, Francis. *An Inquiry into the Original of Our Ideas of Beauty and Virtue*, edited by Wolfgang Leidhold. Indianapolis: Liberty Fund, 2004.

Iigaya, Kiyohito, John P. O'Doherty, and G. Gabrielle Starr. "Progress and Promise in Neuroaesthetics." *Neuron* 108, no. 4 (2020): 594–596. https://doi.org/10.1016/j.neuron.2020.10.022.

Iigaya, Kiyohito, Sanghyun Yi, Iman A. Wahle, Koranis Tanwisuth, and John P. O'Doherty. "Aesthetic Preference for Art Can Be Predicted from a Mixture of Low- and High-Level Visual Features." *Nature Human Behaviour* 5, no. 6 (2021): 743–755.

Jacobellis v. Ohio. 1964, 378 US 184. Supreme Court.

Jacobs, Arthur M. "Towards a Neurocognitive Poetics Model of Literary Reading." In *Cognitive Neuroscience of Natural Language Use*, edited by Roel M. Willems, 135–159. New York: Cambridge University Press, 2015.

Jacobs, Arthur M., Melissa L-H. Võ, Benny B. Briesemeister, Markus Conrad, Markus J. Hofmann, Lars Kuchinke, Jana Lüdtke, and Mario Braun. "10 Years of BAWLing into Affective and Aesthetic Processes in Reading: What Are the Echoes?" *Frontiers in Psychology* 6 (2015): 714.

Jacobs, Arthur M., and Roel M. Willems. "The Fictive Brain: Neurocognitive Correlates of Engagement in Literature." *Review of General Psychology* 22, no. 2 (2018): 147–160.

Jacobsen, Thomas, Ricarda I. Schubotz, Lea Höfel, and D. Yves v. Cramon. "Brain Correlates of Aesthetic Judgment of Beauty." *NeuroImage* 29, no. 1 (2006): 276–285.

Jaeggi, Susanne M., Martin Buschkuehl, Walter J. Perrig, and Beat Meier. "The Concurrent Validity of the N-Back Task as a Working Memory Measure." *Memory* 18, no. 4 (2010): 394–412.

James, Henry. *The Golden Bowl*. New York: Penguin, 2009.

James, William. "What Is an Emotion?" *Mind* 9, no. 34 (1884): 188–205.

Jäncke, Lutz. "Music and Memory." In *Oxford Handbook of Music and the Brain*, edited by Michael Thaut and Donald A. Hodges, 237–262. New York: Oxford University Press, 2019.

Janzen, Thenille Braun, and Michael H. Thaut. "Cerebral Organization of Music Processing." In *The Oxford Handbook of Music and the Brain*, edited by Michael H. Thaut and Donald A. Hodges, 1–41. New York: Oxford University Press, 2019.

Johns, Jasper. *Green Target*. 1955a. Encaustic on newspaper and cloth over canvas. Museum of Modern Art.

Johns, Jasper. *Seven*. 1955. Encaustic and collage on canvas. LACMA.

Johns, Jasper. *Target with Plaster Casts*. 1955b. Encaustic and collage on canvas with objects. Private collection.

Johnson-Laird, Philip N., and Keith Oatley. "Emotions in Music, Literature, and Film." In *Handbook of Emotions*, 4th ed., edited by Lisa Feldman Barrett and Jeannette M. Haviland-Jones, 82–97. New York: Guilford Publications, 2016.

Jones, Mari Riess. "Music as a Stimulus for Psychological Motion: Part I. Some Determinants of Expectancies." *Psychomusicology: A Journal of Research in Music Cognition* 1, no. 2 (1981): 34.

Jones, Mari Riess, and Marilyn Boltz. "Dynamic Attending and Responses to Time." *Psychological Review* 96, no. 3 (1989): 459.

Jones, Robert W. *Gender and the Formation of Taste in Eighteenth-Century Britain: The Analysis of Beauty*. New York: Cambridge University Press, 1998.

Joshua, Mati, Avital Adler, and Hagai Bergman. "The Dynamics of Dopamine in Control of Motor Behavior." *Current Opinion in Neurobiology* 19, no. 6 (2009): 615–620.

Juslin, Patrick N., and Laura S. Sakka. "Neural Correlates of Music and Emotion." In *The Oxford Handbook of Music and the Brain*, edited by Michael H. Thaut and Donald A. Hodges, 285. New York: Oxford University Press, 2019.

Kant, Immanuel. *Critique of Judgment*. Translated by Werner Pluhar. Indianapolis: Hackett, 1987.

Kant, Immanuel. *Observations on the Feeling of the Beautiful and Sublime*. Berkeley: University of California Press, 2003.

Kanwisher, Nancy, and Ewa Wojciulik. "Visual Attention: Insights from Brain Imaging." *Nature Reviews Neuroscience* 1, no. 2 (2000): 91–100.

Kasdan, Anna, and Amy M. Belfi. "Investigating a Self-Reference Effect in Musical Aesthetics." *Experimental Results* 1 (2020).

Kawabata, Hideaki, and Semir Zeki. "Neural Correlates of Beauty." *Journal of Neurophysiology* (2004).

Keen, Suzanne. *Empathy and the Novel*. New York: Oxford University Press, 2007.

Kidd, David Comer, and Emanuele Castano. "Reading Literary Fiction Improves Theory of Mind." *Science* 342, no. 6156 (2013): 377–380.

Killingsworth, Matthew A., and Daniel T. Gilbert. "A Wandering Mind Is an Unhappy Mind." *Science* 330, no. 6006 (2010): 932.

Kim, Hackjin, Ralph Adolphs, John P. O'Doherty, and Shinsuke Shimojo. "Temporal Isolation of Neural Processes Underlying Face Preference Decisions." *Proceedings of the National Academy of Sciences* 104, no. 46 (2007): 18253–18258.

Kirk, Ulrich, Martin Skov, Oliver Hulme, Mark S. Christensen, and Semir Zeki. "Modulation of Aesthetic Value by Semantic Context: An fMRI Study." *NeuroImage* 44, no. 3 (2009): 1125–1132.

Kirsch, Louise P., Cosimo Urgesi, and Emily S. Cross. "Shaping and Reshaping the Aesthetic Brain: Emerging Perspectives on the Neurobiology of Embodied Aesthetics." *Neuroscience & Biobehavioral Reviews* 62 (March 2016): 56–68. https://doi.org/10.1016/j.neubiorev.2015.12.005.

Knutson, Brian, Charles M. Adams, Grace W. Fong, and Daniel Hommer. "Anticipation of Increasing Monetary Reward Selectively Recruits Nucleus Accumbens." *Journal of Neuroscience* 21, no. 16 (2001): RC159–RC159.

Kraxenberger, Maria, and Winfried Menninghaus. "Emotional Effects of Poetic Phonology, Word Positioning and Dominant Stress Peaks in Poetry Reading." *Scientific Study of Literature* 6, no. 2 (2016): 298–313.

Krueger, Joel. "Empathy, Enaction, and Shared Musical Experience: Evidence from Infant Cognition." In *The Emotional Power of Music: Multidisciplinary Perspectives on Musical Expression, Arousal and Social Control*, edited by Tom Cochrane, Bernardino Fantini, and Klaus R. Scherer, 177–196. New York: Oxford University Press, 2011.

Kühn, Simone, and Jürgen Gallinat. "The Neural Correlates of Subjective Pleasantness." *NeuroImage* 61, no. 1 (2012): 289–294.

Kukushkin, Nikolay Vadimovich, and Thomas James Carew. "Memory Takes Time." *Neuron* 95, no. 2 (2017): 259–279.

Kurdi, Benedek, Shayn Lozano, and Mahzarin R. Banaji. "Introducing the Open Affective Standardized Image Set (OASIS)." *Behavior Research Methods* 49, no. 2 (2017): 457–470.

Lang, P., and Margaret M. Bradley. "The International Affective Picture System (IAPS) in the Study of Emotion and Attention." *Handbook of Emotion Elicitation and Assessment* 29 (2007): 70–73.

Laufs, Helmut, K. Krakow, P. Sterzer, E. Eger, A. Beyerle, A. Salek-Haddadi, and A. Kleinschmidt. "Electroencephalographic Signatures of Attentional and Cognitive Default Modes in Spontaneous Brain Activity Fluctuations at Rest." *Proceedings of the National Academy of Sciences* 100, no. 19 (2003): 11053–11058.

Lebreton, Maël, Soledad Jorge, Vincent Michel, Bertrand Thirion, and Mathias Pessiglione. "An Automatic Valuation System in the Human Brain: Evidence from Functional Neuroimaging." *Neuron* 64, no. 3 (2009): 431–439.

Leder, Helmut. "Next Steps in Neuroaesthetics: Which Processes and Processing Stages to Study?" *Psychology of Aesthetics, Creativity, and the Arts* 7, no. 1 (2013): 27.

Leder, Helmut, Claus-Christian Carbon, and Ai-Leen Ripsas. "Entitling Art: Influence of Title Information on Understanding and Appreciation of Paintings." *Acta Psychologica* 121, no. 2 (2006): 176–198.

Leder, Helmut, Juergen Goller, Tanya Rigotti, and Michael Forster. "Private and Shared Taste in Art and Face Appreciation." *Frontiers in Human Neuroscience* 10 (2016): 155.

Leder, Helmut, and Marcos Nadal. "Ten Years of a Model of Aesthetic Appreciation and Aesthetic Judgments: The Aesthetic Episode–Developments and Challenges in Empirical Aesthetics." *British Journal of Psychology* 105, no. 4 (2014): 443–464.

Lee, Hyojun, Amélie Jacquot, Dominique Makowski, Margherita Arcangeli, and Pascale Piolino. "Beauty Is in the Eye of the Beholder: Evidence from a Common Mnemonic Advantage between Aesthetics Judgement and Self-Reference." *PsyArXiv* (2020). https://doi.org/doi:10.31234/osf.io/rw39q.

Leshikar, Eric D., Michael R. Dulas, and Audrey Duarte. "Self-Referencing Enhances Recollection in Both Young and Older Adults." *Aging, Neuropsychology, and Cognition* 22, no. 4 (2015): 388–412. https://doi.org/10.1080/13825585.2014.957150.

Levine, Caroline. *Forms: Whole, Rhythm, Hierarchy, Network*. Princeton, NJ: Princeton University Press, 2015.

Levy, Dino J., and Paul W. Glimcher. "The Root of All Value: A Neural Common Currency for Choice." *Current Opinion in Neurobiology* 22, no. 6 (2012): 1027–1038.

Livingstone, Margaret, and D. H. Hubel. *Vision and Art: The Biology of Seeing*. New York: Abrams, 2008.

Locher, Paul J. "The Aesthetic Experience with Visual Art 'at First Glance.'" In *Investigations Into the Phenomenology and the Ontology of the Work of Art: What Are Artworks and How Do We Experience Them?*, 75–88. New York: Springer 2015.

Locher, Paul, Elizabeth Krupinski, and Alexandra Schaefer. "Art and Authenticity: Behavioral and Eye-Movement Analyses." *Psychology of Aesthetics, Creativity, and the Arts* 9, no. 4 (2015): 356.

Lovejoy, Arthur O. *The Great Chain of Being: A Study of the History of an Idea*. New Brunswick: Transaction Publishers, 2011.

Lüdtke, Jana, Burkhard Meyer-Sickendieck, and Arthur M. Jacobs. "Immersing in the Stillness of an Early Morning: Testing the Mood Empathy Hypothesis of Poetry Reception." *Psychology of Aesthetics, Creativity, and the Arts* 8, no. 3 (2014): 363.

Luhmann, Niklas. *Art as a Social System*. Translated by Eva Knodt. Meridian Crossing Aesthetics. Stanford: Stanford University Press, 2000.

Luo, Cheng, Shipeng Tu, Yueheng Peng, Shan Gao, Jianfu Li, Li Dong, Gujing Li, Yongxiu Lai, Hong Li, and Dezhong Yao. "Long-Term Effects of Musical Training and Functional Plasticity in Salience System." *Neural Plasticity* (2014).

Lutterbie, John. "Feeling Beauty, Time, and the Body in Neuroaesthetics." *Poetics Today* 38, no. 2 (2017): 295–315.

Macdonald, James S. P., Patrick Cavanagh, and Rufin VanRullen. "Attentional Sampling of Multiple Wagon Wheels." *Attention, Perception, & Psychophysics* 76, no. 1 (2014): 64–72.

Maguire, Eleanor A., Katherine Woollett, and Hugo J. Spiers. "London Taxi Drivers and Bus Drivers: A Structural MRI and Neuropsychological Analysis." *Hippocampus* 16, no. 12 (2006): 1091–1101.

Manoliu, Andrei, Valentin Riedl, Andriy Zherdin, Mark Mühlau, Dirk Schwerthöffer, Martin Scherr, Henning Peters, Claus Zimmer, Hans Förstl, and Josef Bäuml. "Aberrant Dependence of Default Mode/Central Executive Network Interactions on Anterior Insular Salience Network Activity in Schizophrenia." *Schizophrenia Bulletin* 40, no. 2 (2014): 428–437.

Marcuse, Herbert. *Eros and Civilization: A Philosophical Inquiry into Freud*. Abingdon: Routledge, 2012.

Marks, David F. "Visual Imagery Differences in the Recall of Pictures." *British Journal of Psychology* 64, no. 1 (1973): 17–24.

Massaro, Davide, Federica Savazzi, Cinzia Di Dio, David Freedberg, Vittorio Gallese, Gabriella Gilli, and Antonella Marchetti. "When Art Moves the Eyes: A Behavioral and Eye-Tracking Study." *PLOS ONE* 7, no. 5 (2012): e37285.

Mastandrea, Stefano, Sabrina Fagioli, and Valeria Biasi. "Art and Psychological Well-Being: Linking the Brain to the Aesthetic Emotion." *Frontiers in Psychology* 10 (2019): 739.

McGrath, Joseph E., Janice R. Kelly, and Diane E. Machatka. "The Social Psychology of Time: Entrainment of Behavior in Social and Organizational Settings." *Applied Social Psychology Annual* (1984).

McLane, Maureen N. *My Poets*. New York: Macmillan, 2012.

McQuire, Marguerite, Lauren McCollum, and Anjan Chatterjee. "Aptness and Beauty in Metaphor." *Language and Cognition* 9, no. 2 (2017): 316–331. https://doi.org/10.1017/langcog.2016.13.

Meade, Adam W., and S. Bartholomew Craig. "Identifying Careless Responses in Survey Data." *Psychological Methods* 17, no. 3 (2012): 437.

Mellet, E., N. Tzourio-Mazoyer, S. Bricogne, B. Mazoyer, S. M. Kosslyn, and M. Denis. "Functional Anatomy of High-Resolution Visual Mental Imagery." *Journal of Cognitive Neuroscience* 12, no. 1 (2000): 98–109.

Mennemeier, Mark S., Anjan Chatterjee, Robert T. Watson, Elie Wertman, L. Philip Carter, and Kenneth M. Heilman. "Contributions of the Parietal and Frontal Lobes to Sustained Attention and Habituation." *Neuropsychologia* 32, no. 6 (1994): 703–716. https://doi.org/10.1016/0028-3932(94)90030-2.

Menninghaus, Winfried, Valentin Wagner, Julian Hanich, Eugen Wassiliwizky, Thomas Jacobsen, and Stefan Koelsch. "The Distancing-Embracing Model of the Enjoyment of Negative Emotions in Art Reception." *Behavioral and Brain Sciences* 40 (2017). https://doi.org/10.1017/S0140525X17000309.

Menninghaus, Winfried, Valentin Wagner, Julian Hanich, Eugen Wassiliwizky, Milena Kuehnast, and Thomas Jacobsen. "Towards a Psychological Construct of Being Moved." *PLOS ONE* 10, no. 6 (2015): e0128451.

Menninghaus, Winfried, Valentin Wagner, Eugen Wassiliwizky, Thomas Jacobsen, and Christine A. Knoop. "The Emotional and Aesthetic Powers of Parallelistic Diction." *Poetics* 63 (2017): 47–59.

Menninghaus, Winfried, Valentin Wagner, Eugen Wassiliwizky, Ines Schindler, Julian Hanich, Thomas Jacobsen, and Stefan Koelsch. "What Are Aesthetic Emotions?" *Psychological Review* 126, no. 2 (2019): 171–195. https://doi.org/10.1037/rev0000135.

Miall, David S., and Don Kuiken. "Foregrounding, Defamiliarization, and Affect: Response to Literary Stories." *Poetics* 22, no. 5 (1994): 389–407.

Miller, George A. "The Magical Number Seven, Plus or Minus Two: Some Limits on Our Capacity for Processing Information." *Psychological Review* 101, no. 2 (1994): 343.

Milton, John. *Paradise Lost*, edited by John Bradshaw. New York: Norton, 1993.

Minka, Thomas. "Automatic Choice of Dimensionality for PCA." *Advances in Neural Information Processing Systems* 13 (2000).

Miron, Marius, Julio J. Carabias Orti, and Jordi Janer Mestres. "Improving Score-Informed Source Separation for Classical Music Through Note Refinement." In *Proceedings of the 16th International Society for Music Information Retrieval (ISMIR) Conference*, edited by M. Müller and F. Wiering. Canada: International Society for Music Information Retrieval, 2015.

Miu, Andrei C., Simina Pițur, and Aurora Szentágotai-Tătar. "Aesthetic Emotions across Arts: A Comparison between Painting and Music." *Frontiers in Psychology* 6 (2016). https://doi.org/10.3389/fpsyg.2015.01951.

Moore, James W., and Sukhvinder S. Obhi. "Intentional Binding and the Sense of Agency: A Review." *Consciousness and Cognition* 21, no. 1 (2012): 546–561.

Moran, Joseph M., William M. Kelley, and Todd F. Heatherton. "What Can the Organization of the Brain's Default Mode Network Tell Us about Self-Knowledge?" *Frontiers in Human Neuroscience* 7 (2013): 391.

Morrison, Toni. *Beloved*. New York: Knopf, 2021.

Moulton, Samuel T., and Stephen M. Kosslyn. "Imagining Predictions: Mental Imagery as Mental Emulation." *Philosophical Transactions of the Royal Society B: Biological Sciences* 364, no. 1521 (2009): 1273–1280.

Myklebust, Nicholas. "'Bergamo on a Postcard'; or, A Critical History of Cognitive Poetics." *Wallace Stevens Journal* 39, no. 2 (2015): 142–156.

Nadal, Marcos, and Anjan Chatterjee. "Neuroaesthetics and Art's Diversity and Universality." *Wiley Interdisciplinary Reviews: Cognitive Science* 10, no. 3 (2019): e1487.

Nadal, Marcos, Gisèle Marty, and Enric Munar. "The Search for Objective Measures of Aesthetic Judgment: The Case of Memory Traces." *Empirical Studies of the Arts* 24, no. 1 (2006): 95–106. https://doi.org/10.2190/5NJ2-7F9J-487P-DCPW.

Nadal, Marcos, and Martin Skov. "Top–down and Bottom–up: Front to Back: Comment on 'Move Me, Astonish Me . . . Delight My Eyes and Brain: The Vienna Integrated Model of Top–down and Bottom–up Processes in Art Perception (VIMAP) and Corresponding Affective, Evaluative, and Neurophysiological Correlates' by Matthew Pelowski et al." *Physics of Life Reviews* 21 (2017): 148–149.

Nakamura, Jeanne, Dwight C. K. Tse, and Shannon Shankland. "Flow: The Experience of Intrinsic Motivation." In *Oxford Handbook of Human Motivation*, 2nd ed., edited by Richard M. Ryan, 169–185. New York: Oxford University Press, 2019. https://doi.org/10.1093/oxfordhb/9780190666453.013.10.

Nehamas, Alexander, and Paul Woodruff, trans. *Plato: Symposium*. Indianapolis: Hackett, 1989.

Nester, Daniel, ed. *The Incredible Sestina Anthology*. Austin: Write Bloody Publishing, 2013.

Ngai, Sianne. *Ugly Feelings*. Cambridge, MA: Harvard University Press, 2005.

Nielsen, F. "Musical Tension and Related Concepts." In *The Semiotic Web*, edited by T. Sebeok and J. Umiker-Sebeok, 491–513. Berlin: Mouton de Gruyter, 1987.

Noë, Alva. *Strange Tools: Art and Human Nature*. New York: Hill and Wang, 2015.

Noguchi, Yasuki, and Miharu Murota. "Temporal Dynamics of Neural Activity in an Integration of Visual and Contextual Information in an Esthetic Preference Task." *Neuropsychologia* 51, no. 6 (2013): 1077–1084.

O'Doherty, John P., Ralf Deichmann, Hugo D. Critchley, and Raymond J. Dolan. "Neural Responses during Anticipation of a Primary Taste Reward." *Neuron* 33, no. 5 (2002): 815–826.

Ogden, Ruth Sarah, Jessica Henderson, Francis McGlone, and Michael Richter. "Time Distortion under Threat: Sympathetic Arousal Predicts Time Distortion Only in the Context of Negative, Highly Arousing Stimuli." *PLOS ONE* 14, no. 5 (2019): e0216704.

O'Sullivan, Noreen, Philip Davis, Josie Billington, Victorina Gonzalez-Diaz, and Rhiannon Corcoran. "'Shall I Compare Thee': The Neural Basis of Literary Awareness, and Its Benefits to Cognition." *Cortex* 73 (2015): 144–157.

Pallesen, Karen Johanne, Elvira Brattico, Christopher J. Bailey, Antti Korvenoja, and Albert Gjedde. "Cognitive and Emotional Modulation of Brain Default Operation." *Journal of Cognitive Neuroscience* 21, no. 6 (2009): 1065–1080.

Panksepp, Jaak. "The Emotional Sources of 'Chills' Induced by Music." *Music Perception* 13, no. 2 (1995): 171–207.

Paolacci, Gabriele, Jesse Chandler, and Panagiotis G. Ipeirotis. "Running Experiments on Amazon Mechanical Turk." *Judgment and Decision Making* 5, no. 5 (2010): 411–419.

Park, Junghyun, Eiko Shimojo, and Shinsuke Shimojo. "Roles of Familiarity and Novelty in Visual Preference Judgments Are Segregated across Object Categories." *Proceedings of the National Academy of Sciences* 107, no. 33 (2010): 14552–14555.

Pascal, Blaise. *Pensées*, edited by Marc Escola. Paris: Flammarion, 1968.

Paulson, Ronald. *The Beautiful, Novel, and Strange: Aesthetics and Heterodoxy*. Baltimore: Johns Hopkins University Press, 2019.

Pearce, Marcus T., Dahlia W. Zaidel, Oshin Vartanian, Martin Skov, Helmut Leder, Anjan Chatterjee, and Marcos Nadal. "Neuroaesthetics: The Cognitive Neuroscience of Aesthetic Experience." *Perspectives on Psychological Science* 11, no. 2 (2016): 265–279.

Pegors, Teresa K., Joseph W. Kable, Anjan Chatterjee, and Russell A. Epstein. "Common and Unique Representations in PFC for Face and Place Attractiveness." *Journal of Cognitive Neuroscience* 27, no. 5 (2014): 959–973. https://doi.org/10.1162/jocn_a_00777.

Pelli, Denis G. "The VideoToolbox Software for Visual Psychophysics: Transforming Numbers into Movies." *Spatial Vision* 10 (1997): 437–442.

Pelowski, Matthew, Patrick S. Markey, Michael Forster, Gernot Gerger, and Helmut Leder. "Move Me, Astonish Me . . . Delight My Eyes and Brain: The Vienna Integrated Model of Top-down and Bottom-up Processes in Art Perception (VIMAP) and Corresponding Affective, Evaluative, and Neurophysiological Correlates." *Physics of Life Reviews* 21 (July 2017): 80–125. https://doi.org/10.1016/j.plrev.2017.02.003.

Pinker, Steven. *The Blank Slate: The Modern Denial of Human Nature*. New York: Penguin, 2003.

Price, Leah. *The Anthology and the Rise of the Novel: From Richardson to George Eliot*. New York: Cambridge University Press, 2003.

Proust, Marcel. *Remembrance of Things Past*. 3 vols., vol. 1. Translated by C. K. Scott Moncrieff. New York: Penguin, 1983.

Raichle, Marcus E. "The Brain's Default Mode Network." *Annual Review of Neuroscience* 38 (2015): 433–447.

Ramachandran, Vilayanur S., and Diane Rogers-Ramachandran. "Phantom Limbs and Neural Plasticity." *Archives of Neurology* 57, no. 3 (2000): 317–320.

Rand, David G. "The Promise of Mechanical Turk: How Online Labor Markets Can Help Theorists Run Behavioral Experiments." *Journal of Theoretical Biology* 299 (2012): 172–179.

Reed, Arden. *Slow Art: The Experience of Looking, Sacred Images to James Turrell*. Berkeley: University of California Press, 2017.

Reeve, Johnmarshall, and Woogul Lee. "Motivational Neuroscience." In *Oxford Handbook of Human Motivation*, 2nd ed., edited by Richard M. Ryan, 355–371. New York: Oxford University Press, 2019. https://doi.org/10.1093/oxfordhb/9780190666453.013.20.

Robbe-Grillet, Alain, and Jasper Johns. *The Target: Alain Robbe-Grillet, Jasper Johns*. Translated by Brian Stoltzfus. Madison, NJ: Fairleigh Dickinson University Press, 2006.

Robinson, Jenefer. *Deeper than Reason: Emotion and Its Role in Literature, Music, and Art*. New York: Oxford University Press, 2005.

Roeske, Tina, Pauline Larrouy-Maestri, Yasuhiro Sakamoto, and David Poeppel. "Listening to Birdsong Reveals Basic Features of Rate Perception and Aesthetic Judgements." *Proceedings of the Royal Society B* 287, no. 1923 (2020): 20193010.

Sachs, Matthew E., Assal Habibi, Antonio Damasio, and Jonas T. Kaplan. "Dynamic Intersubject Neural Synchronization Reflects Affective Responses to Sad Music." *NeuroImage* 218 (September 2020): 116512. https://doi.org/10.1016/j.neuroimage.2019.116512.

Salimpoor, Valorie N., Mitchel Benovoy, Kevin Larcher, Alain Dagher, and Robert J. Zatorre. "Anatomically Distinct Dopamine Release during Anticipation and Experience of Peak Emotion to Music." *Nature Neuroscience* 14, no. 2 (2011): 257.

Salimpoor, Valorie N., Mitchel Benovoy, Gregory Longo, Jeremy R. Cooperstock, and Robert J. Zatorre. "The Rewarding Aspects of Music Listening Are Related to Degree of Emotional Arousal." *PLOS ONE* 4, no. 10 (2009): e7487.

Salimpoor, Valorie N., Iris van den Bosch, Natasa Kovacevic, Anthony Randal McIntosh, Alain Dagher, and Robert J. Zatorre. "Interactions between the Nucleus Accumbens and Auditory Cortices Predict Music Reward Value." *Science* 340, no. 6129 (2013): 216–219.

Salimpoor, Valorie N., David H. Zald, Robert J. Zatorre, Alain Dagher, and Anthony Randal McIntosh. "Predictions and the Brain: How Musical Sounds Become Rewarding." *Trends in Cognitive Sciences* 19, no. 2 (2015): 86–91.

Scarry, Elaine. *The Body in Pain: The Making and Unmaking of the World*. New York: Oxford University Press, 1987.

Scarry, Elaine. *On Beauty and Being Just*. Princeton, NJ: Princeton University Press, 2001.

Schindler, Ines, Georg Hosoya, Winfried Menninghaus, Ursula Beermann, Valentin Wagner, Michael Eid, and Klaus R. Scherer. "Measuring Aesthetic Emotions: A Review of the Literature and a New Assessment Tool." *PLOS ONE* 12, no. 6 (2017): e0178899.

Schoeller, Felix, and Leonid Perlovsky. "Aesthetic Chills: Knowledge-Acquisition, Meaning-Making, and Aesthetic Emotions." *Frontiers in Psychology* 7 (2016). https://doi.org/10.3389/fpsyg.2016.01093.

Schultz, Wolfram, Peter Dayan, and P. Read Montague. "A Neural Substrate of Prediction and Reward." *Science* 275, no. 5306 (1997): 1593–1599.

Schunk, Dale, and Ellen Usher. "Social Cognitive Theory and Motivation." In *Oxford Handbook of Human Motivation*, edited by Richard M. Ryan, 11–26. New York: Oxford University Press, 2019. https://doi.org/10.1093/oxfordhb/9780190666453.013.2.

Seeley, William P. "Art, Meaning, and Aesthetics: The Case for a Cognitive Neuroscience of Art." In *Art, Aesthetics and the Brain*, edited by Joseph P. Hutson, Marcos Nadal, Francisco Mora, Luigi F. Agnati, and Camilo J. Cela-Conde, 19–39. New York: Oxford University Press, 2015.

Shaftesbury, Anthony Ashley Cooper. *Characteristics of Men, Manners, Opinions, Times*, edited by Lawrence Klein. New York: Cambridge University Press, 1999.

Shao, Xi, Wenming Gui, and Changsheng Xu. "Note onset detection based on sparse decomposition." *Multimedia Tools and Applications* 75, no. 5 (2016): 2613–2631.

Shklovsky, Viktor. "Art as Technique." In *Literary Theory: An Anthology*, 3rd ed., edited by Julie Rivkin and Michael Ryan, 208–214. London: Blackwell, n.d.

Shulman, Gordon L., John M. Ollinger, Erbil Akbudak, Thomas E. Conturo, Abraham Z. Snyder, Steven E. Petersen, and Maurizio Corbetta. "Areas Involved in Encoding and Applying Directional Expectations to Moving Objects." *Journal of Neuroscience* 19, no. 21 (1999): 9480–9496.

Silvia, Paul J., and Emily C. Nusbaum. "On Personality and Piloerection: Individual Differences in Aesthetic Chills and Other Unusual Aesthetic Experiences." *Psychology of Aesthetics, Creativity, and the Arts* 5, no. 3 (2011): 208.

Skov, Martin, and Marcos Nadal. "There Are No Aesthetic Emotions: Comment on Menninghaus et al. (2019)." *Psychological Review* 127, no. 4 (2020): 640–649. https://doi.org/10.1037/rev0000187.

Small, Christopher. *Musicking: The Meanings of Performing and Listening*. Middletown, CT: Wesleyan University Press, 1998.

Smallwood, Jonathan, Krzysztof J. Gorgolewski, Johannes Golchert, Florence J. M. Ruby, Haakon G. Engen, Benjamin Baird, Melaina Vinski, Jonathan Schooler, and Daniel S. Margulies. "The Default Modes of Reading: Modulation of Posterior Cingulate and Medial Prefrontal Cortex Connectivity Associated with Comprehension and Task Focus While Reading." *Frontiers in Human Neuroscience* 7 (2013): 734.

Smith, Barbara Herrnstein. *Poetic Closure: A Study of How Poems End*. Vol. 381. Chicago: University of Chicago Press, 1968.

Smith, James C., and Howard D. Baker. "Conditioning in the Horseshoe Crab." *Journal of Comparative and Physiological Psychology* 53, no. 3 (1960): 279.

Smith, Jeffrey K., and Lisa F. Smith. "Spending Time on Art." *Empirical Studies of the Arts* 19, no. 2 (2001): 229–236.

Smith, Lisa F., and Jeffrey K. Smith. "The Nature and Growth of Aesthetic Fluency." In *New Directions in Aesthetics, Creativity, and the Arts*, edited by Paul Locher, Colin Martindale, and Leonid Dorfman, 47–58. New York: Routledge, 2006.

Smith, Stephen M., Peter T. Fox, Karla L. Miller, David C. Glahn, P. Mickle Fox, Clare E. Mackay, Nicola Filippini, Kate E. Watkins, Roberto Toro, Angela R. Laird, and Christian F. Beckmann. "Correspondence of the Brain's Functional Architecture During Activation and Rest." *Proceedings of the National Academy of Sciences* 106, no. 31 (2009): 13040–13045. https://doi.org/10.1073/pnas.0905267106.

Spenser, Edmund. *The Faerie Queene*, edited by Thomas P. Roche Jr. and C. Patrick O'Donnell Jr. New York: Penguin, 1978.

Spreng, R. Nathan, Raymond A. Mar, and Alice S. N. Kim. "The Common Neural Basis of Autobiographical Memory, Prospection, Navigation, Theory of Mind, and the Default Mode: A Quantitative Meta-Analysis." *Journal of Cognitive Neuroscience* 21, no. 3 (2009): 489–510.

Spreng, R. Nathan, W. Dale Stevens, Jon P. Chamberlain, Adrian W. Gilmore, and Daniel L. Schacter. "Default Network Activity, Coupled with the Frontoparietal Control Network, Supports Goal-Directed Cognition." *NeuroImage* 53, no. 1 (2010): 303–317.

Sridharan, Devarajan, Daniel J. Levitin, and Vinod Menon. "A Critical Role for the Right Fronto-Insular Cortex in Switching between Central-Executive and Default-Mode Networks." *Proceedings of the National Academy of Sciences* 105, no. 34 (2008): 12569. https://doi.org/10.1073/pnas.0800005105.

Sripada, Chandra S. "An Exploration/Exploitation Trade-off between Mind Wandering and Goal-Directed Thinking." In *The Oxford Handbook of Spontaneous Thought: Mind-Wandering, Creativity, and Dreaming*, edited by Kieran C. R. Fox and Kalina Christoff, 23–34. New York: Oxford University Press, 2018.

Starr, G. Gabrielle. "Cavendish, Aesthetics, and the Anti-Platonic Line." *Eighteenth-Century Studies* 39, no. 3 (2006): 295–308.

Starr, G. Gabrielle. "Burney, Ovid, and the Value of the Beautiful." *Eighteenth-Century Fiction* 24, no. 1 (2011): 77–104.

Starr, G. Gabrielle. *Feeling Beauty: The Neuroscience of Aesthetic Experience*. Cambridge, MA: MIT Press, 2013.

Starr, G. Gabrielle, and Amy M. Belfi. "Pleasure." In *Further Reading*, edited by Matthew Rubery and Leah Price, 282–293. New York: Oxford University Press, 2020.

Stephens, Greg J., Lauren J. Silbert, and Uri Hasson. "Speaker-Listener Neural Coupling Underlies Successful Communication." *PNAS* 107, no. 32 (2010): 14425–14430.

Stevens, Wallace. *Collected Poetry and Prose*. Edited by Kermode Frank and Joan Richardson. New York: Library of America, 1997.

Stevens, Wallace. *Letters of Wallace Stevens*. Berkeley: University of California Press, 1996.

Stolnitz, Jerome. "On the Origins of 'Aesthetic Disinterestedness.'" *The Journal of Aesthetics and Art Criticism* 20, no. 2 (1961): 131–143.

Stoltzfus, Brian. "Appendix: Target with Objects." In *The Target: Alain Robbe-Grillet, Jasper Johns*, edited by Brian Stoltzfus, 99–104. Madison, NJ: Fairleigh Dickinson University Press, 2006.

Stupacher, Jan, Michael J. Hove, Giacomo Novembre, Simone Schütz-Bosbach, and Peter E. Keller. "Musical Groove Modulates Motor Cortex Excitability: A TMS Investigation." *Brain and Cognition* 82, no. 2 (2013): 127–136.

Supekar, Kaustubh, Lucina Q. Uddin, Katherine Prater, Hitha Amin, Michael D. Greicius, and Vinod Menon. "Development of Functional and Structural Connectivity within the Default Mode Network in Young Children." *NeuroImage* 52, no. 1 (2010): 290–301.

Swift, Jonathan. *The Complete Poems*. New York: Penguin, 1983.

Tournoux, Talairach, and J. Talairach. *Co-Planar Stereotaxic Atlas of the Human Brain*. Stuttgart: Theime, 1988.

Tartt, Donna. *The Goldfinch: A Novel*. Boston: Little, Brown, 2013.

Thakral, Preston P., Lauren R. Moo, and Scott D. Slotnick. "A Neural Mechanism for Aesthetic Experience." *Neuroreport* 23, no. 5 (2012): 310–313.

Ticini, Luca F., Laura Rachman, Jerome Pelletier, and Stephanie Dubal. "Enhancing Aesthetic Appreciation by Priming Canvases with Actions That Match the Artist's Painting Style." *Frontiers in Human Neuroscience* 8 (2014): 391.

Tierney, Adam, and Nina Kraus. "Neural Entrainment to the Rhythmic Structure of Music." *Journal of Cognitive Neuroscience* 27, no. 2 (2014): 400–408.

Tiihonen, Marianne, Elvira Brattico, Johanna Maksimainen, Jan Wikgren, and Suvi Saarikallio. "Constituents of Music and Visual-Art Related Pleasure–A Critical Integrative Literature Review." *Frontiers in Psychology* 8 (2017): 1218.

Tillmann, Barbara, Philippe Albouy, Anne Caclin, and Emmanuel Bigand. "Musical Familiarity in Congenital Amusia: Evidence from a Gating Paradigm." *Cortex* 59 (2014): 84–94.

Tomlinson, Gary. *A Million Years of Music: The Emergence of Human Modernity*. Cambridge, MA: MIT Press, 2015.

Tröndle, Martin, Stéphanie Wintzerith, Roland Wäspe, and Wolfgang Tschacher. "A Museum for the Twenty-First Century: The Influence of 'Sociality' on Art Reception in Museum Space." *Museum Management and Curatorship* 27, no. 5 (2012): 461–486.

Troxler, Ignaz Paul Vital. "Uber Das Vcrschwindern Gegehener Gegenstande Innerhalh Unsers Gesichtskreises." *Ophthalmologische Bibliothek* 2, no. 2 (1804): 1–53.

Tschacher, Wolfgang, Steven Greenwood, Volker Kirchberg, Stéphanie Wintzerith, Karen van den Berg, and Martin Tröndle. "Physiological Correlates of Aesthetic Perception of Artworks in a Museum." *Psychology of Aesthetics, Creativity, and the Arts* 6, no. 1 (2012): 96.

Tsukiura, Takashi, and Roberto Cabeza. "Shared Brain Activity for Aesthetic and Moral Judgments: Implications for the Beauty-Is-Good Stereotype." *Social Cognitive and Affective Neuroscience* 6, no. 1 (2011): 138–148. https://doi.org/10.1093/scan/nsq025.

Tsur, Reuven. *Poetic Rhythm: Structure and Performance: An Empirical Study in Cognitive Poetics*. Portland: Sussex Academic Press, 2012.

Turk, Matija, Ivan Turk, and Marcel Otte. "The Neanderthal Musical Instrument from Divje Babe I Cave (Slovenia): A Critical Review of the Discussion." *Applied Sciences* 10, no. 4 (2020): 1226.

Twombly, Cy. *Untitled*. 1970. Oil-based housepaint and crayon on canvas. 614.1994. Museum of Modern Art, New York.

Ullrich, Susann, Arash Aryani, Maria Kraxenberger, Arthur M. Jacobs, and Markus Conrad. "On the Relation between the General Affective Meaning and the Basic Sublexical, Lexical, and Inter-Lexical Features of Poetic Texts—a Case Study Using 57 Poems of H. M. Enzensberger." *Frontiers in Psychology* 7 (2017): 2073.

Van den Heuvel, Martijn P., René S. Kahn, Joaquín Goñi, and Olaf Sporns. "High-Cost, High-Capacity Backbone for Global Brain Communication." *Proceedings of the National Academy of Sciences* 109, no. 28 (2012): 11372–11377.

Van den Heuvel, Martijn P., and Olaf Sporns. "Rich-Club Organization of the Human Connectome." *Journal of Neuroscience* 31, no. 44 (2011): 15775–15786.

Vartanian, Oshin. "Internal Orientation in Aesthetic Experience." In *The Oxford Handbook of Spontaneous Thought: Mind-Wandering, Creativity, and Dreaming*, edited by Kieran C. R. Fox and Kalina Christoff, 23–34. New York: Oxford University Press, 2018.

Vartanian, Oshin, and Vinod Goel. "Neuroanatomical Correlates of Aesthetic Preference for Paintings." *Neuroreport* 15, no. 5 (2004): 893–897.

Vartanian, Oshin, and Martin Skov. "Neural Correlates of Viewing Paintings: Evidence from a Quantitative Meta-Analysis of Functional Magnetic Resonance Imaging

Data." *Brain and Cognition* 87 (June 2014): 52–56. https://doi.org/10.1016/j.bandc.2014.03.004.

Vendler, Helen. *The Art of Shakespeare's Sonnets*. Cambridge, MA: Harvard University Press, 1997.

Verhavert, San, Johan Wagemans, and M. Dorothee Augustin. "Beauty in the Blink of an Eye: The Time Course of Aesthetic Experiences." *British Journal of Psychology* 109, no. 1 (2018): 63–84. https://doi.org/10.1111/bjop.12258.

Vessel, E. A., and S. Russo. "Effects of Reduced Sensory Stimulation and Assessment of Countermeasures for Sensory Stimulation Augmentation. A Report for NASA Behavioral Health and Performance Research: Sensory Stimulation Augmentation Tools for Long Duration Spaceflight (NASA/TM-2015–218576)." *NASA Center for AeroSpace Information* (2015).

Vessel, Edward A., Ayse Ilkay Isik, Amy M. Belfi, Jonathan L. Stahl, and G. Gabrielle Starr. "The Default-Mode Network Represents Aesthetic Appeal That Generalizes across Visual Domains." *Proceedings of the National Academy of Sciences* 116, no. 38 (2019): 19155–19164. https://doi.org/10.1073/pnas.1902650116.

Vessel, Edward A., Natalia Maurer, Alexander H. Denker, and G. Gabrielle Starr. "Stronger Shared Taste for Natural Aesthetic Domains than for Artifacts of Human Culture." *Cognition* 179 (2018): 121–131.

Vessel, Edward A., and Nava Rubin. "Beauty and the Beholder: Highly Individual Taste for Abstract, but Not Real-World Images." *Journal of Vision* 10, no. 2 (2010): 18.

Vessel, Edward A., G. Gabrielle Starr, and Nava Rubin. "The Brain on Art: Intense Aesthetic Experience Activates the Default-Mode Network." *Frontiers in Human Neuroscience* 6 (2012): 66.

Vessel, Edward A., G. Gabrielle Starr, and Nava Rubin. "Art Reaches within: Aesthetic Experience, the Self and the Default Mode Network." *Frontiers in Neuroscience* 7 (2013): 258.

Vuilleumier, Patrik, and Wiebke Trost. "Music and Emotions: From Enchantment to Entrainment." *Annals of the New York Academy of Sciences* 1337, no. 1 (2015): 212–222.

Walcott, Derek. *Omeros*. New York: Farrar, Straus and Giroux, 2014.

Walls, Elizabeth A., Jim Berkson, and Stephen A. Smith. "The Horseshoe Crab, Limulus Polyphemus: 200 Million Years of Existence, 100 Years of Study." *Reviews in Fisheries Science* 10, no. 1 (2002): 39–73.

Walton, Kendall L. *Mimesis as Make-Believe: On the Foundations of the Representational Arts*. Cambridge, MA: Harvard University Press, 1990.

Wang, Tingting, Lei Mo, Oshin Vartanian, Jonathan S. Cant, and Gerald Cupchik. "An Investigation of the Neural Substrates of Mind Wandering Induced by Viewing Traditional Chinese Landscape Paintings." *Frontiers in Human Neuroscience* 8 (2015): 1018.

Wassiliwizky, Eugen, Thomas Jacobsen, Jan Heinrich, Manuel Schneiderbauer, and Winfried Menninghaus. "Tears Falling on Goosebumps: Co-Occurrence of Emotional Lacrimation and Emotional Piloerection Indicates a Psychophysiological Climax in Emotional Arousal." *Frontiers in Psychology* 8 (2017): 41.

Wassiliwizky, Eugen, Stefan Koelsch, Valentin Wagner, Thomas Jacobsen, and Winfried Menninghaus. "The Emotional Power of Poetry: Neural Circuitry, Psychophysiology and Compositional Principles." *Social Cognitive and Affective Neuroscience* 12, no. 8 (2017): 1229–1240.

Wassiliwizky, Eugen, Valentin Wagner, Thomas Jacobsen, and Winfried Menninghaus. "Art-Elicited Chills Indicate States of Being Moved." *Psychology of Aesthetics, Creativity, and the Arts* 9, no. 4 (2015): 405-416.

Watson, David, and Lee Anna Clark. "The PANAS-X: Manual for the Positive and Negative Affect Schedule-Expanded Form." 1999. https://doi.org/10.17077/48vt-m4t2.

Watson, David, Lee Anna Clark, and Auke Tellegen. "Development and Validation of Brief Measures of Positive and Negative Affect: The PANAS Scales." *Journal of Personality and Social Psychology* 54, no. 6 (1988): 1063.

Wearden, John, Alan O'Donoghue, Ruth Ogden, and Catharine Montgomery. "Subjective Duration in the Laboratory and the World Outside." In *Subjective Time: The Philosophy, Psychology, and Neuroscience of Temporality*, edited by Valtteri Arstila and Dan Lloyd, 287–306. Cambridge, MA: MIT Press, 2014.

Welke, Dominik, Isaac Purton, and Edward A. Vessel. "Inspired by Art: Higher Aesthetic Appeal Elicits Increased Felt Inspiration in a Creative Writing Task." *Psychology of Aesthetics, Creativity, and the Arts* (2021). https://psycnet.apa.org/doi/10.1037/aca0000393.

Wells, H. G. *The Time Machine and the Invisible Man*. New York: Signet, 2007.

Whitlow, Carolyn Beard, and Marilyn Krysl. *Obsession: Sestinas in the Twenty-First Century*. Lebanon, NH: Dartmouth College Press, 2014.

Wilkins, Robin W., Donald A. Hodges, Paul J. Laurienti, Matthew Steen, and Jonathan H. Burdette. "Network Science and the Effects of Music Preference on Functional Brain Connectivity: From Beethoven to Eminem." *Scientific Reports* 4, no. 1 (2014): 1–8.

Winkielman, Piotr, and John T. Cacioppo. "Mind at Ease Puts a Smile on the Face: Psychophysiological Evidence That Processing Facilitation Elicits Positive Affect." *Journal of Personality and Social Psychology* 81, no. 6 (2001): 989.

Wittenbrink, Bernd, and Norbert Schwarz. *Implicit Measures of Attitudes*. New York: Guilford Press, 2007.

Wordsworth, William 1770–1850, and Samuel Taylor 1772–1834. Coleridge. *Lyrical Ballads, 1798*, 2nd ed., edited by W. J. B. (Warwick Jack Burgoyne) Owen. New York: Oxford University Press, 1971.

Xiao, Jianxiong, James Hays, Bryan C. Russell, Genevieve Patterson, Krista A. Ehinger, Antonio Torralba, and Aude Oliva. "Basic Level Scene Understanding: Categories, Attributes and Structures." *Frontiers in Psychology* 4 (2013): 506.

Yue, Xiaomin, Edward A. Vessel, and Irving Biederman. "The Neural Basis of Scene Preferences." *Neuroreport* 18, no. 6 (2007): 525–529.

Zamorano, Anna M., Ignacio Cifre, Pedro Montoya, Inmaculada Riquelme, and Boris Kleber. "Insula-Based Networks in Professional Musicians: Evidence for Increased Functional Connectivity during Resting State fMRI." *Human Brain Mapping* 38, no. 10 (2017): 4834–4849.

Zeki, Semir. *Inner Vision: An Exploration of Art and the Brain*. New York: Oxford University Press, 1999.

Zentner, Marcel, Didier Grandjean, and Klaus R. Scherer. "Emotions Evoked by the Sound of Music: Characterization, Classification, and Measurement." *Emotion* 8, no. 4 (2008): 494.

Zhang, Meichao, Nicola Savill, Daniel S. Margulies, Jonathan Smallwood, and Elizabeth Jefferies. "Distinct Individual Differences in Default Mode Network Connectivity Relate to Off-Task Thought and Text Memory during Reading." *Scientific Reports* 9, no. 1 (2019): 1–13.

Zhang, Wei, Xianyou He, Siyan Lai, Juan Wan, Shuxian Lai, Xueru Zhao, and Darong Li. "Neural Substrates of Embodied Natural Beauty and Social Endowed Beauty: An fMRI Study." *Scientific Reports* 7, no. 1 (2017): 1–12.

Zhao, Xueru, Junjing Wang, Jinhui Li, Guang Luo, Ting Li, Anjan Chatterjee, Wei Zhang, and Xianyou He. "The Neural Mechanism of Aesthetic Judgments of Dynamic Landscapes: An fMRI Study." *Scientific Reports* 10, no. 1 (2020): 1–11.

Zunshine, Lisa. *Why We Read Fiction: Theory of Mind and the Novel*. Columbus: Ohio State University Press, 2006.

Zysset, Stefan, Oswald Huber, Evelyn Ferstl, and D. Yves von Cramon. "The Anterior Frontomedian Cortex and Evaluative Judgment: An fMRI Study." *NeuroImage* 15, no. 4 (2002): 983–991. https://doi.org/10.1006/nimg.2001.1008.

Index